DISCARDED

THE LIFE AND TIMES

OF

THOMAS WILSON DORR,

WITH

OUTLINES OF THE POLITICAL HISTORY

OF

RHODE ISLAND.

Engraved from a Daguerreotype Miniature by A.H. Dick.

T. W. Dorr.

Inaugurated Governor of Rhode Island.

May 3d 1842.

F
83.4
K52
1969

THE
LIFE AND TIMES

OF

THOMAS WILSON DORR,

WITH

OUTLINES OF THE POLITICAL HISTORY

OF

RHODE ISLAND.

BY DAN KING.

Truth shall restore the light by nature given,
And, like Prometheus, bring the fire of heaven!
Prone to the dust Oppression shall be hurled,
Her name, her nature, withered from the world!
CAMPBELL'S DOWNFALL OF POLAND.

↑ 942430

Select Bibliographies Reprint Series

  BOOKS FOR LIBRARIES PRESS
FREEPORT, NEW YORK

First Published 1859
Reprinted 1969

STANDARD BOOK NUMBER:
8369-5071-2

LIBRARY OF CONGRESS CATALOG CARD NUMBER:
74-95071

PRINTED IN THE UNITED STATES OF AMERICA

PREFACE.

The following work is intended to correct some of the prominent mistakes which are found to prevail in regard to the character of that political controversy which took place in Rhode Island in 1841-2. Although some may be of opinion that it is too soon to give that history to the public, and the day may be far distant when it can be written or read without prejudice, yet the author believes that no good cause will suffer by investigation; that it can never be too soon to correct errors and mistakes; that national freedom can only be maintained by the proper diffusion of knowledge, and that in every popular government the respective rights of the people and of their government should be clearly defined and distinctly understood. If popular sovereignty is to be regarded as any thing more than an empty name — if it is in reality the fundamental principle of all free institutions — it should never be lost sight of, but should be constantly watched as the polar star of civil liberty.

The writer is conscious of the perilous position which he has assumed; he knows full well the intensity of those fires which that controversy enkindled, and is aware that beneath their sleeping ashes there may be livid coals which will glow again as soon as stirred. He has no desire to provoke anew those angry feelings which raged with so much fury during the period in question: yet, in obedience to his own convictions of truth and justice, he has plainly and fearlessly made known his own sentiments respecting that controversy and the character of its master spirit — THOMAS WILSON DORR.

TAUNTON, April 1, 1859.

CONTENTS.

CHAPTER I.

The Early History of the Government of Rhode Island and Providence Plantations. 11

CHAPTER II.

The Abrogation of the Royal Charter by the Declaration of Independence. — Its Defects and practical Injustice, and Efforts of the People to bring about a Change. 19

CHAPTER III.

Proceedings of the People in Forming and Adopting a Constitution. 34

CHAPTER IV.

Landholders' Constitution formed and rejected. — Proceedings of the General Assembly. — The Right of the People to form Constitutions considered, and Authorities quoted. . . . 54

CHAPTER V.

The Algerine Act. — Application to the President of the United States for Troops. — Correspondence between the President and Governor King and others. — Mr. Dorr's Election. — His Message, &c. 64

CONTENTS.

CHAPTER VI.

Reasons for believing the Charter Government to be held by a Minority. — The Neglect of the People's Legislature to take Possession of the Public Property, and its Consequences considered. — An Extract from the Journal of the House of Representatives. 97

CHAPTER VII.

The Right of the Charter Government to hold out against the People considered. — Causes of Complaint set forth, &c. — Confidential Letter from President Tyler. 119

CHAPTER VIII.

Mr. Dorr's Visit to Washington and New York. — His Return to Providence. — Attack upon the Arsenal. 125

CHAPTER IX.

Martial Law. — Gov. King's Proclamation. — Gov. Dorr's Return and Proclamations. — Outrages committed under the Pretext of Martial Law. 131

CHAPTER X.

Mr. Dorr's Return. — Proclamation. — Dismisses his Men, and leaves the State. — Proceedings of Charter Troops. — Arrests and Imprisonment of Suffrage Men. 151

CHAPTER XI.

Martial Law. 176

CHAPTER XII.

Commissioners appointed to examine the Prisoners. — Proceedings. — Measures taken to form another Constitution. — Condition of the People at the time. — Constitution declared adopted. 182

CHAPTER XIII.

Mr. Dorr's Return. — His Arrest and Imprisonment. — Trial. — Conviction. — Speech. — Sentence. — Removal to State Prison. 189

CHAPTER XIV.

Reflections. 215

CHAPTER XV.

Resolutions of New Hampshire and Maine concerning Mr. Dorr. 224

CHAPTER XVI.

Report of a Committee of the House of Representatives in the Congress of the United States. — Also, Speech of Hon. Mr. Allen, of Ohio. 230

CHAPTER XVII.

Propositions for the Release of Mr. Dorr, on Condition that he will engage to support the existing Constitution. — He refuses, and is afterwards set at Liberty by an Act of General Amnesty. — Rejoicings and Congratulations, &c. 266

CONTENTS.

CHAPTER XVIII.

An Act of the Rhode Island Legislature to reverse and annul the Judgment of the Supreme Court against Mr. Dorr. . . . 280

CHAPTER XIX.

Sketch of Mr. Dorr's Life. 284

APPENDIX.

Charter of 1643, granted under the Authority of Parliament. . 295

Charter granted by King Charles II. 298

Constitution of the State of Rhode Island and Providence Plantations, adopted by the People December 27th, 28th, and 29th, 1841. 317

Constitution of the State of Rhode Island and Providence Plantations, adopted November, 1842. 346

THE
LIFE AND TIMES
OF
THOMAS WILSON DORR.

CHAPTER I.

THE EARLY HISTORY OF THE GOVERNMENT OF RHODE ISLAND AND PROVIDENCE PLANTATIONS.

SEVENTEEN years have sped their hasty round since the crisis of the great political controversy in Rhode Island, and we have reason to hope that the stormy passions which that occasion generated have in a great measure subsided. Many of the principal actors in those trying scenes have since passed away; the boy who then lay in his cradle has now become a man, and almost an entire new generation has come upon the stage. We have no desire unnecessarily to stir up again the smouldering fires, or to rekindle that angry spirit which raged with so much fury in that eventful period; but it is hoped now, when time has so far quieted the passions and mellowed the feelings, when a sufficient period has been allowed for the exercise of that sober second thought which finally approves of the right and condemns the wrong, we may safely "submit the facts to a candid world." But if we are mistaken — if it is yet too soon — there is still one consolation left, and that is, that the time will some day come, when all the prejudice, and interest, and passion that were developed on that occasion shall have wholly passed away, and nothing but stubborn facts, in all their nakedness, shall imprint their undying images on the page of history. Time will eventually sweep away every minor interest, and every sinister motive, cool every passion, and hush in perpetual silence every angry feeling. Let the present time be thought too soon or too late, the day of assize will assuredly come, and posterity will pass its stern decrees upon all acts that history shall bring before that tribunal.

The history of THOMAS WILSON DORR and his times involves some of the most important principles of civil government. The question is not simply whether Mr. Dorr acted wisely or unwisely, nor whether he and his associates were patriots or felons, but whether the motives by which they were actuated were in accordance with the great principles of American democracy. In order to have a correct and thorough understanding of the subject, we must go back and make ourselves acquainted with the early history of Rhode Island, and the doctrines held by its founders. We must take into consideration the inherent, inalienable natural rights of man, and the purposes for which governments are instituted. We must notice the circumstances under which the government of Rhode Island came into existence, and trace its history down to the period in question.

Let it not be supposed that the great problem that we are to solve has respect only to those few individuals who were actively engaged in the controversy, or that it is confined to the territory of Rhode Island, or to any number of states, or even the United States. It involves the principles of popular sovereignty — the right of the people themselves, in their own time, and in their own way, to set up a new government or change an old one. This is the most grave of all political questions, and deserves to be well considered by every American citizen; its importance cannot be confined to any age or country, but it must concern all men throughout all time. The first settlers of the American colonies repudiated the aristocratic doctrines of the mother country, and held that the people should be considered as the true source of all civil power. This principle is fully developed in the early history of Rhode Island. Perhaps no man ever entertained more liberal views of civil and religious freedom than Roger Williams; and for the sole purpose of enjoying that freedom, he and his associates planted their infant colony upon the borders of Narragansett Bay. Here they sought to establish and perpetuate the true principles of rational liberty. The settlement was commenced in 1636, and the following is one of their earliest records: —

"We, whose names are hereunder, desirous to inhabit in the town of Providence, do promise to subject ourselves, in active or passive obedience, to all such orders or agreements as shall be made for public good of the body in an orderly way, by the major assent of the present inhabitants, masters of families, incorporated together into a *town-fellowship*, and such *others whom they shall admit unto them,* only in civil things."

This compact plainly indicates their civil and religious sentiments. They declared that in all civil things the majority should govern, but left every one at liberty to follow the dictates of his own conscience in all matters of religion. About the year 1637, another settlement was commenced on the Island of Rhode Island by a Mr. Coddington and his associates. Among their early records it appears that, " At a General Court of Elections, it was ordered and unanimously agreed, that this government was a democracy, or popular government, and that the power to make laws and depute magistrates to execute them, was in the body of freemen, orderly assembled, or a major part of them."

Smarting with the rigor of Puritan intolerance, they became extremely anxious to guard their own colony against any encroachments upon their religious freedom; therefore, in 1638, it was ordered by the General Court, " None shall be received as inhabitants or freemen, to build or plant upon the island, but such as shall be received in, by consent of the body, and do submit to the government that is or shall be established according to the word of God."

It is obvious that the sole purpose for which this order was made was to exclude from that community all who were not supporters of their own doctrine of religious liberty. Freedom of opinion in all matters of conscience was made the test; no other qualification was required.

In 1644, the towns of Providence, Portsmouth, and Newport, which had thus far been separate settlements or townships, were united under one government, by a charter which Roger Williams, through the aid of Sir Henry Vane, obtained from the Parliament under the Commonwealth of England. This charter conferred upon the inhabitants " full power and authority to govern and rule themselves, by such a form of civil government as, by voluntary consent of all or the greatest part of them, shall be found most serviceable in their estates and condition " — provided such form of civil government " be conformable to the laws of England, so far as the nature and constitution of the place will admit."

This charter, which will be found in the Appendix, No. 1, left the colonists free to maintain their principles of religious liberty, and by an early act of their General Court, it was ordered that " all men may walk as their consciences persuade them, every one in the name of his God." Bancroft, describing the condition of Rhode Island under the first charter, says, " All men were equal; all might meet in the public assemblies; all might aspire to office; the people for a season constituted its own tribune, and every public law required confirmation in the primary assemblies. The government of Rhode Island and Providence Plantations continued under this charter until 1663, when the inhabitants of the colony, fearing that a commission which had been obtained from Cromwell's Parliament, whilst Charles II. was in exile, might not be respected by him on his return to the throne, petitioned the King, and at length, through the agency of Mr. John Clarke, obtained a new charter, having the broad seal of the crown, and the signature of the secretary affixed. For this second charter, see No. 2 of the Appendix.

On looking over the early history of Rhode Island and Providence Plantations, we find that, at first, two little distinct democratic communities were established, one at Providence, and the other on the Island of Rhode Island. In a few years we find that by consent of a majority of the inhabitants in both settlements, without ceremony or form of law, the two colonies were merged in one, under a British charter, in conformity to which a government was organized and continued until about the year 1663. Then, again, a portion of the inhabitants, without any legal forms or provisions, but by general consent, made application to the King of Great Britain for a new charter, which was to make radical and important changes in their system of government. Their request was granted, and Mr. Baxter proudly returned with the royal document. And how was it adopted? Not by a formal vote in town meeting, but the people, hearing the good news, ran together at Newport, and received it by one spontaneous acclamation. This charter was a written compact between Great Britain and the colonists; it implied allegiance on the one part, and protection on the other. The colony became a British province, its inhabitants were British subjects, and all the authority of the government under the charter was derived from the British crown. This good old charter, as it has often been called, continued in full force and virtue until the tie which bound the colony to the mother country was severed by a sovereign act of the people when they declared themselves independent. As soon as that was done — as soon as Rhode Island, with her sister colonies, declared herself absolved from all connection with Great Britain, and assumed to be an independent state — in that hour the good old charter died, and forever after became a dead letter. Here was a complete abrogation of all its constitutional authority, and political power returned to the people at large. Under these circumstances a majority of the inhabitants of the colony, in accordance with those democratic principles which had marked all their former proceedings, might have instantly set themselves at work to form and establish a written constitution. But like a clap of thunder war broke upon them, and they had no quiet hours to deliberate upon a constitution. Rhode Island was of easy access to the British navy, and British troops were soon quartered in her bosom; public and private concerns were swallowed up in the spirit of heroism; they left "the deer and the steer, and their nets and barges," and rushed to the defence of their common country; and nobly did they acquit themselves.

Rhode Island soldiers mingled in every conflict; her Spartan bands fought with a courage and determination never surpassed; free as water they poured their blood upon the altar of their country, and without a murmur cheerfully sacrificed their lives in the great cause of freedom; and through all future time that state may well be proud of the part she bore in the American Revolution.

CHAPTER II.

THE ABROGATION OF THE ROYAL CHARTER BY THE DECLARATION OF INDEPENDENCE. ITS DEFECTS AND PRACTICAL INJUSTICE, AND EFFORTS OF THE PEOPLE TO BRING ABOUT A CHANGE.

As we have said before, all the authority of the British government in Rhode Island became extinguished as soon as the people refused to recognize it, and declared the colony independent; but if any one should be disposed to deny that, there can certainly be no doubt that the absolution was fully consummated by the treaty of peace made in 1783. Whatever period may be fixed upon as that of the full emancipation of the inhabitants of the colony from the government of Great Britain, that was the time when the official authority of all who held under the charter ceased and terminated ; that was the time when all political power returned to the people ; the officers of the government, in its several departments, became tenants at will, and liable at any time to be ejected by the people in the exercise of their natural and unalienable rights; and if at that time, as they had twice done before, they had of their own accord, without any legal provision, met and conferred together in order to devise some plan by which the sentiments of the whole people, or the major part of them, should be ascertained and made known, and, if finally a decided majority had manifested their wishes by adopting, in a regular public manner, a written constitution for the government of the state, such constitution would have been of undoubted validity, and every where acknowledged as the supreme law of the state. But we have been told that when the authority of Charles II. ceased, it vested immediately in the legislature. Could that be so? Does the agent retain power after the authority of the principal who granted it ceases? Certainly not. That would be a violation of every principle of law and reason. It must therefore be acknowledged that there was a time, after the abrogation of the charter, when the people of Rhode Island might have proceeded in their own way to form and adopt a constitution. They were no longer a colony of Great Britain, but of themselves an independent, sovereign state. Yet they suffered the government to go on in form and name as though the old, defunct parchment still retained its original validity; and from 1776 to 1841 the people made no efficient effort to establish a written constitution.

Now, if, in 1776, the inhabitants, or a major part of them, might rightfully and properly have proceeded, in their own way, and formed a written constitution, when, we ask, did that right cease? When was it forfeited? Why might not the inhabitants of that territory as well and as rightfully proceed, in their original, sovereign capacity, to form and establish a written rule of government in 1841, as at any former period? It is said to be a maxim in the English government, that " time does not run against the King." By this rule, in a democratic government, time does not run against the people, and, therefore, what they had a right to do in 1776, they had a right to do in 1841.

But we are told that a government once established cannot be rightfully changed otherwise than through the government itself. According to that doctrine, as soon as a government of any sort is once set up, whatever may be its effects or tendencies, the people lose all control over it, and are forever bound to yield obedience to it, unless, by humbling themselves, they can induce the powers that be to modify it. These are not democratic, but despotic, doctrines, and they ill become the American Republic.

We are told that when the people wish to bring about a change in their government, they must do it in a constitutional manner, and proceed according to prescribed forms. This might be true to a certain extent, when the state already had a written constitution which contained provisions for its amendment. But Rhode Island can hardly be said to have had a constitution at the time the controversy broke out. After the people, by their declaration of independence, had annulled the authority of the royal charter, they never proposed to adopt that instrument as the constitution of the state; and if they had done so, it would have afforded them no relief, because it contained no provision for any change. That power was vested exclusively in the British crown. The people themselves could never change it; therefore no such provision was made.

Under these circumstances, the people must either

yield an abject submission to a government which was little better than usurpation — a government which acknowledged no constitutional limits to its authority, and denied the natural rights of men — or they must seek relief by an appeal to a majority of the people in their sovereign capacity. They chose the latter; and although the result was disastrous to some of its principal agents, yet the time will come when the world will applaud their course, and justify their conduct.

We shall now proceed to point out some of the principal causes which induced the people to desire a reform.

And first, it was thought to be inconsistent with the honor and dignity of the people of a sovereign state to suffer the government to be regulated by a musty charter, which never had any authority except as a commission from a British King. After the authority of the crown was repudiated, the legislature assumed absolute and unlimited power; that body claimed the right to regulate the elective franchise, and made and unmade their own electors; it held and exercised a most improper and dangerous influence over the judiciary by making the judges dependent on that body for their annual election. This was the precarious tenure by which every judge in the state held his office.

In such a condition, there could be no safe and independent judiciary. Both the judges and the causes which they were to determine became the sport of party controversies. It has been elsewhere eloquently said, " A judge should sit serenely above all the storms of political strife, that he may rightly divide the justice of the law between man and man; he should have nothing to hope from party ascendency, and nothing to fear from the fall of political friends."

The Hon. William E. Goddard, late Professor of Moral Philosophy in Brown University, in an address delivered at the inauguration of the legislature under the present constitution, at Newport, May 3, 1843, made use of the following language, as appears from a printed report of that address : —

"In truth, my fellow-citizens, without a judiciary which feels itself to be independent of the legislative power, no constitution is worth the parchment upon which it is engrossed. Without a judiciary there can be no freedom under a popular government. Without such a judiciary, civilization in its higher forms can make no advance."

And, strange as it may seem, this declaration was publicly and solemnly made by one who eulogized the old royal charter, and bitterly opposed the people's constitution.

The restriction of the privilege of suffrage to freeholders and their eldest sons excluded from voting quite a large class of citizens, and incidentally became the cause of much fraud and corruption at the polls. In 1841, and for many years previous, the right to vote was limited by law to such only as could show a deed of some freehold estate, supposed to be worth one hundred and thirty-four dollars, and the eldest sons of such freeholders. In times of strong party excitement, a great portion of the unscrupulous non-freeholders were qualified to vote by sham deeds of estates in which they really had no interest; and to so great an extent was this fraud carried, that in many towns it was supposed that one fourth of all who voted in town meeting were so qualified. In many instances one sham deed, by qualifying the father, made two voters by qualifying his eldest son at the same time. It will be recollected, also, that many of those who consented to be thus qualified were not of the most reliable class of citizens, because many high-minded men despised such dishonest means.

When her brave soldiers returned from the war of the revolution, scarred, broken down, and exhausted by their long service in the cause of their country, a great majority found themselves excluded and shut out from all participation in that government for which they had labored so ardently, and sacrificed so much. They found the government a landed oligarchy, and because they had become poor in the service of their country, and had little left but worthless continental paper, although they had been victorious abroad, they found themselves outlawed at home. They were told that non-freeholders were not considered as citizens, that they had no natural rights, and that the word *people* meant those, and those only, who had been made such by legislative enactment.

As agriculture declined, and commercial, mechanical, and manufacturing employments increased, the number excluded from the privilege of voting was continually on the increase, so that some in every town, and large numbers of good citizens in many towns, were cut off from the privilege of voting. Many of these disfranchised citizens owned large amounts of personal estate;

among them were men of learning, enterprise, and character. In many towns they paid a large share of the taxes, and throughout the state they constituted by far the largest portion of the military; they were required by law to purchase and provide themselves with arms and military equipments, to perform duty at stated times in every year, and to hold themselves in readiness for any service which the state authorities might require of them; and yet, for all this, they received no compensation, but were denounced by the charter authorities as the *rabble*, that had no interest in the government of their country.

The charter legislature claimed to be the sovereign power of the state, and exercised unrestricted control over the elective franchise; and although in 1841, only real estate of the value of one hundred and thirty-four dollars was required to make a freeman, yet the amount required had formerly been much higher. In 1729, two hundred pounds, or more than six hundred dollars, was required, and in 1746, the legislature passed an act restricting the right to vote to those only who at the time of their voting possessed in their own right real estate of the value of four hundred pounds, or something more than thirteen hundred dollars; yet the right of primogeniture was always respected, and the eldest sons of qualified freeholders were always allowed to vote; and this feudal right was continued by the charter government up to the time of the present constitution.

There can be no more dangerous feature in any government than the control of the elective franchise by the legislature; because, in that case, there is no legal impediment between freedom and despotism.

But the denial of the right to vote was not the only disability to which non-freeholders were subjected. A non-freeholder, by himself, without the aid of some freeholder, was not protected by the laws of the state; he could not commence or maintain any action for the collection of a debt, and if he was assaulted and wounded in his person, he could have no process against the offender, unless some freeholder would consent to indorse his name upon the back of the writ. By statute this was required in every case before a non-freeholder could pray out a writ, and without such indorsement the law afforded him no protection whatever. Again, non-freeholders were not allowed to serve as jurors, yet they were required in all cases to be tried by juries composed exclusively of freeholders; the non-freeholder, therefore, was not tried by a jury of his peers, but by a privileged class to which he did not belong. This was a flagrant violation of the great principle of common law, which allows every man to be tried by his equals.

It is said that the charter of Charles II. was first drawn up in Rhode Island, according to the views and wishes of the principal inhabitants, and subsequently carried to England to receive the royal signature; and there is little doubt that the assignment of representatives to the several towns was fair, and based upon the population at that time. Newport, which had the largest number of inhabitants, was allowed six; Portsmouth, Warwick, and Providence, being perhaps about equal in population, were each allowed four; and, that none should be unrepresented, every other town was allowed two representatives. But, in 1841, almost two centuries had passed since the adoption of the charter, and the population had so changed as to make that allotment very unequal. From the census of the United States for 1840, it appears that the town of Providence had at that time more than forty thousand inhabitants, which was very near one third of the whole population of the state at that time; yet Providence was allowed but four representatives in the legislature, whilst every small town continued to send two. Several of these towns had each less than one thousand inhabitants, and by comparing the census of the state with the charter, it is seen that less than one third of the inhabitants of the state under the charter elected a majority of the representatives in the legislature. And if we examine the subject still more closely, we shall find that a little more than one third of that third, or one ninth of the whole number of inhabitants, might control the legislature. According to the census of 1840, the number of white male citizens over twenty-one years of age was about twenty-five thousand; and we find from authentic returns, that the whole number of votes polled that year for presidential electors was eight thousand six hundred and sixty-two. This, we believe, was the largest vote ever polled under the charter. By this it appears that only about one third of all the male citizens over twenty-one years of age were voters, and this third in the small towns, as we said before, elected a majority of the House of Representatives.

Under these circumstances the intelligent, liberal-minded young men felt aggrieved; and it is said that some even removed out of the state for no other reason than because they were held as vassals at home. When they looked abroad, they saw no such invidious distinction in any other state. They found non-freeholders and young men respected as citizens, and often occupying responsible official stations. The disparaged condition of non-freeholders in Rhode Island was dishonorable to the state, and humiliating to its citizens; it repressed emulation and discouraged enterprise.

Now, under all the circumstances which have been mentioned, it may well be supposed that an intelligent people, who were jealous of their rights, would be very desirous to bring about important changes in the government; and a history of their proceedings shows that to have been the case. Soon after the revolution, Congress recommended to the several states to organize governments and form constitutions which should be adapted to the great change which had taken place in their condition, and nearly all the states complied with the recommendation. A committee was soon after appointed by the General Assembly of Rhode Island to take the matter into consideration; but it does not appear that they made any report. In 1797, the necessity of forming a constitution was zealously urged by some of their ablest statesmen. In 1811, the subject was again brought before the legislature, and an act extending the right of suffrage passed the Senate, but was rejected in the House. Again, in 1820, the subject was agitated; and a convention was holden in the county of Providence to consider what measures should be made use of to bring about the desired reform. It was there declared " *that a free people have for more than forty years submitted to a species of government in theory, if not always in practice, as despotic as that of the autocrat of the Russias.*"

And, speaking of the General Assembly, they said, " That omnipotent body should consider that the *people* are competent to form a convention for themselves, and that any longer delay on the part of the legislature would be likely to produce such a result."

In 1824, a convention, called the "Freemen's Convention," met and formed a constitution. This constitution did not answer the demands of the people; it made no extension of the right of suffrage, but proposed, by a constitutional enactment, to place relief beyond the power of the legislature. This constitution was submitted to the "freemen" only, and by them rejected.

In 1829, several petitions and memorials, asking for a republican constitution and an extension of suffrage, were presented to the legislature. These memorials contained, in all, the names of about two thousand men, who certified that they were permanent residents of the state; many of the signers were freeholders, and known to be of good standing in the community. These memorials were referred to a committee, of whom the Hon. Benjamin Hazard, of Newport, was chairman. That committee made a very long report, which was printed and extensively circulated. The committee, in their report, assumed a tone of authority which was evidently designed to repress the efforts of the people, and give them to understand that the General Assembly would never make any concessions to them. Although the committee knew, and every body knew, that every other state in the Union had long since given their musty charters to the moles and the bats, and were governed by written constitutions, which the people had formed and adopted for themselves, yet the committee proceeded to say of the charter of Charles II., " No constitution before or since the revolution has been framed — none can be framed — more free and popular."

The committee well knew that the charter government in Rhode Island was the subject of ridicule abroad; but their report goes on to say, " Let strangers, if they please, treat this instrument with levity, and hold it up as a reproach to the state, but let *us* continue to be proud of it." The committee say that they cannot understand the meaning of the term " natural rights," and declare that the only political *right* which belongs to men in society is the *right to comply with the demands of their rulers.* They declare that " the whole science of legislation and jurisprudence is exercised in application to the rights of property," and that those who have little or no property have " no claims upon us more than the rights of hospitality, and the protection of our laws." The committee go on to argue the feudal right of the eldest son to vote, to the exclusion of the younger brothers; and although it was held that the sovereign power of the state was fixed in the General Assembly, yet they declared in their report that that body had no power to grant the relief which the petitioners asked for. The report says, "If the representatives of the people, chosen for the ordinary purposes of legislation, could assume a control over the right of suffrage, to limit, curtail, or extend it at will, they might on the one hand disfranchise any portion they pleased of their own electors, and thereby deprive them of power ever to remove their representatives, and therefore reduce the government to a permanent aristocracy."

Now, the committee who made that report, and held up to the petitioners the danger that would attend the exercise of that power by a legislative body, knew very well, at the same time, that their own General Assembly had claimed and exercised that same unjust and dangerous power for nearly two hundred years; and it was nothing less than gross insult and mockery to foist upon the petitioners the tissue of reproach and falsehood of which that report was made up.

In conclusion, the committee say, "We ought to recollect that all the evils which may result from an extension of suffrage will be evils beyond our reach. We shall entail them upon our latest posterity without remedy. Open this door, and the whole frame and character of our institutions are changed forever."

We have been thus particular in noting that report, because it was intended as a final answer to all applications for the extension of suffrage, or a written constitution. It was considered at the time to be a masterly production, and held by the government to be perfectly orthodox in sentiment. A very able member of the legislature at that time made the following declaration in the House of Representatives: "Sir, I conceive that this body has the same power over the non-freeholders of this state that *the Almighty has over the universe.*"

In 1832, the same subject was agitated without effect. In 1834, a constitutional party was organized, which, after struggling two or three years, was abandoned. In the mean time another "freeholders'" convention was called to draught a constitution. This convention, by a vote of about ten to one, refused to extend the right of suffrage, and after a session of two or three weeks, dismissed the whole subject and returned home. Thus matters went on until 1840, and nothing was accomplished. For nearly half a century the people had been struggling against the tyranny of an unauthorized legislature, in fruitless endeavors to obtain a republican constitution, that should protect them from the abuses of power, and guarantee equal rights to all the citizens. During that half century, the government had succeeded in baffling every effort of the people. Time after time the disfranchised, in the language of humble supplicants, implored the government to recognize them as citizens, and grant them relief. Time after time, they were driven away, as from the throne of a despot, and obliged to abandon their efforts in hopeless despair. One class of applicants became worn out, and retired — others followed them — again and again the people renewed their efforts with the same mortifying result, and a whole generation passed away in fruitless endeavors to establish a republican form of government.

The people of Rhode Island, a quiet, peace-loving,

law-abiding community, submitted to the tyranny, whilst they still clung to their own anchor of hope, confiding in the justice of their cause, and looking to an overruling Providence for ultimate success. When, we ask, in the history of the whole world, has an enlightened people borne so long and so much?

CHAPTER III.

PROCEEDINGS OF THE PEOPLE IN FORMING AND ADOPTING A CONSTITUTION.

THE extraordinary excitement which attended the presidential election, in 1840, for a time overcame all local interests, and nearly all those who had previously composed the suffrage party were drawn into the ranks of one or the other of the two great contending parties. But as soon as that election was over, and its temporary enthusiasm quieted, the disfranchised, with other liberal-minded citizens of the state, returned again to the consideration of a written constitution. To the friends of suffrage the field now appeared clear of almost all other political controversies, and all seemed to say, " Now is the day and now is the hour " to strike for constitutional liberty. The subject assumed a grave aspect, and engaged the serious attention of the people of the whole state. Men of the highest legal attainments, who were not influenced by selfish motives, entered into the interests of the suffrage party, and the best judges of constitutional matters, in and out of the state, decided that the people of Rhode Island had an undoubted right to form and adopt a written constitution, without the concurrence of the legislature. The people were assured that the American governments were founded upon popular sovereignty, and that the expressed will of a decided majority of the people must be regarded as the supreme law of the state.

The course of the suffrage party now seemed clear. A large association was organized in Providence, and auxiliary associations were soon formed in other parts of the state. At the January session of the General Assembly, 1841, a memorial, numerously signed, was received from the town of Smithfield, asking for an addition to the number of her representatives in the legislature. Upon that memorial the House passed the following resolution : —

Resolved, by the General Assembly, (the Senate concurring with the House of Representatives therein,) That the freemen of the several towns in this state, and of the city of Providence, qualified to vote for general officers, be, and they are hereby, requested to choose, at their semi-annual town or ward meetings in August next, so many delegates, and of like qualifications, as they are now respectively entitled to choose representatives to the General Assembly, to attend a convention to be holden at Providence on the first Monday of November, 1841, to frame a new constitution for this state, either in whole or in part, with full powers for this purpose ; and if only for a constitution in part, that said convention have under their especial consideration the expediency of equalizing the representation of the towns in the House of Representatives.

It will be seen that none but qualified *freemen* were allowed to vote for delegates to that convention.

The action of the legislature upon that petition plainly showed a fixed determination to yield nothing to the people, and the friends of reform became satisfied that nothing could be gained by applications to the General Assembly, and therefore resolved, as a last resort, to carry their cause before the whole people of the state. Accordingly, a mass meeting was convened in the city of Providence, on the 18th of April, 1841. Here several thousands assembled, and in a quiet and orderly manner, conferred together upon the great question at issue. This mass convention adjourned to meet at Newport on the 5th of May following. The adjourned meeting was numerously attended, and a large number of highly respected freeholders were among its most active members. The following preamble and resolutions were passed at that meeting : —

Whereas, It is the undeniable right of the people, at all times, peaceably to assemble for consultation and conference touching the government under which they live, and which they assist in supporting ; and independently to utter and set forth, on such occasions of meeting together, their views, sentiments, and plans relative to the correction, as well of defects in the organization of government, as of faults in the administration of the same : We, a portion of the people of this state, now assembled at Newport in mass convention, from all parts of the state, and acting on behalf of the great body of our unenfranchised fellow-citizens, do declare their and our opinions and purposes in the following resolutions : —

1. *Resolved*, That it is repugnant to the spirit of the Declaration of American Independence, and derogatory to the character of Rhode Island republicans, to acknowledge the charter of a British King as a constitution of political government. While we venerate the illustrious names of Roger Williams and John Clarke, to whose untiring ability and perseverance the colony

of Rhode Island was indebted for this grant from the throne of England, so well adapted at the time to the wants of his majesty's subjects, and so liberal in its concessions, — we are at the same time aware that in almost all respects, excepting the immortal declaration and guarantee of religious freedom, it has become insufficient and obsolete; that it should be laid aside in the archives of the state, and no longer be permitted to subsist as a barrier against the rights and liberties of the people.

2. *Resolved*, That, in the opinion of this convention, on the occurrence of the American revolution, when the ties of allegiance which bound the subjects of this colony to the throne of England were dissolved, the rights of sovereignty, in accordance with the principles of republican government, passed to the whole body of the people of this state, and not to any special or favored portion of the same; that the whole people were, and are, the just and rightful successors of the British King, and as such were and are entitled to alter, amend, or annul the form and provisions of government then and now subsisting, with the sole restriction imposed by the constitution of the United States; and, in their original and sovereign capacity, to devise and substitute such a constitution as they may deem to be best adapted to the general welfare.

3. *Resolved*, That no lapse of time can bar the sovereignty inherent in the people of this state; and that their omission to form a constitution, and their toleration of the abuses under which they have so long labored, are to be regarded as proof of their long suffering and forbearance, rather than as arguments against their power and their capacity to right themselves, whenever, in their opinion, redress from the governments at present subsisting is hopeless.

4. *Resolved*, That the time has now fully arrived for a vigorous and concentrated effort to accomplish a

thorough and permanent reform in the political institutions of this state.

5. *Resolved,* That a system of government under which the legislative body exercise power undefined and uncontrolled by fundamental laws, according to its own " especial grace, certain knowledge, and mere motion," and limits and restricts, and makes and unmakes, the people at its pleasure, is anti-republican, and odious in its character and operations, at war with the spirit of the age, and repugnant to the feelings of every right-minded Rhode Island man, and ought to be abated.

6. *Resolved,* That the public good imperatively requires that the powers of the legislature, and rights of the citizens, should be defined and fixed by a written state constitution.

7. *Resolved,* That the representation of the towns in the General Assembly, as originally established by the provisions of the charter of King Charles II., had refference to the then existing population of the same, and was at that time not unfairly adjusted to it; but that, by the great increase of population in the towns, the existing apportionment has become exceedingly unequal and unjust in its operations; and that a new assignment of representatives among the towns, according to population, will be an indispensable article in a constitution for this state. A majority of the representatives to the General Assembly are now elected by towns containing less than one third of the population of the state, and some of the towns from twice to twenty times what they are entitled to under the just principles of distribution above named — an inequality not uncommon in the monarchies of Europe, but with the single exception of Rhode Island, unknown in the United States.

8. *Resolved,* That, at the foundation of this state, and long after, property in land was not only the principal property of the citizens, but was so easily attainable, that a landed qualification for voters (first definitely

established in the colony by the legislature in 1724) excluded only a small portion of the people from political power; but that the circumstances of the people have since greatly changed, and the existing qualification for voting has the effect, contrary to the designs of those who first established it, of excluding the great majority of sixteen thousand, or twenty-five thousand, over the age of twenty-one years, from all political privileges, and participation in the affairs of government; and that, although we entertain a high and becoming respect for farmers, and their just influence in the state, we are not insensible to the merits of their younger sons — of the mechanics, the merchants, the workingmen, and others — who own no land ; and that we are of opinion that the longer continuance of a landed qualification for voters is a great injustice, and is contrary to the spirit and principles of a republican government; and that a constitution for this state will be altogether insufficient, unsatisfactory, and impracticable, that does not restore to the body of the people of this state the rights and principles of American citizens.

9. *Resolved*, That a continuance of the provisions of the charter relating to representation, and of the act of the legislature requiring a freehold estate to entitle a citizen to vote for public officers, has the effect not only to vest the control of the General Assembly, as we have before seen, in less than one third of the population, but as the voters in this third are only a third part of the whole number of male adult citizens, this further effect also — the most odious of all — of placing the control of the Assembly and the state in one ninth part of its adult population; or, in other words, in the hands of less than three thousand men out of twenty-five thousand who are over twenty-one years of age.

10. *Resolved*, That such a state of things is a bold and hardy defiance of all popular rights, and is a total

departure from the principles advanced at the first session of the General Assembly in the year 1647, who then solemnly declared and voted that the government of this state should be a democracy.

11. *Resolved*, That the American system of government is a government of men, and not of property; and that while it provides for the ample protection and safe enjoyment and transmission of property, it confers upon it no political advantages, but regards all men as free and equal, and exacts from them no price for the exercise of their birthright; and that, therefore, the undoubted rights and privileges of the people, as well as the true honor and prosperity of the state, can only be completely obtained and permanently insured by a written constitution, whose framers shall be chosen from the people of the towns, in proportion to population, and which shall be approved and ratified by the people at large; and that, in the exercise of this high act of sovereignty, every American citizen, whose actual permanent residence or home is in this state, has a right to participate. And we accordingly pledge ourselves individually to each other, and collectively to the public, that we will use our unremitting exertions for such a constitution, in the way that has been described.

12. *Resolved*, That we disclaim all action with or for any particular party in this great question of state rights, reserving to ourselves individually our own opinions on all matters of state or national politics, which we call upon no man to sacrifice; and that we heartily invite the earnest coöperation of men of all political parties in the cause which we have at heart, and which we believe to be the cause of liberty, equality, and justice to all men.

13. *Resolved*, That the General Assembly should have called the convention to frame a constitution in such a manner as to apportion the delegates to the convention among the several towns, according to popula-

tion, and to give to every American citizen as aforesaid the right of voting for delegates, and for the constitution which may be proposed for the ratification of the people.

14. *Resolved,* That the friends of reform in each town be requested forthwith to establish an association for the purpose of a better organization for correspondence, and generally for the promotion of the objects of this convention.

15. *Resolved,* That a state committee of eleven persons be appointed by this convention to correspond with the associations of the several towns, and to carry forward the cause of reform and equal rights, and to call a convention of delegates to draught a constitution at as early a day as possible.

16. *Resolved,* That the state committee be requested to obtained, without delay, a list of all the citizens in the several towns who are ready to vote for and sustain a constitution based on the principles hereinbefore declared, and to present the same at the adjourned meeting.

17. *Resolved,* That the state committee be requested to prepare and send forth an address to the people of this state on the subjects contained in the foregoing resolutions, and to report proceedings at an adjourned meeting.

18. *Resolved,* That a copy of these resolutions be transmitted to the governor, to the lieutenant governor, and to each member of the Senate and House of Representatives, whose attention is especially and respectfully asked to the resolution relative to the call of the convention for framing a constitution.

19. *Resolved,* that the support and patronage of all the friends of reform are urgently requested in behalf of the " New Age," a newspaper exclusively devoted to the cause which we have this day assembled to promote.

20. *Resolved,* That these resolutions be signed by the president and secretaries of the convention, and published in the several newspapers throughout the state, and that the publishers be requested to give them a gratuitous insertion in their respective papers.

21. *Resolved,* That this convention, when it adjourns, will adjourn to meet at Providence, on the 5th day of July next.

When the General Assembly held their session in June following, several leading members of the suffrage party came to the conclusion that if the legislature would adopt a resolution authorizing non-freeholders to vote for delegates to the convention which was to meet in November following, it would be advisable to postpone any further action until that convention should have met. Accordingly, the Hon. Samuel Y. Atwell, then a member of the House, was requested to use his exertions for that purpose; and in compliance with that request, the records of that session show that Mr. Atwell, then chairman of the judiciary committee, did report a bill which provided that all who had paid a town or state tax, on real or personal estate, within one year, should be allowed to vote for delegates to that convention. This proposition, after a spirited debate, was rejected by a vote of fifty-two to ten. This showed plainly enough that non-freeholders could expect no relief from the General Assembly.

And, on the 5th of July following, a large mass meeting was held by adjournment in the city of Providence, by which the following resolutions were adopted: —

Resolved, That on this, the anniversary (5th July,

1841) of our national independence, we recur, with emotions of deep and patriotic gratitude, to the principles, the measures, and the men of the American revolution.

Resolved, That the doctrines of liberty and equality, first promulgated in modern times by the immortal founders of our state, and re-asserted by the illustrious author of the Declaration of Independence, lie at the foundation of all that is just and free in our political institutions; and that the vindication of these doctrines, when impaired, and the development of them in all their force and effect, are duties of the most sacred and imperative obligation, and enjoined upon us by the venerable fathers, who, being dead, yet speak to us, by our character as republicans and as men, and by our regard to the rights and interests of our successors.

Resolved, That, in the language of Jefferson, "It is not only the right, but the duty, of those now on the stage of action, to change the laws and institutions of government, to keep pace with the progress of knowledge, the lights of science, and the amelioration of the condition of society;" — and that "nothing is to be considered unchangeable but the inherent and unalienable rights of man."

Resolved, That the political institutions of this state have long since lost their character of liberty and equality which belong to a republic; and that, inasmuch as, in the words of Washington, "the basis of our political institutions is the right of the people to make and to alter their constitutions," it has now become the duty of the people of Rhode Island, acting upon the principles which have been recited, and animated by the example of their patriotic ancestors, to apply with a firm hand, without unnecessary delay, and in their original and sovereign capacity, the necessary corrective to existing political evils, by the formation and adoption of a written republican state constitution.

Resolved, " That we unanimously and cordially reaffirm the views, sentiments, and plans " set forth in their resolutions by the convention of the friends of equal rights, held at Newport on the 5th day of May last; and that, inasmuch as the General Assembly of this state, at their last session, in June, have finally decided that the freeholders are exclusively the people of Rhode Island, and have denied to the great majority of the people, so far as it is in their power thus to deny, any participation in the convention to be held in November next, the time has now fully arrived for the people, in their original and sovereign capacity, to exercise their reserved rights; and that we hereby approve the call by the state committee of the people's convention, on the basis of the resolutions aforesaid, at an early day, for the formation of a constitution.

Resolved, That when the constitution, so framed, shall be adopted by a majority of the whole people of the state, by their signatures or otherwise, as the convention may provide, we will sustain and carry into effect said constitution, by all necessary means; and that, so far as in us lies, we will remove all obstacles to its successful establishment and operation : and we hereunto solemnly pledge ourselves to each other and the public.

Resolved, That we hail with pleasure the presence among us of the venerable remnants of our revolutionary worthies ; and entertain the hope that they may be spared to witness another anniversary, when they will be deemed not only worthy of shedding their blood for the defence of their country, but of voting for their rulers, and of taking an equal share of the concerns of government.

Resolved, That we enter our solemn protest against the principles upon which the landholders' convention is called, as by that call a large majority of the people of this state are excluded from a participation in the choice of delegates to frame a constitution, by the provisions of which they are to be governed.

Resolved, That we deny the authority of the legislature to proscribe or prevent any portion of our fellow-citizens, who are permanent residents of this state, from a participation in the organization of the government, which is to affect the rights and privileges of all.

Resolved, That it is contrary to the spirit of a republican government for a minority to make laws that shall bind the majority ; and that we will resist to the utmost of our ability a government that shall not acknowledge the just rights of the whole people.

Resolved, That we will use all honorable means within our power to have every American citizen, who is a permanent resident in this state, represented in the convention for framing a constitution that shall define the powers of the legislature, and secure to the people the free exercise of their rights and privileges.

A state committee, composed of the following gentlemen, was elected : —

Newport County, . . { Charles Collins, Dutee J. Pearce, Silas Sisson.

Providence County, . { Samuel H. Wales, Benjamin Arnold, Jr., Welcome B. Sayles, Henry L. Webster, James B. Stiness, Metcalf Marsh.

Bristol County, . . . { Benjamin M. Bosworth, Samuel S. Allen, Abijah Luce.

Kent County, ... { Emanuel Rice, Silas Weaver, John B. Sheldon.

Washington County, . { Sylvester Himes, Wager Weeden, Charles Allen.

This committee met at Providence, on the 20th of July, and proceeded, according to instructions, to issue a call for the election of delegates, to take place on the 28th day of August following, to attend a convention to be holden at the state house in Providence, on the first Monday of October, for the purpose of framing such a democratic constitution as is guaranteed to every state in the Union by the constitution of the United States, and laying it before the people of the state for their adoption or rejection. The following votes were also passed : —

Voted, That every American male citizen, of twenty-one years of age and upwards, who has resided in this state one year preceding the election of delegates, shall vote for delegates to the convention called by the state committee, to be held at the state house in Providence, on the first Monday in October next.

Voted, That every meeting holden for the election of delegates to the state convention shall be organized by the election of a chairman and secretary, whose certificate shall be required of the delegates.

Voted, That each town of one thousand inhabitants, or less, shall be entitled to one delegate ; and for every additional thousand, one delegate shall be appointed ; and the city of Providence shall elect three delegates from each ward in the city.

Voted, That the chairman and secretary be directed

to cause one thousand handbills to be printed and distributed through the state, containing the call for a convention of delegates.

Voted, That the proceedings of this meeting be signed by the chairman and secretary, and be published.

On motion, voted, That this meeting stand adjourned, to meet at this place on the 1st day of September, at 11 o'clock, A. M.

In compliance with the foregoing recommendation, regularly-organized town meetings were held in all the towns in the state, on the 28th of August, and delegates were chosen to meet in convention at the time specified to form a constitution.

The delegates so elected met in convention at the state house, in the city of Providence, on the first Monday of October, 1841, and proceeded to form a constitution, which they caused to be published and circulated in every part of the state for examination. The convention then adjourned to meet again at the same place, on the 16th of November. The convention assembled according to adjournment, and after making some slight amendments, ordered the constitution, as finally agreed upon, to be again published, and afterwards to be submitted to the people for their adoption or rejection, on the 27th, 28th, and 29th of December following. The convention then adjourned to meet again on the 12th of January, 1842.

Perhaps no abler deliberative assembly than that which met to form the People's Constitution ever convened in the State of Rhode Island. The members received no compensation for their services — they met and labored for the sole purpose of forming for the people of the state a written constitution, adapted to their condition and wants.

The constitution was again printed and freely circulated throughout the state, and on the 27th, 28th, and 29th of December following, regularly-organized, open town meetings were held in all the towns of the state for its adoption or rejection. Never, before or since, was so large a vote polled in the State of Rhode Island in favor of any one object. Every American citizen over twenty-one years of age, who had resided in the state one year previous to the time of voting, was allowed to vote, by indorsing his name on the back of his ballot. Throughout the whole state, these meetings were conducted in a quiet and orderly manner. Every person who voted certified upon his ballot whether he was or was not qualified by statute to vote. Free from all the side issues, which often bias men in party contests, every voter was now at liberty to declare the honest sentiments of his heart.

The secretaries of all the town meetings held as aforesaid, preserved and forwarded to the constitutional convention all the ballots which were received in open town meeting; and on the 12th day of January, 1842, the convention reassembled and proceeded to count the ballots so returned, when it was found that 13,944 votes had been given for the constitution, and 52 only against it. Of the whole number who voted, 4960 were freeholders, who were qualified by statute to vote. It therefore appeared that a decided majority, not only of all the male citizens of the state over twenty-one years of age, but also a majority of all the qualified voters, had given their votes for the constitution. From the census of the United States for 1840, it appears, as near as can be ascertained, that the whole number of males in the state at that time over twenty-one years of age, was about 25,000. Now, if we deduct from that number all who were under guardians, the insane, and the idiots, and also those who had not resided in the state one year previous to the time of voting, the whole number of those who were competent to vote would not probably exceed 20,000; and of that number nearly 14,000 voted for the constitution. Again, we find that about 5000 of that 14,000 were qualified to vote, by statute; and by examining the annexed schedule, furnished by the secretary of state, we shall be satisfied that a good majority of all the qualified freemen voted for the constitution.

State of Votes for General Officers in the Elections, from 1832 to 1841, inclusive.

STATE OF RHODE ISLAND AND PROVIDENCE PLANTATIONS, } Secretary's Office, January 6, 1844.

I, Henry Bowen, secretary of said state, and keeper [L. S.] of the records and the seals thereof, do certify, that the whole number of votes for general officers, as reported by the counting committee appointed by the General Assembly at the May session, for the years after named, was as follows, viz. : —

For the year 1832, five thousand six hundred and fifteen.

For the year 1833, seven thousand three hundred and one.

For the year 1834, seven thousand two hundred and thirty-four.

For the year 1835, seven thousand six hundred and seventy-four.

For the year 1836, seven thousand one hundred and sixty-eight.

For the year 1837, four thousand two hundred and seventeen.

For the year 1838, seven thousand seven hundred and forty-six.

For the year 1839, six thousand two hundred and seventy-three.

For the year 1840, eight thousand two hundred and ninety-two.

For the year 1841, two thousand seven hundred and thirteen.

All which appears of record.

This vote gave the fullest assurance that a very large majority of all the people of the state were in favor of the constitution, and the convention therefore proceeded to declare it adopted, and issued and caused to be published the following proclamation: —

STATE OF RHODE ISLAND AND PROVIDENCE PLANTATIONS.

A PROCLAMATION.

Whereas the convention of the people of this state, at their last session, in the city of Providence, on the 13th day of January, A. D. 1842, passed the following resolutions, to wit: —

"Whereas, by the return of the votes upon the constitution proposed to the citizens of this state by this convention, on the 18th of November last, it satisfactorily appears that the citizens of this state, in their original and sovereign capacity, have ratified and adopted said constitution by a large majority; and the will of the people thus decisively made known, ought to be implicitly obeyed and faithfully executed : —

"We do, therefore, resolve and declare, that said constitution rightfully ought to be, and is, the paramount law and constitution of the State of Rhode Island and Providence Plantations.

"And we do further resolve and declare, for ourselves, and in behalf of the people whom we represent, that we will establish said constitution, and sustain and defend the same by all necessary means.

"*Resolved,* That the officers of this convention make proclamation of the return of the votes upon the constitution, and that the same has been adopted and has become the constitution of this state, and that they cause said proclamation to be published in the newspapers of the same."

Now, therefore, in obedience to the above vote of said convention, we, the undersigned, officers of the same, do hereby proclaim and make known to all the people of this state, that said constitution has been adopted by a large majority of the votes of the citizens of this state; and that said constitution of right ought to be, and is, the paramount law and constitution of the State of Rhode Island and Providence Plantations.

And we hereby call upon the citizens of the state to give their aid and support in carrying said constitution into full operation and effect, according to the terms and provisions thereof.

Witness our hands, at Providence, in said state, this 13th day of January, A. D. 1842.

JOSEPH JOSLIN,
President of the Convention.

WAGER WEEDEN,
SAMUEL H. WALES, } *Vice Presidents.*

WM. H. SMITH,
JOHN S. HARRIS, } *Secretaries.*

The constitution provided that the new government should commence and be organized at the expiration of the then existing political year. Article XIV. contained the following provisions : —

The present government shall exercise all the powers with which it is now clothed, until the said first Tuesday of May, one thousand eight hundred and forty-two, and until their successors, under this constitution, shall be duly elected and qualified.

All civil, judicial, and military officers now elected, or who shall hereafter be elected by the General Assembly, or other competent authority, before the said first Tuesday of May, shall hold their offices, and may exercise their powers, until that time.

All laws and statutes, public and private, now in force, and not repugnant to this constitution, shall continue in force until they expire by their own limitation, or are repealed by the General Assembly. All contracts, judgments, actions, and rights of action, shall be as valid as if this constitution had not been made. All debts contracted, and engagements entered into, before the adoption of this constitution, shall be as valid against the state as if this constitution had not been made.

The convention, before they adjourned, directed the committee which counted the votes to present to his excellency the governor a certified copy of the same, and also an attested copy of the constitution which the people had adopted, with a request that he should communicate the same to the two Houses of the General Assembly then in session.

That communication was made accordingly, signed by the following committee : —

William James, *Chairm.*
John R. Waterman,
Dutee J. Pearce,
David Daniels,
Oliver Chace, Jr.,
Robert R. Carr,
Ariel Ballou,
Thomas W. Dorr,
Samuel T. Hopkins,
Alfred Reed,
Wm. C. Barker,
Abner Haskell,
Alexander Allen,

Willard Hazard,
Welcome Ballou Sayles,
Sylv. Himes,
Israel Wilson,
Jonathan Remington,
Christ. Smith,
Elisha G. Smith,
Samuel Luther,
Erasmus D. Campbell,
Nathan Bardin,
Joshua B. Rathbun,
Nathan A. Brown.

Wm. H. Smith, } *Secretaries.*
John S. Harris,

PROVIDENCE, *January* 13, 1842.

Every step that had been taken had been done openly and boldly, with all due respect to the existing government. No attempts were made to disturb or invalidate any acts of the existing legislature, or other laws of the state, unless they should be found inconsistent with the constitution. The new government was not intended to *overthrow*, but to *succeed* the old. No state constitution was ever formed and adopted in a more quiet and orderly manner, or met a more hearty approval from the people. But it soon became evident that those who held the government would not willingly surrender their authority. The constitution and its framers and advocates were treated with a haughty contempt, and all available means were made use of to deter the people from supporting it.

CHAPTER IV.

LANDHOLDERS' CONSTITUTION FORMED AND REJECTED. PROCEEDINGS OF THE GENERAL ASSEMBLY. THE RIGHT OF THE PEOPLE TO FORM CONSTITUTIONS CONSIDERED, AND AUTHORITIES QUOTED.

IN the mean time the landholders' convention, which was composed of delegates chosen only by freemen, met and formed their constitution, which was ordered to be submitted to such only as were ascertained to be entitled to vote under its provisions. The 21st, 22d, and 23d days of March, 1842, were fixed upon for its adoption, and the General Assembly, at their January session, ordered five thousand copies of that constitution to be printed, and with twenty-five thousand ballots, to be distributed throughout the state, and the most strenuous efforts were made by the charter government to induce the people to go forward and adopt it. At length the time for voting arrived, the polls were kept open three days, and when the votes came to be returned and counted, it was found that this constitution had been rejected by a majority of six hundred and seventy-five votes. The result of this contest may justly be considered as a second demonstration in favor of the people's constitution.

As we have said before, the convention which

counted the votes given for the people's constitution communicated their doings to the legislature then in session in Providence, and thereupon the Hon. Samuel Y. Atwell, then a member of the House, and one of the most able and high-minded statesmen that Rhode Island has ever had, introduced a bill which provided for the surrendering of the charter government at the expiration of that political year to the government that was to be organized at that time under the constitution which had been adopted. An opportunity was now offered the charter authorities honorably and quietly to surrender the government to the rightful authorities. Such had been the case at every change that had before taken place in the government of that state. When the first charter was received, each of the colonial governments readily and cheerfully surrendered to the government under the charter; and again, when the government under the first charter was superseded by the charter from Charles II., the old government surrendered its authority to the new one the very next day after the charter was received. Therefore, in compliance with former usage, and by every principle of law and reason, — by every principle of honor, justice, and humanity, — every member of that legislature was bound to support the resolution offered by Mr. Atwell.

But that proposition was unceremoniously rejected; and when doubts were expressed about the majority of votes given for the people's constitution, Mr. Atwell proposed to the legislature to go into an examination of those votes, which had been carefully preserved by the convention, and were tendered to the General Assembly for that purpose. That proposition was treated with scorn, and promptly rejected. The legislature held that it was of no consequence whether a majority had or had not voted for the constitution. We may well presume that every member of the legislature was perfectly satisfied that votes enough had been given for it, and that nothing could be gained by an investigation. At the same time the Assembly saw that if they should take that issue, and find the votes correctly returned and counted, that body would be expected to yield up its authority.

The refusal to examine the votes was an implied acknowledgment of their correctness, and therefore the legislature were driven to the necessity of resting their case upon another horn of the dilemma. The whole of the proceedings of the people in the formation and adoption of their constitution were declared void *ab initio* for want of legislative authority, and this is the point upon which the whole case, with all its consequences, rests; it therefore deserves to be duly considered. Had the legislature any authority to require or authorize the people to form and adopt a constitution? The charter gave them no such authority, nor had the people at any time or in any manner conferred such power upon the General Assembly; therefore, if the legislature had pretended to have or exercise any such authority, it would have been usurpation, and in itself illegal. Those who knew any thing about it, knew very well that the Assembly had no power to pass any act that should be of binding force, or confer upon the people any legal power to take measures for forming a constitution. It will be seen by an examination of the doings of the legislature at the January session, 1841, that the act of that session relative to the calling of a convention was merely advisory; it did not order or direct, but *requested* the " freemen " to meet and choose delegates to form a constitution. The words " *Be it enacted,*" in themselves, are of no authority, therefore all that was done by that act was simply to recommend to the " freemen " to take the course pointed out; nobody was bound by it, and a refusal to comply would have been no breach of law. Nor had the eighty-four individuals who composed that Assembly any more right to *request* the " freemen " so to proceed, than the same number of respectable individuals in private life; therefore the town meetings that were held pursuant to that *request*, were just as illegal as the meetings which were held for a similar purpose in compliance with the *request* of a mass convention; and, therefore, if the landholders' constitution had been adopted, it would have had no more authority than that which the people did adopt. Nor does the validity of a constitution depend at all upon any initiatory measures; it is the *adoption* alone which gives it authority. But there is another feature in the case. The call of the Assembly was directed to the *freemen* only, and these, as we have seen, constituted only about one third of the people, so that the invitation was not extended to all the people, or a majority, but to a known minority; so that a majority of the people could not, if they chose, comply with the request. They were, therefore, left free to take their own course, without any legislative instruction. But we are told that the people are not the *people* in a legal sense; that men have no natural inherent rights, but that political rights are gifts from the government, and bestowed upon such only as the government sees fit to point out as objects of favor.

This is anti-republican doctrine, and directly opposite to the declared principles upon which all the American governments are founded. If this doctrine is true, the Declaration of American Independence is a lie, and the patriots of the revolution shed their blood for nothing. Some appear to be unable to understand that men have certain natural rights which are before, and independent of, all social compacts. They cannot understand that the consent of the governed is the only true source of political power; yet no philosophical problem is capable of clearer demonstration. All who are the subjects of a government possess an indefeasible right to give or withhold their consent. A consideration of the greatest good of the greatest number has led to the adoption of the rule that the will of the majority should be considered the will of the whole, and be obeyed accordingly; and so long, therefore, as any government enjoys that consent, it may justly exercise its authority; but whenever that consent is decidedly withheld, the government becomes arbitrary and unjust. Tyrants may cavil at this, and interested men find many objections; but it is nevertheless the true doctrine of American democracy. In its commencement, every free government has been established by mutual agreement. The compact formed on board the Mayflower is a good example, and the colonies established by Roger Williams at Providence, and by John Clarke at Newport, were of the same character. Such were also many other infant settlements in this country. The records of the colony of Roger Williams for many years show that the declaratory clause in their legislative proceedings was, " It is agreed," instead of " Be it enacted," as now used. Although those who held the government of Rhode Island under the charter, in 1841–2, resorted to the sacrilegious measure of denying the truths set forth in the Declaration of American Independence, yet the whole frame of government in the United States, and every single state, rests upon that declaration of rights as upon a corner stone which can never be overthrown, except with the freedom of the government. In our statute books, it takes precedence of every other document; its principles are incorporated into every state constitution; and at every returning anniversary in every town, city, and hamlet throughout the United States, it is publicly read and renewedly and solemnly acknowledged as the basis of our political faith. At such a time, to deny or doubt its truth would be regarded as political infidelity, and bring upon every such individual the hatred and scorn of every true American. It is idle to say that that instrument was a revolutionary document, and that we have no further use for it, or that it was made up of rhetorical flourishes and unmeaning declamations. Its principles, which were true then, are true now, and will continue to be so to the end of time. Tyrants may storm and rave against them — despotism may crush them out or bury them in obscurity — ignorance or irresolution may allow them to be forgotten or trampled upon; but the truths themselves, as irrefragable as the doctrine of the solar system, will remain forever. If any one state more than another cherished these principles, it was Rhode Island. They governed her earliest institutions, and are recognized in all her subsequent history, and were publicly proclaimed by a solemn enactment of her General Assembly in 1776. So jealous was that state of those rights, and so anxious to guard them against any innovation, that her delegates in Congress would not ratify the constitution of the United States until they had filed with it the following declaration : —

We, the delegates of the people of the State of Rhode Island and Providence Plantations, duly elected and met in convention, having maturely considered the constitution for the United States of America, agreed to on the seventeenth day of September, in the year one thousand seven hundred and eighty-seven, by the convention then assembled at Philadelphia, in the Commonwealth of Pennsylvania, (a copy whereof precedes these presents,) and having also seriously and deliberately considered the present situation of this state, do declare and make known, —

I. That there are certain natural rights, of which men, when they form a social compact, cannot deprive or divest their posterity ; among which are the enjoyment of life and liberty, with the means of acquiring, possessing, and protecting property, and pursuing and obtaining happiness and safety.

II. That all power is naturally vested in, and consequently derived from, the people ; that magistrates, therefore, are their trustees and agents, and at all times amenable to them.

III. That the powers of government may be reassumed by the people whensoever it shall become necessary to their happiness.

The suffrage party did not ignorantly and rashly adopt the course which they pursued in order to establish a written constitution. The subject was thoroughly examined and considered by all its leading members, and the decisive step was not taken until all other means had failed. They saw the course which they had marked out justified by the history of their own government; they saw the principles which they had adopted publicly incorporated into the constitutions of more than twenty of their sister states; they consulted able jurists in different parts of the United States; they also found themselves justified by the written declarations of the ablest statesmen and highest judges. Mr. Jefferson said, "It is not only the *right*, but the *duty*, of those now on the stage of action to change the laws and the institutions of government, to keep pace with the progress of knowledge, the light of science, and the amelioration of the condition of society. Nothing is to be considered unchangeable but the inherent inalienable rights of man." Justice Iredell, of the Supreme Court of the United States, declared that "the people may remodel their government whenever they think proper, without the consent of the government itself, not merely because it is oppressively exercised, but because they think another form is more conducive to their welfare."

Justice Wilson, one of the signers of the Declaration of Independence, and a member of the convention that framed the constitution of the United States, and afterwards one of the judges of the Supreme Court, says, "Of the right of a *majority* of the *whole people* to change their government *at will* there is no doubt." Again he says, "The people may change their constitution *whenever* and *however they please.*"

The late Hon. Thomas H. Benton said in the Senate of the United States, "The people of any state may at any time meet in convention without a law of their legislature, and without any provision, or against any provision, in their constitution, and may alter or abolish the whole frame of government as they please."

The convention which formed the present constitution of the State of Virginia, by a vote of sixty-eight to twenty-five, decided that no clause providing for amendments, should be inserted in their constitution, because it was held " that a majority of the people had the power at any time and in any manner they pleased to amend that constitution, or make a new one." By that act sixty-eight men, nearly three fourths of the whole number of the members of that convention, solemnly declared that the people themselves could not be bound by any constitutional provisions, but might at any time, and without any law, amend that constitution, or make a new one. Among those who voted with the majority were Chief Justice Marshall and Ex-President Madison, and, strange as it may seem, the name of John Tyler, who was afterwards president of the United States, appears in the same catalogue; and if he had not forgotten his own solemn act in that instance, he would never have been induced to lend the military forces of the United States to overthrow a constitution which a large majority of the whole people of a sovereign state had adopted.

A long catalogue of illustrious names of the highest authority might be produced to show that Mr. Dorr and the suffrage party had an undoubted right to take the course which they did in forming and adopting a constitution, and in setting up a government under it.

This step was not taken unadvisedly; it was no quixotic enterprise, or sudden ebullition of passion, nor was it occasioned by slight causes which had just transpired, but was a course to which the people were driven by a long train of abuses and insults, "all tending to the same end." The great body of those who voted for the people's constitution, honestly relying upon the justice of their cause, anticipated little or no opposition to its final accomplishment; they supposed that they were doing what they had an undoubted right to do, and they expected to receive the approbation of all intelligent men; they could not believe that a constitution, so just in its provisions, so well adapted to the condition and wants of the people, and so urgently demanded by so decided a majority, would be resisted with the bayonet. But the result showed that they counted too much upon the honor and magnanimity of their opponents, and far too much upon their own firmness and fidelity.

CHAPTER V.

THE ALGERINE ACT. APPLICATION TO THE PRESIDENT OF THE UNITED STATES FOR TROOPS. CORRESPONDENCE BETWEEN THE PRESIDENT AND GOVERNOR KING, AND OTHERS. MR. DORR'S ELECTION. HIS MESSAGE, ETC.

As soon as it was ascertained that the landholders' constitution had been rejected, an extra session of the General Assembly was called, and convened in Providence, on the 28th of March, at which time the following act was passed : —

An Act in relation to Offences against the Sovereign Power of this State.

Whereas in a free government it is especially necessary that the duties of the citizen to the constituted authorities should be plainly defined, so that none may confound our regulated American liberty with unbridled license ; and whereas certain artful and ill-disposed persons have, for some time past, been busy with false pretences amongst the good people of this state, and have formed, and are now endeavoring to carry through, a plan for the subversion of our government under assumed forms of law, but in plain violation of the first principles of constitutional right, and many have been deceived thereby ; and whereas this General Assembly, at the same time that it is desirous to awaken the honest and well meaning to a sense of their duty, is resolved by all necessary means to guard the safety and honor of the state, and, overlooking what is past, to punish such evil doers, in future, in a manner due to their offences:

Be it enacted by the General Assembly as follows: —

SECTION 1. All town, ward, or other meetings of the freemen, inhabitants or residents of this state, or of any portion of the same, for the election of any town, county, or state officer or officers, called or held in any town of this state, or in the city of Providence, except in the manner, for the purposes, at the times, and by the freemen by law prescribed, are illegal and void; and that any person or persons who shall act as moderator or moderators, warden or wardens, clerk or clerks, in such pretended town, ward, or other meetings hereafter to be held, or in any name or manner, receive, record, or certify votes for the election of any pretended town, county, or state officers, shall be deemed guilty of a misdemeanor, and be punished by indictment with a fine not exceeding one thousand nor less than five hundred dollars, and be imprisoned for the term of six months: *Provided, however*, that this act is not intended to apply to cases in which, by accident or mistake, some prescribed form or forms of calling town or ward meetings of the freemen of the several towns of this state, and of the city of Providence, shall be omitted or overlooked.

SEC. 2. Any person or persons who shall in any manner signify that he or they will accept any executive, legislative, judicial, or ministerial office or offices, by virtue of any such pretended election in any such pretended town, ward, or other meeting or meetings, or shall knowingly suffer or permit his or their name or names to be used as a candidate or candidates therefor, shall be adjudged guilty of a high crime and misdemeanor, and be punished by indictment in a fine of two thousand dollars, and be imprisoned for the term of one year.

SEC. 3. If any person or persons, except such as are duly elected thereto, according to the laws of this state, shall under any pretended constitution of government for this state, or otherwise, assume to exercise any of the legislative, executive, or ministerial functions of the offices of governor, lieutenant governor, senators, members of the House of Representatives, secretary of state, attorney general, or general treasurer of this state, or within the territorial limits of the same, as the same are now actually held and enjoyed, either separately or collectively, or shall assemble for the purpose of exercising any of said functions, all and every such exercise of or meeting for the purpose of exercising all, any, or either of said functions, shall be deemed and taken to be a usurpation of the sovereign power of this state, and is hereby declared to be treason against the state, and shall be punished by imprisonment during life, as is now by law prescribed.

SEC. 4. All offences under this act shall be triable before the Supreme Judicial Court only. Any person or persons arrested under the same, and also for treason against the state, may be imprisoned or held in custody for trial in the jail of such county of the state as the judge or justice issuing the warrant may order or direct; and the sheriff or other officer charged with the service of such warrant, shall, without regard to his precinct, have full power and authority to take such person or persons and him or them to commit to any county jail in this state, which may be designated by such judge or justice; and it shall be the duty of all sheriffs, deputy sheriffs, town sergeants, constables, and jailers, to govern themselves accordingly. All indictments under this act, and also all indictments for treason against this state, may be preferred and found in any county of this state, without regard to the county in which the offence was committed; and the Supreme Judicial Court shall have full power, for good cause, from time to time, to remove for trial any indictment which may be found under this act, or for treason against the state, to such county of the state as they shall deem best for the purpose of insuring a fair trial of the same, and shall, upon the conviction of any such offender or offenders, have full power to order, and from time to time to alter the place of imprisonment of such offender or offenders to such county jail within this state, or to the state prison, as to them shall seem best for the safe custody of such offender or offenders, any act, law, or usage to the contrary notwithstanding.

While this act, in the spirit of the Furies, outrages all moral considerations, it is believed also to be contrary to the common law of all civilized nations, and in direct violation of the constitution of the United States. This act was immediately published and circulated throughout the state, its framers hoping that it would so terrify the people as to prevent them from proceeding to elect a legislature under their constitution.

Now, why was the charter government so extremely anxious to defeat that constitution? Did they not know that the people had publicly and positively declared it to be their will that a government should be organized, and go into operation according to its provisions? And was it not the solemn duty of every good citizen of Rhode Island, whether in or out of office, quietly and cheerfully to yield obedience to that known will? Or was there any thing in the constitution itself to which any serious objections were made? Certainly not; because the charter party, in urging the people to vote for the landholders' constitution, had declared that the latter was "just about the same thing as that adopted by the people, and that all the essential difference was, that one was *legal*, while the other was not." All at once the charter government became very sensitive about nice technical points of law; they would have nothing done illegally, and, therefore, they set at nought the will of the people, and set up their own as the supreme law; yet, as has already been shown, the General Assembly, under the charter, could not, by any act of binding force, prescribe the mode by which the people must proceed in order to form a written constitution, and, therefore, any democratic constitution regularly formed and adopted by the people was just as legal and binding without as with any such legislative provision. It should be understood that, although the legislative power was nominally in the General Assembly, yet there were powers outside which often, to a great extent, controlled that body, so that after all, the General Assembly was little more than the mouthpiece of an aristocracy, invisible to the masses; when, therefore, we speak of the General Assembly, it should be remembered that its members were not always their own keepers.

After the General Assembly had passed the act aforesaid, sometimes called the "Algerine Act," the charter authorities looked about to ascertain how far its menaces would go to deter the people from sustaining their own constitution. It soon became apparent that, although a portion of the irresolute and timid might be terrified and induced to abandon their course, yet that a majority at least would remain faithful. Every charter functionary was on the *qui vive*. Something more must be done, or the government under the new constitution would go quietly into operation. Samuel Ward King was the acting governor of the state, but his authority was only nominal; for not only behind him, but above, around, and beneath the throne, were powers greater than his. Any one may command a ship in a calm, but when the storms come and the winds blow, the old salts take her in charge. On the 4th of April, 1842, about two weeks before the time appointed for the election of state officers under the constitution, his excellency Governor King despatched the following letter to the President of the United States : —

PROVIDENCE, *April* 4, 1842.

SIR : The State of Rhode Island is threatened with domestic violence. Apprehending that the legislature cannot be convened in sufficient season to apply to the government of the United States for effectual protection in this case, I hereby apply to you, as the executive of the State of Rhode Island, for the protection which is required by the constitution of the United States. To communicate more fully with you on this subject, I have appointed John Whipple, John Brown Francis, and Elisha R. Potter, Esquires, three of our most distinguished citizens, to proceed to Washington, and to make known to you, in behalf of this state, the circumstances which call for the interposition of the government of the United States for our protection.

I am, sir, very respectfully,
Your obedient servant,
SAMUEL W. KING,
Governor of Rhode Island.
THE PRESIDENT OF THE UNITED STATES.

On the same day the governor wrote another long letter to the president, informing him that the gentlemen whom he had commissioned to proceed forthwith to Washington, and crave audience with the president, were "three of the most distinguished citizens of the state," also notifying the president of the imminent danger which the crazy old charter government was in. He stated that notwithstanding the act which his legislature had passed, "in relation to the sovereign power of the state," the suffrage party appeared determined to sustain their constitution; that "in some portions of the state, and in the city of Providence particularly, they might constitute a majority of the physical force." And he urges the president to provide immediate measures to prevent the government from passing into the hands of the people. He says, "The protective power would be lamentably deficient, if the beginning of strife which is like the letting out of waters, cannot be prevented, and no protection can be afforded the state until, to many, it would be too late."

The commission proceeded to Washington with all possible haste, procured an interview with the president, and at length succeeded in making him believe that he was the rightful arbiter between contending governments in a sovereign state, and that it was a duty incumbent on him to employ the military forces of the United States to sustain a minority government holding under a dead charter, and to overthrow a republican government, which the sovereign people had ordained and established. The gentlemen commissioners returned with the glad news, and it was soon proclaimed that the president of the United States would furnish such troops as the charter government might require to sustain itself against the people's constitution.

This information was immediately spread over the state, and the most strenuous efforts were made to induce suffrage men to believe that an army of national troops, with bristling bayonets, only waited the call of the governor to strike down every man who dared to go forward and vote for officers under the people's constitution.

Now, why were all these unparalleled efforts made at home and abroad to defeat the government under the people's constitution? Was there any thing essentially wrong in that document, or in the proceedings which had taken place under it? Did the new government threaten to overthrow or disturb any wholesome and cherished institutions of the state? Certainly not. No objections were made or fears raised on any of these accounts. But the old government brought all their ostensible opposition to a single focus; their sensibilities had become very acute, and they saw, as they pretended, with deep concern, that the people's constitution was *illegal!* And if that party are to be believed, it was on that single ground that they opposed it. Now, if we trace back their own history a few years, we shall find that, in 1832, this same charter government, to all intents and purposes, legally fell through and terminated, and every particle of legislative authority under that instrument came to a final end. And if the coalition which controlled the state had been half as scrupulous in 1832, as they professed to be in 1842, the whole government should have been surrendered, like a sinking ship to the underwriters. The facts are these. The charter required that the governor, lieutenant governor, and the ten senators, or assistants, as they were called, should be "newly chosen" every year. Therefore, on the first Wednesday of May annually, the official functions of the governor and Senate for the previous year expired, and the "newly-elected" incumbents, whether they were the same or different individuals, were engaged and sworn to discharge the duties of their respective offices for the ensuing year, and no longer. Now, it so happened, that in 1832 there was no election of governor, lieutenant governor, or Senate for that entire year. The House of Representatives had no authority except in concurrence with the Senate. Therefore the State of Rhode Island and Providence Plantations was destitute of a legislature.

The good old charter had aborted, and the government had expired. Where were the fastidious "law and order" men at that time, and what did they do in that extremity? Why, they declared that the government must not thus unceremoniously fall through, and the dear people be put to the trouble of instituting a government *de novo*; therefore they brought back the last year's governor, and last year's senators, placed them in their seats, and ordered them to go on as if nothing had happened, until a new election could be brought about. Might not the whole people, if they had thought proper, during this interregnum have rallied round and formed a constitution, and set up a government in room of the charter government? And if they had done so, would the national executive have sent his troops to demolish such a democracy? Would he rashly have stained his own hands with the blood of men striving for freedom? When we recollect that Andrew Jackson, and not John Tyler, was president of the United States at that time, the question is answered; he would have taken upon himself the responsibility of sustaining the democracy of the people against all its enemies.

Notwithstanding the combined efforts of the state and national authorities to terrify the people, and induce them to abandon their constitution, when the third Wednesday of April arrived, regularly-organized town meetings were held, and a full complement of state officers elected. And on the 3d day of May following, the members elect of the legislature, as required by their constitution, met in the city of Providence. Eight or nine hundred state troops in uniform, and two or three thousand citizens, attended the procession. As it had been previously ascertained that the charter authorities had closed and barred the state house, the people's legislature proceeded to hold their session in another place. On counting the votes, it was found that the whole number, 6359, had been given for Thomas Wilson Dorr, of Providence, for governor, and that Amasa Eddy, Jr., had been also elected to the office of lieutenant governor, William H. Smith, secretary, and Jonah Titus, attorney general. These officers were then duly sworn, as provided in the constitution.

As soon as the ceremonies of inauguration were completed, the governor was requested to notify the president of the United States of the organization of a government under the constitution, and also to notify the presiding officers of both Houses of Congress of the same fact, and request them to lay the information before their respective Houses; and also to notify the governors of the several states of the same, to be communicated to their legislatures.

In the afternoon of the same day Governor Dorr delivered the following Message to both Houses in joint session: —

SENATORS AND REPRESENTATIVES:

It is with no ordinary emotions that I proceed to discharge the duties imposed upon me by the constitution of this state, in submitting such suggestions for your consideration as the occasion requires.

This is the first session of a legislature ever convened under a written constitution of government, proceeding from the people of Rhode Island. That a majority of the people should have been so long debarred from a participation in those rights which are elsewhere so well recognized, and that we have been so slow in arriving at a point long since attained in other states, are facts ill adapted to elevate our feelings of state pride, as successors of those venerated men who here proclaimed, for the first time, the just principles of religious and political freedom which are now the common inheritance of American citizens. On the other hand, the peculiar circumstances in which the people of this state have been placed, and the extraordinary difficulties with which they have had to contend, render the establishment of their constitution a subject of the deepest satisfaction to the people themselves, and to all who sympathize in the progress of rational liberty. If the people of Rhode Island are true to themselves, the democracy of Roger Williams has this day been restored in the place where it originated. The sacred fire, so long extinguished, has been rekindled upon our altar. The sovereignty of the people has been vindicated. The distinctions of caste and privilege have been abolished. Our institutions are rendered conformable to the standard of our sister republics. While the rights of those heretofore denominated the freemen of the state have not been impaired, the rights of others have been placed on a sure basis, by constitutional provisions securing the common welfare of the whole people.

On this peculiar occasion, it is due to ourselves, and to our fellow-citizens abroad, who entertain so lively an interest in our affairs, to pass briefly in review the history of our proceedings, and to submit them to the scrutiny of public opinion — the arbiter of political questions in a free country, and to which, in the confidence inspired by a righteous cause, we are ever ready to appeal. The idea of imposing a government on the people of this state by mere power, and without right, is one which will be promptly discarded by the constitutionalists of Rhode Island. They maintain the ground that they are not only a majority, but that they have proceeded rightfully to alter and reform their government, according to well-defined principles in our republican system.

The people of Rhode Island have, for many years past, complained of manifest defects in their form of government; the most serious of which were the limitation of the right of suffrage, an unequal representation, and the absence of all fundamental laws to limit and regulate the powers and functions of the General Assembly. The operation of the suffrage law of this state has for a long time excluded from the right of voting three fifths of its adult population. The largest vote ever polled by the freeholders was at the election of the president in 1840, when eight thousand six hundred and sixty-two votes were cast, in a total adult male population, of permanently resident citizens of the United States, exceeding twenty-three thousand. It is impracticable for the disfranchised majority, even if of pecuniary ability and so disposed, to qualify themselves as voters upon real estate. Although the Senate, consisting of ten members, was elected upon general ticket by the freemen at large, yet a majority of the House of Representatives was chosen by towns containing less than one third of the population of the state; so that the conjoint effect of suffrage and representation in this state has been to place all political power in the hands of a minority of its citizens, and to hold out the greatest temptation to that minority to resist all changes which would divest the few of the exclusive control of affairs. But if these evils had not existed, if suffrage had been extended, and representation had been equalized, still the want of fundamental laws to regulate the legislature itself, and to protect the citizen against legislative tyranny or caprice, would alone have afforded ample justification to the strong impulse among the people in favor of a state constitution — such a constitution as should define the rights of the citizen, establish the departments and powers of government, and lay down definite and permanent rules for its administration, to which all might appeal.

The charter government of this state had no counterpart in any state of the Union. We have never had a constitution, in the American sense of the term. The substitutes for it were a charter granted by Charles II. of England; various statutes to explain, define, and alter the charter, and to supply its deficiencies; and certain usages; all which, taken together, composed our form of government, and were all subject to the will and pleasure of the General Assembly.

The charter of 1663 was the creation, in ordinary form, of a political corporation, with general powers of self-government to the colony; and it granted to the colonists the utmost freedom in all religious concernments. The zeal and perseverance manifested by Roger Williams and John Clarke in obtaining this charter entitle them to our lasting gratitude. Our ancestors declared themselves a democracy long before the date of the charter, and they lived as such under it; and, although their proceedings were subject to the government at home, they enjoyed their institutions, with little interruption, to the time of the revolution. It is not the charter with which we find fault. In the day when it was granted, it was a noble monument of freedom, and well adapted to the circumstances of the people at the time. It has long since performed its office, and ought to have been laid aside in the colonial archives when our connection with the mother country was severed. It is the action of the General Assembly under this charter, and since the revolution of 1776, which has occasioned all our difficulties. It has been in the power of the General Assembly, at any moment, by their entire control over the right of suffrage, and by extending it, to remove every existing cause of complaint among the people; inasmuch as a liberal extension would have led to the adoption of a liberal constitution. The charter empowers the Assembly to admit persons free of the company, and prescribes no terms or qualifications whatever. Before this charter, and under that of 1643, the rule of admission was "being found meet for the service of the body politic."

After the charter of 1663, the laws make mention of "competent estates," without defining their nature or amount; and in 1666 the admission of the freemen was transferred, for greater convenience, to the several towns, who were authorized to make admission of those who were "deserving thereof." It was not till the year 1724, eighty-eight years after the settlement of the state, that a definite property qualification was established by a law of that year, which enacted that no man should be admitted a freeman unless possessed of a freehold estate of the value of one hundred pounds, or forty shillings a year, or unless he were the oldest son of such freeholder. The amount of the qualification was afterwards raised to two hundred, then to four hundred pounds; and in the year 1762 it was diminished to forty pounds, equivalent, in our present currency, to one hundred and thirty-four dollars, at which point it has ever since remained.

Whatever may have been the original inducement for the passage of such a law, it does not appear to have been regarded at the time as a serious inconvenience, any more than such a law would be regarded in any state purely agricultural. At the time of the revolution, and for some years subsequent, the voters of the state were a majority of the inhabitants. The state became deeply involved in the war of the Revolution. The attention of the people was turned from their own institutions to matters of more general and absorbing interest; and the old charter system remained, as before, the government of the state. As population increased, and the inhabitants became more and more diverted from agriculture to other pursuits, the evil of this system became more manifest — the number of voters bearing a constantly decreasing proportion to the whole number of adult male citizens. The vote polled fifty years ago, at ordinary elections, was not, as has been stated, two thousand less than the average vote at our elections at the present day, in a population nearly double in numbers.

A political injustice so marked as this did not fail to suggest the proper remedy by an extension of suffrage. In the course of time, the apportionment of representatives, which was fairly made in the charter, according to population, had become extremely unequal. A movement in favor of a constitution was made near the close of the last century, but without any practical results. In the year 1811 a bill to extend suffrage to all citizens who paid taxes and performed military duty was passed in the Senate, but was lost in the House of Representatives. In the year 1819, and the three following years, the subject of a state constitution was again agitated, and the oppressive inequality of our present system was clearly demonstrated, but with the usual want of success. In 1824 a convention of the freemen was called by the General Assembly to form a constitution. This convention proposed to the freemen a constitution which redressed, in part, the inequalities of our representation; but a resolution to extend suffrage to others besides landholders received only three votes. This constitution was voted down by a large majority.

In 1829 a renewed interest upon the question of their rights was awakened among the disfranchised inhabitants, especially in the city of Providence. Frequent meetings were held, and a petition numerously signed was addressed to the General Assembly. It was so far deemed worthy of notice as to be referred to a committee, and to be made the subject of a report, drawn up by a very distinguished member of the House of Representatives. This committee treated the application of the petitioners with scorn and contumely; described them as a low and degraded portion of the community; and reminded them that, if they were dissatisfied with the institutions of the state, they were at liberty to leave it. The report was received and printed, and considered, with much exultation, as the most effective rebuke ever administered to the advocates of liberal suffrage in Rhode Island.

In 1832 an attempt to obtain a participation in the elective right shared a similar fate.

In 1834 a party was organized for the express purpose of accomplishing the same object by direct political action on the electors of the state. After a resolute struggle of four years, this party became extinct, without having apparently created much impression upon the freemen, or having tended, in any perceptible degree, to change their fixed determination never to abandon the existing suffrage laws.

But the movement of this party gave occasion for some alarm; and the General Assembly forthwith called a convention of freemen, who met at Providence, in September, 1834, to propose amendments to the existing institutions of the state, or to form a constitution, as they might deem expedient. A motion to extend suffrage beyond the landed qualification was decisively negatived, only seven members voting in its favor. The convention was unable to maintain a quorum, and adjourned without proposing a constitution, or any part of one, to their constituents.

A whole generation had thus passed away in fruitless efforts to obtain, as a grant from the chartered authorities, those rights which are every where else, throughout the length and breadth of this great republic, regarded as the birthright of the people. The legislature had been repeatedly approached in terms of respectful petition, and the applicants had been driven away as intruders upon the vested rights of the ruling political class. The General Assembly, which was invested with as full power to alter the law of suffrage in favor of the people, as to establish the law originally, without any prescription in the charter, had turned a deaf ear to the reiterated and most earnest remonstrances of a long injured and oppressed majority.

The conventions of the freemen had manifested, if possible, a still greater hostility to the claims of the majority. The anxious inquiry of the people began to be raised — Is there no remedy for these manifest grievances? Must we submit forever to be trodden under foot by men no better than ourselves? Is the law of a minority, who happen to possess the control of a state, like the laws of the Medes and Persians, to be the immutable standard of right and justice, in despite of all the changes which have been occasioned by time and circumstances in the condition of the state and its inhabitants? Was this designed to be a government of the few, or of the many? Have we gained or lost by the boasted emancipation of our state from colonial subjection? Questions like these were naturally interchanged among those who felt the pressure of a common injustice; and they became bound together in attachment to a common cause, and in a struggle for the same just and equal rights. And who were these men? They were the younger sons of farmers, the great body of the mechanics and of the workingmen of the state.

They found among their number nearly all the surviving patriots of the revolution, who felt themselves impelled to assert, in the period of venerable age, the same cause to which they had devoted the freshness and vigor of their youthful days. The men thus hopelessly disfranchised were those to whom the defence of the country is committed in time of war, who protect the community against the ravages of conflagration, who sustain their equal amount of the burdens of community, and who sustain, by indirect taxation, the government of the United States. They were sensible of no inferiority of nature or condition, which marked them for the subjects rather than the citizens of a nominally republican government. They were the descendants of ancestors who had proclaimed to the world, for the first time in its history, the first principles of a democratic government, or of the men who contributed their substance, their honor, and their lives to the freedom and independence of their country. Could they hesitate in the course which they were bound to pursue? It was idle to tell them that they were well governed, and that the existing authorities were better qualified to provide for their interests, than they were to take care of themselves. They felt in their inmost hearts the proud response of American freemen, conscious of their rights, and daring to maintain them.

While it is the right of a British subject to be well governed, they believed it to be the right of American citizens to govern themselves; and they determined to remove the badge of servitude fastened upon them by a landed oligarchy.

In the latter part of the year 1840, an association of mechanics, mostly non-freeholders, was organized in this city, for the final attainment of their political rights; and similar associations were soon formed in many other towns of the state. A portion of the members of these associations, still retaining a hope that the General Assembly might lend an ear to the remonstrances of the people, presented once more a petition at the January session, 1841, for a redress of their political grievances. The petition was not acted upon. At the same session, a memorial from the town of Smithfield, praying for an increase in its representation, received the attention of the House, and a committee once more reported a bill for a freemen's convention to form a constitution. The experience of the past had forbidden disfranchised citizens to expect, from a convention so organized, any favorable result; and they soon after proceeded to call a mass convention of the people to consider the condition and prospects of their cause. This convention met in Providence on the 18th of April, 1841. A second mass convention was held at Newport on the 5th of May, when it was resolved that a convention of the people at large should be called for the formation of a republican constitution; and a state committee was appointed to issue the call. The General Assembly met in May, 1841, and passed a law for the more equal apportionment among the towns of the delegates to the freeholders' convention in November. At the adjourned session in June, a bill was introduced in the House to admit tax-payers to vote with the freemen in the choice of delegates to the November convention. This bill was negatived by the same decisive vote that had been before given against all propositions for an extension of suffrage.

On the 5th of July, 1841, the Newport mass convention held an adjourned meeting at Providence, and, having become satisfied that there was no longer any hope from the General Assembly, issued instructions to the state committee to proceed forthwith in the call of a popular convention; which instructions were complied with, by issuing to all the towns in the state a request to elect delegates, in the proportion, as nearly as possible, of one to every thousand inhabitants, to assemble at Providence in October for the purpose aforesaid. Meetings of the citizens were duly held, pursuant to notice, in nearly all the towns of the state, in the latter part of August, moderators and clerks were appointed, and delegates were elected in the usual form for such occasions. A large majority of the delegates assembled in convention, at Providence, on the 4th day of October; and, after having formed the plan of a constitution, adjourned till the next month, in order that their labors might be submitted to the investigation of the public. The convention reassembled in November; and after making several amendments, finally passed upon the constitution, and proposed it for adoption, or rejection, to the adult male population, who were citizens of the United States, and had their permanent residence, or home, in the state. The question upon the constitution was taken on the days appointed in the same, in the month of December, 1841; and the result was, the adoption of the constitution by a large majority.

The freeholders' convention met in November, and, after preparing the plan of a constitution — in which, however, there were some provisions proposed only, and not acted upon, — adjourned to the month of February, 1842. Their adjournment took place prior to the second meeting of the convention of the people. The freeholders' convention, at their first session, extended suffrage beyond the existing freehold qualification, to the possessors of personal property of the value of five hundred dollars. This convention met again, according to adjournment, in February, completed their constitution, and submitted it to those of the people who were qualified to vote under it; by whom, in the month succeeding, it was rejected.

This constitution was voted against by a large majority of the friends of the people's constitution — not because it was made by the freemen, and not by themselves, but because its leading provisions were unjust and anti-republican, and tended to prolong, under a different guise, some of the greatest of those evils which had been the occasion of so much complaint under the old charter system. It is a fact which challenges contradiction, and is familiar to every man in this state, that the friends of political reform and equal rights have ever been desirous, previous to the adoption of their constitution, that all changes in their form of government should be made through the action of the Assembly, or the body of the freemen. The course adopted by them during a long series of years — their respectful applications to the Assembly — their delay in the call of a popular convention, until every probability of redress had been cut off, and patience had ceased to be a virtue, will satisfy all candid men that the minority are in the wrong on this point, and that the people have pursued the only course consistent with a proper regard to their rights as citizens of a free country.

Two questions here arise, to which it is our duty to reply — a question of right, and a question of fact. Had the people of this state a right to adopt a constitution of government in the mode they have pursued? and, if so, have they adopted this constitution by a majority of their whole number?

That the sovereignty of this country resides in the people, is an axiom in the American system of government, which it is too late to call in question. By the theory of other governments, the sovereign power is vested in the head of the state, or shared with him by the legislature. The sovereignty of the country from which we derive our origin, and, I may add, many of our opinions upon political subjects inconsistent with our present condition, is in the king and Parliament; and any attempt on the part of the people to change the government of that country would be deemed an insurrection. There all reform must proceed from the government itself, which calls no conventions of the people, and recognizes no such remedy for political grievances. In this country, the case is totally the reverse. When the revolution severed the ties of allegiance which bound the colonies to the parent country, the sovereign power passed from its former possessors — not to the general government, which was the creation of the states; nor to the state governments; nor to a portion of the people; but to the whole people of the states, in whom it has ever since remained. This is the doctrine of our fathers, and of the early days of the republic, and should be sacredly guarded as the only safe foundation of our political fabric. The idea that government is in any proper sense the source of power in this country, is of foreign origin, and at war with the letter and spirit of our institutions. The moment we admit the principle that no change in government can take place without permission of the existing authorities, we revert to the worn-out theory of the monarchies of Europe: and whether we are the subjects of the Czar of Russia, or of the monarch of Great Britain, or of a landed oligarchy, the difference to us is only in degree; and we have lost the reality, though we may retain the forms, of a democratic republic. If the people of Rhode Island are wrong in the course they have pursued, they will nevertheless have conferred one benefit upon their countrymen by the agitation of this question, in dissipating the notion that the people are the sovereigns of the country, and in consigning to the department of rhetorical declamations those solemn declarations of 1776, which are repeated in so many of the state constitutions, and which are so clearly and confidently asserted by the most eminent jurists and statesmen of our country.

By sovereign power, we understand that ultimate power, which must be vested somewhere, and which prescribes the form and functions of government. It is, of course, superior to the legislative power, which can be properly exerted only according to rules laid down for its action, in that expression of the sovereign will called a constitution. This sovereignty is a personal attribute, and belongs to the man himself, and not to the soil or property with which he may be endowed. It is a power seldom visible; which ought to be, and can be, but rarely exerted. The making and altering of laws, which lie at the foundations of society, should be a work of great care and caution; and when done, ought to be well done, that it may be effectual and permanent. It is our misfortune in this state, that as no expression of the sovereign will has been, until recently, made in the adoption of a constitution, and no index of this will constantly before the public eye, the distinction between the two powers has become obliterated among us; and the legislature has been regarded not only as the immediate acting power, but as the sole power of the state; and all who maintain the right of the people, in their original, sovereign capacity, to alter the present government, and render it conformable to their just rights, have been represented as hostile to law and order, and as putting in jeopardy the stability of government. On the other hand, we contend that the people have a right to change the government when necessary to their welfare; that they are the judges of that necessity; that "time does not run against the people, any more than against the king," and that they have not forfeited this right by any acquiescence; that a power to assent, involves another to dissent; that even if a past generation had surrendered to a minority their political rights, (which they never have done,) they did not, and could not, bind their successors, or prevent them from reassuming their sovereignty.

If time permitted, I should take great satisfaction in laying before you the most abundant evidence that these are the well-recognized principles of our republican system, and are not to be regarded as revolutionary.

The Declaration of American Independence asserts that governments derive their just powers from the consent of the governed, and that it is the right of the people (meaning the whole people, the governed) to alter or abolish their government whenever they deem it expedient, and to institute new government, laying its foundations on such principles, and organizing its powers in such form, as to them shall seem most likely to effect their safety and happiness. This Declaration was expressly adopted by the General Assembly of this state in July, 1776.

The constitutions of many of the states, while they contain specific provisions for the mode of their amendment, set forth, in the strongest terms, the right of the people to change them as they may deem expedient.

Any other construction would render a portion of the declarations of rights in these constitutions entirely nugatory.

The convention which framed the constitution of the United States acted as the representatives of the sovereignty of the people of the states, without regard to the limitation attempted to be imposed by the Congress of the confederation. That the whole people, by an explicit and authentic act, — the great body of society, — have a right to make and alter their constitutions of government, is a principle which has been laid down by the fathers of the constitution, and the ablest expounders of our political institutions — by Washington, Hamilton, and Madison. The strong opinions of Jefferson on this point are too well known to need a particular repetition.

Chief Justice Jay says, "At the revolution the sovereignty devolved on the people; and they are truly the sovereigns of the country." "The citizens of America are equal as fellow-citizens, and as joint tenants in the sovereignty."

Justice Wilson, of the same court, says, "Of the right of the majority of the whole people to change their government, at will, there is no doubt." It is this "one great principle, the vital principle," "which diffuses animation and vigor through all the others." He says, "The principle I mean is this — that the supreme or sovereign power of society resides in the citizens at large; and that, therefore, they always retain the right of abolishing, altering, or amending their constitution, at whatever time, and in whatever manner, they shall deem expedient." "In our government, the supreme, absolute, uncontrollable power remains in the people. As our constitutions are superior to our legislatures, so the people are superior to our constitutions." The consequence is, that the people may change the constitution, whenever and however they please. This is a right of which no positive institutions can deprive them.

Mr. Rawle, a distinguished commentator on the constitution of the United States, in speaking of the mode of amending a constitution, remarks, "The people retain — the people cannot, perhaps, divest themselves of

— the power to make such alterations." "The laws of one legislature may be repealed by another legislature, and the power to repeal them cannot be withheld by the power that enacted them. So the people may, on the same principle, at any time alter or abolish the constitution they have formed. If a particular mode of effecting such alterations have been agreed upon, it is most convenient to adhere to it; but it is not exclusively binding."

It is impossible to misunderstand language like this. It might be suggested that the people referred to are those who are recognized as voters by constitution or laws; but the language used is too clear to admit of such an interpretation. It is the whole people, the people at large, who have the right to change the institutions under which they live. Nor is this a dangerous doctrine in its practical application. This, I believe, is the only state in which the majority of the whole people do not partake of the electoral privilege. All other states have written constitutions, with precise provisions for their amendment. It is hardly possible for a case to occur in any other state, which would require the interposition of the people in any other than the prescribed mode. In all others suffrage has been enlarged, and all complaints respecting a limitation of suffrage or inequality of representation have been redressed without any very protracted delay. The constitution will here also be regarded as a final measure. While we assert the sovereign right of the people in our own case, and presume not to limit its exercise under possible exigencies not now foreseen, and of which every generation must judge for itself, we have no reason to believe that Rhode Island will be an exception to the general rule in other states, or to doubt that its constitution will become a permanent as well as paramount law, to be altered or amended according to its prescribed mode.

But, whatever opinions may be entertained respecting

the right of the whole people to change a constitution in any other than the prescribed mode, where such a mode exists, there is a point in our case to which the attention of every one should be closely invited. Until the adoption of the present constitution, there has been no mode prescribed in this state, either by the charter or by any law or usage, for amending our form of government. The charter contains no such direction; being a royal grant, the power to amend by a supplemental charter remained in the grantor, and needed no specification. The charter contains a very general authority to make all necessary laws; but they must be consistent with the royal prerogative, and with the rights of Parliament. The power of amending the charter passed over to the people of the state, as an incident to their sovereignty, at the revolution.

In the absence of any such provision, it is a totally unfounded assumption in the charter Assembly to pretend that the proceedings of the people are null and void for want of a compliance with law, when no legal or other provision exists upon the subject. All that the General Assembly have ever done, has been to request, in their own form, the freemen to assemble and elect delegates to form a constitution.

The freemen, if they saw fit, might at any time have chosen such delegates, without such a request, in their own form, and with an equally valid effect. Is it not apparent that the people at large have a still greater right to do the same thing in this state? They have demanded in vain that any valid legal objections to their proceedings should be produced. It is to the last degree ungenerous and unjust that the freemen should set up their own neglect in years past to provide a constitutional mode of amendments as a bar to the action of the people, in the only mode in which they can act at all. When any disposition is manifested to amend our constitution in a different mode from that prescribed in it, it will be time for alarmists to suggest the danger and instability that may possibly occur from any irregular action of the people.

But was this sovereign power of the people exercised, in fact, by a majority of the whole people of the state? We assert, with entire confidence, that it was. The voting was conducted as fairly as at any election ever held in this state. All challenges of voters were received and entertained. The moderators of the meetings, who received the votes, were not under oath; neither are those of the freemen's meetings. The town clerks, and wardens, and ward clerks, in the city of Providence, act under an engagement; and this is the only difference between the meetings of the freemen and those of the people. This difference will create no serious objection, when it is stated that the name of every man who voted for the people's constitution was written on his ticket; and that the ticket of every man who did not attend the polls on the three last of the six days of voting, in addition to his signature, was attested by that of some person who voted at the polls on the three first days. These proxy votes were but a small portion of the whole. Still further: the name of every man who voted was registered; and a copy of the register in every town and ward was duly certified with the votes. All the votes have been preserved in their envelopes for any subsequent reference. The votes were duly returned to the people's convention, and were examined and counted by a large committee. The committee reported that, as nearly as could be ascertained, the number of males in this state over the age of twenty-one years, citizens of the United States, and permanently resident, deducting persons under guardianship, insane, and convict, was 23,142, of whom a majority is 11,572; and that the people's constitution received 13,944 votes — being a majority of 4747. After making every reasonable allowance for questionable votes, from which no election can be entirely free, it is impossible to entertain a reasonable doubt that a large majority of the whole people fairly voted for this constitution. The report of the counting committee was transmitted to the General Assembly at the January session, 1842, and a motion was made to inquire into the return of the votes polled; but it was negatived, as usual, by a large majority.

An attempt to impeach the return has been made, by drawing an unfavorable inference from the subsequent diminished vote against the constitution of the freeholders. But the attempt fails at once, when it is understood that a considerable number of those who voted for the people's constitution, and are now friendly to it, voted also for the freeholders' constitution, as a mode of obtaining a part of their rights and of terminating all controversies. Many who voted for the first-named constitution were excluded from a vote against the second by its suffrage provisions; and there were others who were qualified, but declined to vote at all.

At the election of state officers under the people's constitution, there were no opposing candidates; and, notwithstanding the powerful influences brought to bear upon the election, there was a larger vote by 1600 than was polled for the officers of our opponents at the election held by the freemen. At this election, a portion of those freeholders who are the friends of the people's constitution, and who had voted for officers at the election held under that constitution on Monday, voted again for a constitutional candidate, and have been very strangely claimed, in consequence, by the party who sustain the old charter system.

When the constitution of the people is examined, without reference to its origin, it is found that there are few objections made against it. It guards with great care all civil and political rights; it establishes as equal a representation as the circumstances of the state will permit, and a Senate to be chosen in districts under such an appointment as to secure to a majority of the population a majority of its members. The freeholders' constitution, on the other hand, was rejected for many reasons — one of which was its defective provisions relating to suffrage, and its exclusion of the vote by ballot. The main objection was, that it entirely abolished the majority principle in our government. Under it, both the House of Representatives and the Senate were to be elected by towns and districts containing less than one third of the inhabitants of the state. The senators were also assigned to the districts, without scarcely any reference to their population.

By the nature of the provisions relative to amendment, any subsequent improvement of this instrument was rendered nearly impracticable.

At the session of the Assembly in March, 1842, the people's constitution came under the consideration of that body, twice ratified — directly by the votes of the people in its favor, and indirectly by the rejection of another instrument. But these repeated manifestations of the popular will were totally disregarded. A bill to conform the general election to the provisions of this constitution, and another to submit it to those who were qualified to vote under the constitution of the freeholders, were promptly rejected. A proposition was made to extend suffrage; and a second proposition was offered at the adjourned session in April, for the call of another convention to form a constitution — the delegates to which convention were to be voted for by a constituency not much extended beyond the present freeholder. Both propositions shared the fate of the preceding.

Your attention will be required to the force law and resolutions recently adopted by the General Assembly for the suppression of the constitution. Laws like these, which violate in some of their provisions the well-known privileges enjoyed by the subjects of the

British monarchy, could hardly find favor in the land of Roger Williams. These enactments have been regarded by the considerate men among our opponents as most impolitic and unjust, and by the people as null and void, because conflicting with the paramount provisions of the constitution.

Military preparations have been made by direction of the Assembly, and the people have been consequently put upon the defensive. But this is not the age nor the country in which the will of the people can be overawed or defeated by measures like these. There is reason to believe that a letter addressed to Governor King by the president of the United States was written under a mistake of the facts, occasioned by the misrepresentation of the character, motives, and objects of the constitutionalists of this state.

Our fellow-citizens in other states will perceive, from the exposition which has been made, without further comment, that the people of this state are engaged in a just and honorable cause, and that they have taken the only course for the attainment and security of their just rights.

We are assembled in pursuance of the constitution, and under a sacred obligation to carry its provisions into effect. Knowing the spirit which you have manifested throughout this exciting controversy; the moderate, but determined, course which you have pursued; your love of order, and respect for all constitutional laws, and for the rights of all other persons, while engaged in the acquisition of your own, I hardly need to remind you of your duty to cast behind you all injuries or provocations, and to leave them to the retributive justice of public opinion, which will ultimately appreciate every sincere sacrifice to the cause of truth, of freedom, and humanity. Entertaining the deep and earnest conviction that we are engaged in such a cause, and conscious of our own imperfections, let us implore the favor of that gracious. Providence which guided the steps of our ancestors, upon this our attempt to restore, and permanently secure, the blessings of that well-ordered and rational freedom here established by the patriotic founders of our state.

The provisions in the constitution, relating to the security of the right of suffrage against fraud, and to the registration of voters, will require your immediate action. The state demands of its government an economical administration of affairs, and will justly complain of any increase of its ordinary expenses at the present period.

I cannot more appropriately conclude this communication than in the words of the constitution, which declares that "no favor or disfavor ought to be shown in legislation towards any man, or party, or society, or religious denomination. The laws should be made, not for the good of the few, but of the many; and the burdens of the state ought to be fairly distributed among its citizens."

THOMAS W. DORR.

PROVIDENCE, R. I., *May* 4, 1842.

Rhode Island, at this moment, presented a strange anomaly. While the legislature at Providence were holding a regular session, as provided by the constitution, the old charter General Assembly was sitting at Newport. There were two separate Assemblies, sitting at the two capitals, and exercising distinct legislative functions; each claiming to be the legitimate government. In view of what has been stated, it must be apparent that the people of the state had declared it to be their wish and determination, that the old charter government should cease, and come to a full end, on the 3d of May of that year, and that the government under their constitution should take its place, and be organized in its stead; and to that unmistakable expression of the people's will every good citizen was bound to yield. But all history shows that when men, either justly or unjustly, become clothed with political authority, they part with it with extreme reluctance; physical force has almost always been necessary to transfer political power from one class of men to another. The natural propensity of mankind was strengthened in this case by another consideration. The state had, for a long time, been governed exclusively by freeholders, and those who held important offices in the government of the state had always opposed every effort made by the non-freeholders to obtain their political rights; and as the number of non-freeholders was known greatly to exceed the number of freeholders, it required no prophet to tell that unless the non-freeholders could be brought to accept the franchise as a special favor from the government, the old official incumbents would not be likely to be retained in office. This was the source, and the only source, of that danger, which the Rhode Island authorities saw and so much feared; not a danger which threatened the interests of the state or the people, but which threatened to bring down the office holders from their high places, and consign them to private life. Such men now entertained a most fastidious regard for "law and order," and were sorely pained at the thought that the state was in danger of being disgraced by allowing the sovereign people to wrest the government from their hands, and place it in the hands of men of their own choosing.

CHAPTER VI.

REASONS FOR BELIEVING THE CHARTER GOVERNMENT TO BE HELD BY A MINORITY. THE NEGLECT OF THE PEOPLE'S LEGISLATURE TO TAKE POSSESSION OF THE PUBLIC PROPERTY, AND ITS CONSEQUENCES CONSIDERED. AN EXTRACT FROM THE JOURNAL OF THE HOUSE OF REPRESENTATIVES.

We have seen that, as early as the 4th of April, 1842, two or three weeks before an election took place under the people's constitution, the chief magistrate of the State of Rhode Island applied to the president of the United States for assistance to put down the government which the people were preparing to organize under the constitution which they had just adopted. The charter authorities well knew that theirs was a minority government, and they were well aware of their inability to resist the free will of an intelligent people, and therefore took the early precaution to engage assistance from abroad, notwithstanding they had at the same time the full possession of all the public property — the control of the treasury, the keys of the state house and court rooms, the command of the arsenal, and the control of the prisons — notwithstanding they had both the sword and purse firmly clinched in their own hands. With all these advantages on their side, they publicly declared to the president and to the world that, unless they had assistance from abroad, their government was in danger of being overthrown by the people under their own constitution. These facts, which cannot be denied or hushed out of sight, go to establish the point, beyond all controversy, that the number in favor of the people's constitution far exceeded the number of those who were opposed to it. It is obvious that while the people were left free to follow the plain dictates of their own convictions, — before they were drawn away by promises, or terrified by threats, — three fourths, at least, chose to lay aside the old charter, and submit the government of the state to a written constitution of their own making. The wonder is, that an intelligent and resolute people did not sooner rise in their might and shake off the cords by which they were enslaved.

On the day previous to the organization of the legislature under the people's constitution, Mr. Dorr and the members elect of his legislature held a special meeting for deciding upon measures proper to be pursued. It had been already ascertained that the state house in Providence had been closed and barred against them, and the great question to be settled was, Should they proceed to take immediate possession of that, and all the other public property of the state, or should they suffer it to remain in the hands of their opponents? Mr. Dorr strongly urged the propriety and necessity of taking the former course; and it is presumed that no one now, friend or foe, will say that that advice was not judicious; but he and others, who thought as he did, were overruled, and that all-important step was not taken. Here was a fatal mistake, which no subsequent measures could remedy. Had Mr. Dorr's advice prevailed, the people's government would by that single step have become master of the forces and finances of the state, and instead of being a government in form only, it would have been a government in fact and in power, respected at home and abroad, and might have regarded with indifference any measures which the national executive might adopt. For nearly half a century the people of Rhode Island had been striving to obtain their just political rights. The momentous question had become wrapped up in the decision of a single hour — the die was cast, and the cause was ruined. This was the cruel rock upon which the ship was lost. From that moment an unbroken train of disasters followed. Had the course been pursued which Mr. Dorr pointed out, no important opposition would have been made to his government, and many of those, who, in his reverses, were most anxious to destroy him, would have been among the foremost to seek for honor and patronage under his government.

No one who witnessed the powerful military escort and long procession of citizens which attended the inauguration of the government under the people's constitution could doubt for a moment the ability of Governor Dorr at that time to take undisputed possession of all the public property of the state. Those who voted for the members of that legislature expected that they would really and fully assume and exercise all the powers and functions of a *de facto* government.

This was their imperious duty. No timid, irresolute man, no one panting for empty distinction, should have been there to assume the responsibilities of that important occasion: this was no time for vain show and empty boasting. None but men of high motives and undaunted courage should have mingled in the deliberations of that momentous crisis. Before the legislature convened, many honest but timid men had become terrified and induced to desist from all further proceedings; and now, when the whole party saw their legislature ingloriously shrink away into a private hall to exercise the high functions of a state legislature, they were disappointed and disheartened. The tide, which before had only slackened, instantly began to ebb with irresistible force. High-minded men could not be proud of a government so meek and so powerless; they could not be persuaded that this was the government for which they had labored so ardently; and in view of that spectacle, hundreds retired in disgust from the party. The following is an extract from the Journal of the House of Representatives, which met in Providence on the 3d day of May, 1842.

JOURNAL OF THE HOUSE OF REPRESENTATIVES of the State of Rhode Island and Providence Plantations, first held in the City of Providence, under the Constitution of said State, on Tuesday, the 3d day of May, in the year 1842.

On this third day of May, 1842, (being the first Tuesday of said May,) the House of Representatives of said state, elected under and by virtue of the constitution of said state, met, and proceeded to its organization by a vote that the Hon. Dutee J. Pearce, of Newport, take the chair for that purpose.

The towns and representative districts were called, and the credentials of their respective representatives, in the following order, were presented : —

City of Providence:
First representative district. — William M. Webster.
Second representative district. — Samuel H. Wales, J. F. B. Flagg.
Third representative district. — William Coleman, John A. Howland.
Fourth representative district. — Perez Simmons, Frederick L. Beckford.
Fifth representative district. — Benjamin Arnold, Jr., Franklin Cooley.
Sixth representative district. — William L. Thornton, John S. Parkis.
Newport. — Dutee J. Pearce, Robert R. Carr, Henry Oman, Daniel Brown.
Warwick. — John G. Mawney, Sylvanus C. Newman, Isbon Shearman, Alanson Holley.
Portsmouth. — Thomas Cory, Parker Hall.
Westerly. — William P. Arnold, Thomas G. Hazard.
New Shoreham. — Simeon Babcock, Jr., George E. S. Ely.
Smithfield. — Elisha Smith, Nathaniel Mowry, Welcome B. Sayles, William B. Taber.
Charlestown. — Joseph Gavit, Job Taylor.
Scituate. — Simon Mathewson, David Phillips, 3d, James Yeaw.
North Providence. — Stephen Whipple, Robert G. Lewis, Alfred Anthony.
Richmond. — Wells Reynolds, George Niles.
North Kingstown. — Sylvester Himes, Samuel C. Cottrel.
Exeter. — George Sprague, Cranston Blevin.
Tiverton. — Charles F. Townsend.
Bristol. — William Munro, Jeremiah Bosworth.

Warren. — Elisha G. Smith, Jeremiah Woodmancy.
Barrington. — Nathaniel Smith.
Glocester. — Jeremiah Sheldon, George H. Brown.
Cumberland. — Nelson Jencks, Columbia Tingley, Barton Whipple.
East Greenwich. — Peleg R. Bennet, Sidney Tillinghast.
West Greenwich. — Nathan Carr, Peter T. Brown.
Coventry. — George Fairbanks, Israel Johnson.
Foster. — Obadiah Fenner, Anan Aldrich.
Burrillville. — Alfred L. Comstock, Esten Angell.
Cranston. — Ebenezer Barney, Albion N. Olney.
Johnston. — Ephraim Winsor, Edwin C. Kelley.

Upon a call of the names returned by the credentials, as aforesaid, all were present and answered, excepting Mr. Samuel C. Cottrel, of North Kingstown. Sixty-six members were present and answered.

A quorum being ascertained to be present, the chairman announced the fact; and thereupon Welcome B. Sayles, Esq., a representative from the town of Smithfield, was nominated, and duly elected speaker by a unanimous vote.

The speaker, on taking the chair, made a short but pertinent speech, returning thanks for the honor conferred upon him; and thereupon engaged himself to the faithful discharge of his duties in the words and as required by the constitution, and in the presence of the House.

The speaker called every member by the list returned, and those present were engaged in the manner and form and in the words prescribed in the constitution.

John S. Harris and Levi Salisbury were unanimously elected clerks, and were duly engaged by the speaker.

On motion of Mr. Pearce, it was *Voted*, that Messrs. Cooley, S. H. Wales, Elisha Smith, Lewis, Simmons, George H. Brown, and Jencks, from the county of

Providence; Daniel Brown and Townsend, of the county of Newport; Himes and Arnold, of the county of Washington; Tillinghast, Holley, and Newman, of the county of Kent; and Bosworth and E. G. Smith, of the county of Bristol, be a committee to count the votes for governor, lieutenant governor, secretary of state, general treasurer, attorney general, sheriffs, and senators, and report the result.

The towns and representative districts were called, to return the votes of the electors for governor, &c., when no returns were made by the following towns: Portsmouth, Hopkinton, South Kingstown, Little Compton, Middletown, and Jamestown. Said votes were delivered to the aforesaid committee to count and report.

The House took a recess for one hour.

At three o'clock, P. M., the speaker resumed the chair.

Gilbert Chace, Esq., a representative from the town of Newport, appeared, produced his credentials, and was qualified by the speaker.

Mr. Simmons, on behalf of the committee appointed to count the votes, made the following report, which was received.

HOUSE OF REPRESENTATIVES, *May* 3, 1842.

The committee to whom was referred the counting of the votes given at the election under the constitution, April 18, 1842, for governor, lieutenant governor, senators, secretary of state, general treasurer, and attorney general, and also the votes for sheriffs in the several counties, respectfully report, —

That the whole number of votes given in for governor is 6359; that of this number 6359 were given in for Thomas W. Dorr, of Providence, and he is therefore elected.

That the whole number of votes given in for lieutenant governor is 6361; that of this number 6361 were given in for Amasa Eddy, Jr., of Glocester, and he is therefore elected.

That the whole number of votes given in for secretary of state is 6360; that of this number 6360 were given in for William H. Smith, of Providence, and he is therefore elected.

That the whole number of votes given in for attorney general is 6360; that of this number 6360 were given in for Jonah Titus, of Scituate, and he is therefore elected.

That the whole number of votes given in for general treasurer is 6360; that of this number Joseph Joslin, of Newport, received 6360, and is therefore elected.

That in the first senatorial district the whole number of votes given in for senator is 820; that of this number 820 are for Eli Brown, of Providence, and he is therefore elected.

That in the second senatorial district the whole number of votes given in for senator is 1315; that of this number 1315 are for Hezekiah Willard, of Providence, and he is therefore elected.

That in the third senatorial district the whole number of votes given in for senator is 652; that of this number John Paine received 652, and is therefore elected.

That in the fourth senatorial district the whole number of votes given in for senator is 907; of which Abner Haskell received 907, and is therefore elected.

That in the fifth senatorial district the whole number of votes given in for senator is 856; of which Solomon Smith received 856, and is therefore elected.

That in the sixth senatorial district the whole number of votes given in for senator is 648; of which 648 are for Benjamin Nichols, and he is therefore elected.

That in the seventh senatorial district the whole number of votes given in for senator is 237; of which 237 are for John Wood, of Coventry, and he is therefore elected.

That in the eighth senatorial district the whole number of votes given in for senator is 324; of which Benjamin Chace received 324, and is therefore elected.

That in the ninth senatorial district 119 votes were given in for senator; of which 119 are for John B. Cook, and he is therefore elected.

That in the tenth senatorial district 234 votes were given in for senator; of which Joseph Spink received 234 votes, and is therefore elected.

That in the eleventh senatorial district 135 votes were given in for senator; of which 135 were for William James, and he is therefore elected:

That in the twelfth senatorial district 210 votes were given in for senator; of which Christopher Smith received 210, and is therefore elected.

That in Providence county the whole number of votes given in for sheriff is 4718; that of this number 4717 are for Burrington Anthony, and he is therefore elected.

That in Newport county the whole number of votes given in for sheriff is 444; all for Joshua B. Rathbone, and he is therefore elected.

That in Bristol county the whole number of votes given in for sheriff is 210; all for Nathan Bardin, and he is therefore elected.

That in Kent county the whole number of votes given in for sheriff is 613; all for Hazard Carder, and he is therefore elected.

That in Washington county the whole number of votes given in for sheriff is 307; all for Benjamin Blevin, and he is therefore elected.

That no votes were received in season to be counted by the committee from the towns of Hopkinton, Little Compton, Jamestown, New Shoreham, and Portsmouth; in the two last towns votes were polled, but not returned to the House of Representatives.

Respectfully submitted.   FRANKLIN COOLEY,
For the Committee.

Voted, That Messrs. Pearce, B. Arnold, Jr., and Mawney, be a committee to inform the governor, lieutenant governor, secretary of state, attorney general, general treasurer, and the senators elect, of their election, and learn of them at what time they will be ready to take the oath of office.

Mr. Pearce, from the committee appointed to inform the general officers and senators of their election, made report: That they had waited upon the governor, lieutenant governor, secretary of state, attorney general, and senators Brown, Willard, Haskell, Paine, S. Smith, Nichols, Chace, James, and C. Smith, and that they had severally signified the acceptance of their respective offices, and would immediately be engaged by oath; that the general treasurer was not present, and John Wood of the seventh district, Joseph Spink of the tenth district, and John B. Cooke of the ninth district, were not present, and it is said had declined to serve.

The governor, Thomas W. Dorr; the lieutenant governor, Amasa Eddy, Jr.; William H. Smith, secretary of state; Jonah Titus, attorney general, came into the House, and severally took the oath prescribed in the constitution, administered by the speaker in the presence of the House.

Eli Brown, senator of the first district; Hezekiah Willard, senator of the second district; John Paine, senator of the third district; Abner Haskell, senator of the fourth district; Solomon Smith, senator of the fifth district; Benjamin Nichols, senator of the sixth district; Benjamin Chace, senator of the eighth district; William James, senator of the eleventh district; Christopher Smith, senator of the twelfth district, severally came into the House, and took the oath of office prescribed in the constitution, administered by the speaker in the presence of the governor, lieutenant governor, and of the House.

Voted, That Messrs. Simmons and Pearce be a committee to wait upon the governor, with such others as the Senate may add, and inquire whether he has any communication to make to the General Assembly. The vote came down concurred, with the addition of Eli Brown, senator of the first district, to said committee.

Mr. Pearce, from the committee to ask the governor if he has any communication to make to the General Assembly, reported : That the governor would forthwith, in person, meet the two Houses, and communicate a message.

The two Houses having joined, the governor, in person, communicated his message.

The governor, lieutenant governor, and Senate returned from the House.

Mr. Simmons offered a set of rules, which were read and voted to be laid on the table.

Mr. Simmons, of Providence, offered the following resolutions, to wit: —

Resolved, That the governor be requested to inform the president of the United States that the government of this state has been duly elected and organized under the constitution of the same, and that the General Assembly are now in session and proceeding to discharge their duties according to the provisions of said constitution.

Resolved, That the governor be requested to make the same communication to the president of the Senate and to the speaker of the House of Representatives, to be laid before the two Houses of the Congress of the United States.

Resolved, That the governor be requested to make the same communication to the governors of the several states, to be laid before the respective legislatures.

The resolutions above were read twice and voted unanimously, and sent up for concurrence.

Mr. Pearce offered the following resolution, to wit : —

Resolved, That the governor be requested to make

known, by proclamation to the people of this state, that the government under the constitution thereof has been duly organized, and calling upon all persons, both civil and military, to conform themselves to said constitution and to the laws enacted under the same, and to all other jurisdiction and authority under and by virtue of the same.

Read twice, and voted to pass unanimously, and sent up for concurrence.

Mr. Brown, of Glocester, moved than when this House adjourn, it will adjourn to meet at this place at nine o'clock, A. M., and that, in the mean time, the sheriff be directed to prepare the state house for the reception of this House.

The motion, after debate, was adopted.

Mr. Simmons, of Providence, offered the following act, to wit: —

Be it enacted by the General Assembly as follows: —

The act entitled "An act in relation to offences against the sovereign power of the state," passed at the March adjourned session of the General Assembly, 1842, is hereby repealed.

Read once; and, on the second reading, Mr. Olney, of Cranston, moved to lay the bill on the table until to-morrow.

The motion was negatived without a count.

The bill passed as an act, and was sent up for concurrence.

The secretary of state returned the resolutions voted by this House to inform the president, Congress, &c., of our organization, duly concurred in by the Senate and approved by the governor.

The secretary of state also returned a resolution voted by this House to request the governor to issue his proclamation, &c., duly concurred in by the Senate and approved by the governor.

The secretary of state also returned the bill repealing the act entitled "An act in relation to offences against the sovereign power of the state," duly concurred in and approved by the governor.

The house adjourned until nine o'clock to-morrow morning.

Attest: J. S. HARRIS, *Clerk.*

WEDNESDAY MORNING, MAY 4, 1842.

The House met at nine o'clock, A. M. The speaker in the chair.

The House is called to order. The roll is called, and a quorum is present.

Mr. Olney, of Cranston, addressed a note to the speaker, asking to be excused from attending in his seat to-day, in consequence of severe sickness in his family.

Voted to excuse Mr. Olney.

Mr. Wales, of Providence, offered the following resolution, to wit:—

Resolved, by this General Assembly, (the Senate concurring with the House of Representatives therein,) That a committee of   be appointed to proceed to Newport, and to request a conference with a similar committee of the General Assembly now convened at that place, for the immediate and honorable adjustment of the controversy now existing in this state.

This resolution was read; and, after debate, was, on motion, voted to be laid on the table.

Mr. Jencks, of Cumberland, offered a bill entitled "An act providing for the registration of electors, and directing the manner of voting by ballot in town and ward meetings."

Read; and, on motion, it is voted to take said bill up and pass upon it by sections.

The first section is read, and passed to be enacted.

The second section is read, and passed to be enacted.

The third section is read, and passed to be enacted.

The fourth section is read, amended, and passed to be enacted.

The fifth section is read, amended, and passed to be enacted.

The sixth section is read, and blanks are filled, and passed to be enacted.

The seventh, eighth, and ninth sections are read, and passed to be enacted.

The bill, as engrossed, passed to be enacted, and sent up for concurrence.

Mr. Brown, of Glocester, moved a bill entitled "An act to revive the charter of Glocester and Burrillville Greene Artillery."

The above bill was read twice, and passed to be enacted, and sent up for concurrence.

Mr. Pearce presented a bill entitled "An act to repeal an act entitled 'An act in amendment of an act entitled An act to prevent routs, riots, and tumultuous assemblies, and the evil consequences thereof,'" passed by the General Assembly at their April session, 1842.

Read twice; and, after debate, the same passed to be enacted, and sent up for concurrence.

Joseph Joslin, the general treasurer elect, came into the House, and having signified his acceptance of said office, took the oath in the words and form prescribed by the constitution, administered in the presence of the House.

Voted, on motion of Mr. Pearce, That Messrs. Simmons, Brown of Glocester, Gavitt, Cory, Holley, and Bosworth, be a committee to report a bill fixing the pay of members of both Houses at one dollar per day.

Mr. Pearce presented a bill entitled "An act to repeal certain resolutions passed by the General Assembly at their April session, 1842." The resolutions to authorize the governor to preserve the public property, to recall any arms loaned by the General Assembly, to authorize the governor to fill vacancies in the offices of the militia, and the appointment of a board of counsellors, were read, and passed to be enacted, and sent up for concurrence.

On motion, the rules of the House were taken up, and being read under each head, were debated, amended, and passed, as they appear on the files of the House.

Mr. Simmons, of Providence, from the committee on the compensation of the members of the General Assembly, reports the following bill, to wit: —

Be it enacted by the General Assembly as follows, to wit: —

SECTION 1. The several members of the Senate and House of Representatives shall hereafter receive, as a compensation for their services, the sum of one dollar for each day in which they shall be in actual attendance during any session of the Assembly.

SEC. 2. The several members of the Senate and House of Representatives shall be entitled to receive the sum of ten cents per mile, each way, for their travel, in attending at each session.

The above bill is read, debated, and passed to be enacted, and sent up for concurrence.

Voted, That Messrs. Arnold of Providence county, Arnold of Washington county, Pearce of Newport county, Bosworth of Bristol county, and Newman of Kent county, be a committee to consider to what time it is proper for the Assembly to adjourn.

Adjourned until two o'clock, P. M.

J. S. HARRIS, *Clerk.*

AFTERNOON SESSION.

The House met at two o'clock, P. M. The speaker in the chair.

Upon a call of the roll, a quorum is present.

Mr. Gavitt offered the following joint resolution, to wit: —

Resolved, by the House of Representatives, (the Senate concurring herein,) That Messrs. Simmons of Providence, and Mowry of Smithfield, be a committee to demand, receive, and transfer the records, books, and papers, appertaining to the office of the secretary of state, and transfer the same from Henry Bowen, late secretary of state, to his successor, William H. Smith.

Voted, and sent up for concurrence.

The committee on the time to which the legislature should adjourn, report by Mr. Arnold, and recommend that the General Assembly hold an adjourned session on the first Monday of July. Report accepted; and it is voted, that when this General Assembly adjourn, (the Senate concurring herein,) it will meet again on the first Monday in July next.

Resolutions drawn and sent up.

Mr. Pearce offered the following resolutions, to wit: —

Resolved, That the governor be further requested to call on all persons who are, or may become, indebted to the state, to make payment to the duly appointed officers and agents, under the provisions of said constitution; and to make known to all persons that no payment to any other officers or agents than those aforesaid will be considered as a discharge of their obligations.

Resolved, That the governor be requested to call on all persons who are in possession, or have charge of any of the public property, to deliver the possession or charge of said property to the authorities and officers acting under the constitution and laws of the state.

Read and passed, and sent up for concurrence.

The act repealing the amendment to the riot act, passed this morning, came down concurred in by the Senate, and approved by the governor.

The act providing for the registration, &c., of voters, came down with an amendment, changing the time, &c., of registry.

Voted to concur with the Senate in the amendment.

On motion, it is voted that the two Houses join in committee to proceed upon the election of officers.

Mr. Brown, of Glocester, moved the following bill, to wit: —

Be it enacted by the General Assembly as follows:—

SECTION 1. If any person or persons, or body corporate, from whom any sum or sums of money may become due and payable to the general treasurer of this state, elected under the provisions of the constitution of this state, as adopted by the people thereof, according to the provisions of the act to which this is in addition, or of other acts in addition or amendment to the same, should refuse or neglect to pay said sum or sums of money as by law directed, he or they so refusing and neglecting shall be liable to pay interest for the retainer of such sum or sums of money, at and after the rate of one per cent. of the amount due for each month's neglect and refusal as aforesaid.

SEC. 2. If any person or persons, or body corporate, holding in their possession any other money or property whatsoever belonging to the state, shall refuse to pay over and deliver the same to any officer or agent of the state duly authorized to receive the same, after being duly required hereto, he or they so refusing shall be liable to be sued therefor in any court of competent jurisdiction, in the name of the general treasurer aforesaid; and on rendition of judgment in any such case against the defendant or defendants, the court before whom such judgment may be rendered shall assess damages thereon at double the amount of the money or value of the property found due, with costs.

Read, and passed to be enacted, and sent up for concurrence.

The act reviving the charter of the Greene Artillery, came down concurred, and approved by the governor.

The act repealing the act establishing volunteer police companies in Providence, came down concurred, and approved by the governor.

The act repealing certain resolutions passed in April last, investing the governor with great power, and appointing his council, came down concurred, and approved by the governor.

The two Houses having joined, on motion, his honor the lieutenant governor was called to preside.

The elections of all civil officers were postponed until the next session of the General Assembly.

Several military officers were appointed, the record of which will appear on the secretary's minutes. The two Houses separated.

The act submitted to enable the governor to appoint and commission officers, and to organize the militia, was taken up, debated, and committed to Mr. Brown of Glocester.

Mr. Brown made report, that the act referred to him, giving the governor certain power in appointing and organizing the militia, is unconstitutional, and asks to be discharged from the further consideration of the same.

Voted to discharge the committee, and the act is laid on the table.

Mr. Brown offered the following resolution, to wit : —

Resolved, That the thanks of this House are due to their constituents, civil and military, for the zeal they have displayed, and efficient aid rendered, in assisting this General Assembly in organizing the government under the constitution. Voted unanimously.

Mr. Simmons offered a resolution authorizing the governor to send commissioners to Washington, to make known to the president our position, &c. Voted that the same be laid upon the table.

Mr. Simmons moved the following resolution, viz. : —
Resolved, by the House of Representatives, (the Senate concurring herein,) That Messrs. Pearce and Chace be a committee to demand, receive, and transfer all the moneys, bonds, securities, records, books, and papers, and every other article appertaining to the office of the general treasurer of this state, from Stephen Cahoone, late treasurer, to Joseph Joslin, his successor.

Voted, and sent up for concurrence.

Mr. Wales moved the following act, to wit: —

Be it enacted by the General Assembly as follows : —

SECTION 1. The charter of the United Independent Company of Volunteers, of the city of Providence, is so amended as that said company is authorized to receive and enrol additional members to the number of two hundred, exclusive of commissioned officers.

Voted to be enacted, and sent to the Senate for concurrence.

Voted that the House take a recess for one hour, it being now 5 o'clock, P. M.

At 6 o'clock, P. M., the House reassembled.

The speaker and a quorum present.

The act authorizing the volunteer company to increase the number of their men, came down concurred, and approved by the governor.

The resolutions transferring the effects of the offices of the late secretary of state and general treasurer, came down concurred, and approved by the governor.

The act to collect the revenue, and secure the payment to, and the possession of the state's property, and the consequences and liability in paying and delivering the same to officers under the constitution, came down concurred, and approved by the governor.

The act relating to the pay and travel of the members of the General Assembly, came down concurred, and approved by the governor.

The act relating to the duties of those indebted to the state, (marked No. 1,) came down concurred, and approved by the governor.

The resolution to adjourn until the first Monday in July next, came down concurred.

Mr Taber, of Smithfield, moved the following bill : —

Be it enacted by the General Assembly as follows : —

SECTION 1. In all elections of the captains and subalterns of militia companies, at their annual elections, the elections shall be made by the members of said companies delivering their votes, with the name of the person voted for thereon, to the officer of the company in command on the day of election; and all companies who may have neglected to choose their officers at their last annual election, may proceed to choose the same as aforesaid, on any day before the next annual election.

SEC. 2. The chartered military companies who have not made their returns, may make the same at any time previous to the next adjourned session of this Assembly.

SEC. 3. The governor is hereby authorized to commission the officers chosen by volunteer companies in this state for a term not exceeding one year from this time.

Voted to be enacted, and sent up for concurrence.

Mr. Simmons, of Providence, moved the following resolution, viz. : —

Resolved, by the House of Representatives, (the Senate concurring therein,) That the governor be authorized to appoint suitable persons as commissioners in behalf of this state, to proceed to Washington, to make known to the president of the United States, that the people of this state have formed a written constitution, and elected officers, and peaceably organized a government under the same, and that said government is now in full operation.

Voted, and sent up for concurrence.

Mr. Nathaniel C. Smith, a member from Barrington, sent to the speaker his resignation.

Voted, That the same be accepted, and that the speaker issue his warrant to the electors of said town, requiring them to elect another representative in his place.

George Niles, a member from Richmond, resigned his seat.

Voted, That the same be accepted, and that the speaker issue his warrant to the electors of said town, requiring them to elect another representative in his place.

Voted, That the clerks be directed to make out certificates of attendance for the pay of each member, according to the act of this session; and to deliver the same to them respectively.

On motion of Mr. Pearce, Mr. Simmons was appointed a committee to wait upon the governor, and inform him that this House is ready to adjourn if he has no further communications to make to them.

Mr. Simmons, the committee appointed to wait upon the governor, made report that he had performed that duty, and that the governor had nothing further to communicate.

The act relating to the election of military officers, to commissioning the same, and to charter companies, came down concurred, and approved by the governor.

The resolution appointing commissioners to proceed to Washington, came down concurred, and approved by the governor.

Voted, That John S. Harris be allowed, and paid out of the treasury, for his services as clerk this session, six dollars.

Voted, That Levi Salisbury be allowed, and paid out of the treasury, for his services as clerk this session, six dollars.

Voted, That Burrington Anthony be allowed, and paid out of the treasury, for attendance as sheriff, and other expenses this session, the sum of five dollars and fifty cents.

Voted, That Seth Howard be allowed, and paid out of the treasury, for attendance of himself and other officers at this session, the sum of ten dollars.

On motion of Mr. Newman, of Warwick, it is unanimously *Voted,* That the thanks of this House be presented to the Speaker for the able, dignified, and impartial manner in which he has presided over its deliberations.

Voted and resolved, That all officers not reëlected, and in whose places others have not been appointed, be, and they are hereby, continued in their respective offices until the adjourned session of this General Assembly, to be holden at Providence on the first Monday in July, 1842, with as full power and authority as they have at any time had.

Voted and resolved, That all business lying before this Assembly unfinished, be referred to the adjourned session to be holden on the first Monday in July, 1842; that the secretary cause the acts, orders, and resolutions passed at this session, to be published, with a suitable index, and distributed according to law; and that this Assembly be, and the same is hereby, adjourned to the first Monday in July, 1842, then to convene in the city of Providence.

Voted to be enacted, and sent up for concurrence.

The vote of adjournment came down concurred; and thereupon, the speaker informed the House that they were adjourned accordingly.

Attest: J. S. HARRIS, *Clerk.*

CHAPTER VII.

THE RIGHT OF THE CHARTER GOVERNMENT TO HOLD OUT AGAINST THE PEOPLE CONSIDERED. CAUSES OF COMPLAINT SET FORTH, ETC. CONFIDENTIAL LETTER FROM PRESIDENT TYLER.

It has already been shown that on the 3d of May, 1842, there were two organized political governments in Rhode Island, each claiming the exclusive right to the exercise of legislative functions; they could not both be right. One claimed under an exploded British charter, which the people had never adopted, and which no free, intelligent people ever would adopt; the government under which had been held by sufferance after the royal parchment had become a dead letter. The other claimed to derive its authority directly from the people. A very large majority of the whole people had, in the exercise of their inalienable sovereignty, conferred upon the latter legislative powers, and by the same act had forever abrogated and withdrawn all authority from the former. Under the charter the whole government of Rhode Island expired and was renewed every year, and the duties and powers of all officers, from the highest to the lowest, ceased and terminated at the end of every year, if they were not reëlected, and the government under the people's constitution was intended to commence at the time the old government expired by its own limitation. The charter legislature was nothing more than a tenant at will. This being the case, it follows of course that the government which had been set up by the people themselves had an undoubted right to make use of all necessary means to sustain itself. The people had committed their political interests to this new legislature, and it had become the duty of that legislature to protect and defend them. This each member of that legislature had sworn to do; therefore if any government ever had a right to defend and sustain itself by physical power, the people's legislature had that right, and must stand perfectly justified in the use of any measures necessary for that purpose. The question is simply this, Was the people's government set up upon the true principles of American democracy? The advocates for the charter government have told us that the people had no right to set up a government or to take any measures for that purpose without permission from the General Assembly. We have seen that fourteen thousand out of twenty thousand gave their votes for the constitution under which the people's government was organized; but we are told that that is of no consequence so long as the legislature did not give the people a license to proceed in the manner they did, and that therefore the old government must be considered as the rightful government until the General Assembly should authorize the people to set up a different form of government. Now if a government which had been set up by three fourths of the people was illegal and void because the legislature refused to sanction it, then if every man in the state, except the eighty-four who composed the General Assembly of the State of Rhode Island in 1841, had voted for the people's constitution and agreed to support it, it would still have been just as illegal, and the eighty-four men who composed that legislature might just as rightfully have declared the whole proceedings of the people void, and still claimed their right to rule the state, and have called upon the president of the United States, or any foreign power, to sustain them; and if, by means of menaces from abroad, and concessions and promises at home, that body found themselves able to subdue the people, they would maintain their power by the same right that the charter government was maintained in 1842. If three fourths of the people could not rightfully set up a government without the consent of the legislature, then *all* the people could not. It was upon that ground alone that the charter government held on to power in 1842; and we ask if there is a single unprejudiced individual living under the democratic institutions of the United States, who has any claim to common sense, who agrees to that doctrine? But we are told that the people of Rhode Island had no reason to complain of the government under the charter. Has it not been shown that more than half of the male citizens of that state over twenty-one years of age were by law excluded from all participation in the affairs of the government, whilst at the same time they were required by law to do duty in military and fire companies, and also to pay their full proportion of all public taxes? Has it not been shown also that the laws of that state gave non-freeholders no remedy against any wrongs that they might sustain unless they obtained the assistance of freeholders? Has it not been shown that they were denied the right of trial by a jury of their peers?

If they were satisfied to be thus disparaged and outlawed, why did they petition the legislature, time after time, during almost half a century? What was meant by the petition presented to the General Assembly in 1829, signed by two thousand citizens? What meant the suffrage organizations throughout the state in 1838 and 1839? What brought together the immense mass meetings in the summer of 1841? For what purpose did ten or twelve thousand men meet in convention in the city of Providence? What did these people mean by their loud complaints against the oppressive acts of the charter government, and what did their strong resolutions declare?

Is it not true that "all experience hath shown that mankind are more disposed to suffer, while evils are sufferable, than to right themselves by abolishing the forms to which they are accustomed"? And might not the disfranchised citizens of Rhode Island have said, in the language of their revolutionary fathers, "In every stage of these oppressions we have petitioned for redress in the most humble terms; our repeated petitions have been answered only by repeated injury."

Although the president was over-persuaded and misadvised, yet the following "private and confidential" letter to Governor King, dated May 9, 1842, shows that he was desirous that the controversy should be amicably settled by the parties themselves.

May 9, 1842.

Sir: Messrs. Randolph and Potter will hand you an official letter; but I think it important that you should be informed of my views and opinions as to the best mode of settling all difficulties. I deprecate the use of force, except in the last resort; and I am persuaded that measures of conciliation will at once operate to produce quiet. *I am well advised,* if the General Assembly would authorize you to announce a general amnesty and pardon for the past, without making any exception, upon the condition of a return to allegiance, and follow it up by a call for a new convention upon somewhat liberal principles, that all difficulty would at once cease. And why should not this be done? A government never loses any thing by mildness and forbearance to its own citizens; more especially when the consequences of an opposite course may be the shedding of blood. In your case, the one half of your people are involved in the consequences of recent proceedings. Why urge matters to an extremity? If you succeed by the bayonet, you succeed against your own fellow-citizens, and by the shedding of kindred blood; whereas, by taking the opposite course, you will have shown a paternal care for the lives of your people. My own opinion is, that the adoption of the above measures will give you peace, and insure you harmony. A resort to force, on the contrary, will engender, for years to come, feelings of animosity.

I have said that I *speak advisedly.* Try the experiment; and if it fail, then your justification in using force becomes complete.

Excuse the freedom I take, and be assured of my respect.   John Tyler.

Governor King, *of Rhode Island.*

But the charter authorities, elated with the idea of putting down the suffrage party by force of arms, were not inclined to make any concessions or adopt any conciliatory measures, and the president's advice was disregarded.

CHAPTER VIII.

MR. DORR'S VISIT TO WASHINGTON AND NEW YORK. HIS RETURN TO PROVIDENCE. ATTACK UPON THE ARSENAL.

IMMEDIATELY after the adjournment of the constitutional legislature, Mr. Dorr proceeded to Washington, and laid his case before the chief magistrate and heads of the departments. But he soon found, to his mortification, that the administration had become strongly prejudiced against him in consequence of misrepresentations which had been made by the envoys of the charter government.

Southern men had become imbittered against him and his cause by being told that it was wholly an anti-slavery movement. This was false; not a particle of abolitionism was mingled in the controversy. At home the vilest slanders and most egregious falsehoods were conjured up and put in circulation by the obsequious minions of power; the desk and the forum assisted to give them currency, and they were echoed and reëchoed from high places. At one time it was rumored that Mr. Dorr was coming with murderous legions from abroad, and at another that he and his men intended to rob all the banks in the state, to pillage and burn the city of Providence, and ravish its fair inhabitants.

Such reports were not only entirely without foundation, but so extremely absurd and improbable, that no honest man ought to have given them currency. Again, to pacify the people, they were told that the government had consented to accede to their demands, and would, as soon as possible, give them a *legal* constitution, with free suffrage, and about every thing else they asked for.

On his return from Washington, Mr. Dorr was received in the city of New York with strong demonstrations of respect and confidence, and was assured that, if the president should oppose him with the national soldiery, that city would furnish troops enough to withstand all that the general government might send. Returning home, Mr. Dorr arrived at Stonington on Sunday morning, the 15th of May. As soon as it was known that he was at Stonington, a large party of citizens, with about thirty men under arms, proceeded to that place to greet him and renew their assurances of fidelity. On his arrival in Providence, he was met by a large escort of military and private citizens; a splendid barouche drawn by four fine white horses had been prepared for his reception, and as the procession moved through the principal streets of the city, shouts of welcome were heard on all sides. The pageant appeared more like the triumphant entry of a victor than that of a returning exile. The multitude thronged about his person to greet and encourage him, and renew again and again their promises of fidelity. But alas! many of these promises were hollow and false, and made by irresolute, fickle-minded men, who did not know themselves; and Mr. Dorr was destined soon to witness scenes of an opposite character. During his absence, a large number of arrests were made under what was denominated the Algerine laws. Alarmed and disheartened, nearly all the members of his legislatures who had not been arrested, soon resigned.

These resignations fell upon the ears of Mr. Dorr like the rumblings of an earthquake. No language can describe the emotions of his heart, when, in that critical moment, he saw the pillars upon which he had rested for support shaken and falling thick around him. It required the firmness of a Cato to withstand the shock. But relying on the justice of his cause and the rectitude of his own intentions, and still confiding too much, far too much, in the integrity and fidelity of the people, he never faltered for a moment; whatever his reason and his conscience told him was right he would do to the utmost of his power, and whatever was wrong he would not do. Call this obstinacy, or wilfulness, or by whatever name you please, it is nevertheless the most prominent trait in the character of every truly great man. It required no ordinary heroism to sustain the mind under reverses like these. He that could remain firm and unmoved, self-poised and self-sustained, in a crisis like this, must possess a transcendent moral magnanimity.

During Mr. Dorr's absence, the charter authorities were busily occupied in making preparations to resist, by force of arms, the constitutional government. Military companies were reorganized, filled up, and drilled, and required to be in readiness to obey any orders which might be given them. It had become apparent to every one that the existing political controversy would never be settled without a resort to arms. When Mr. Dorr became advised of the notes of preparation in progress against him, he saw that a crisis had arrived when decisive measures must be taken. The state arsenal, in the vicinity of the city, was an object of indispensable importance; this was a strong stone building, containing, at that time, six or eight pieces of ordnance, with a great part of the muskets and ammunition belonging to the state. An additional guard had recently been placed within it, of which Mr. Dorr had not been advised; but he saw at once that he must gain possession of that, or abandon his position immediately. This was a most trying moment. A large number of those men upon whose courage and counsel he had depended had left him and retired. The whole responsibility of a cause which fourteen thousand men had instituted was now thrown upon the shoulders of a single individual. He must give up the cause, and retire in disgrace, or make an attempt to take possession of the arsenal. The hearty greetings and imposing demonstrations with which he had been met on his return to the city seemed to give him assurance that the people were determined to sustain him. Who could have witnessed the long procession of men, both armed and unarmed, that escorted him through the city the day before, and heard their cheerful greetings and repeated assurances of fidelity, and not have believed that any assistance which he might require would be forthcoming at the first call? He could not and he would not cease to confide in the integrity of his friends. On the morning of the 17th of May, Mr. Dorr issued his orders to the military of the several towns to repair forthwith to head quarters and wait further orders. That call met with but a very imperfect response, and many who did obey it departed before evening. At one of the clock on Wednesday morning, May 18th, the signal for an attack upon the arsenal was given by the firing of an alarm gun. After nearly an hour's delay, Mr. Dorr found that only about two hundred and fifty men waited his command. At the head of that little band, armed with muskets and two pieces of artillery, he marched on foot, stationed his forces in front of the arsenal, and summoned its commander to surrender. The summons was returned with an indignant refusal. The night was so extremely dark that it was difficult for friends and foes to distinguish each other, and it was soon found that Mr. Dorr's two pieces of artillery had been rendered inefficient by unseen hands, and he and his small force returned to head quarters without firing a single gun. When morning came, and it was satisfactorily ascertained that Mr. Dorr's forces had dispersed, several companies of militia, armed with muskets and field pieces, marched boldly up to his head quarters; but before their arrival Mr. Dorr left in company with a friend, and fortunately escaped the grasp of his enemies. Thus ended a bloodless tragedy, which had caused the city of Providence dire forebodings. This transaction has been the subject of animadversion and ridicule, and Mr. Dorr's conduct looked upon as the feat of a maniac. But it should be recollected that it is much easier to find fault than to command a burning steamer. Mr. Dorr, by the resignation and desertion of his men, had been unexpectedly forced into the perilous position which he occupied; he made no pretensions to military knowledge or skill, but a tremendous responsibility was thrown upon him, and he was not the man to shrink from it; and if he did not display the wisdom and acumen of a veteran officer no one need be surprised. It is easy now to see that the attack upon the arsenal was injudicious; but this point is more easily decided now than it could have been at that moment. Mr. Dorr was not aware of the defection which was rapidly taking place in the suffrage ranks; he had an overweening confidence in the integrity and fidelity of mankind; he had not yet learned by his own sad experience that "all men are liars." He was not aware of the power of the arsenal to resist attacks. He did not stop to consider the force which the charter government could almost instantly bring against him. But he vainly imagined that a large portion of all the military of the state would rally around his standard at the first call. Yet when the signal was given and the demand made, like the "spirits of the vasty deep," they were called, but did not come.

CHAPTER IX.

MARTIAL LAW. GOV. KING'S PROCLAMATION. GOV. DORR'S RETURN AND PROCLAMATIONS. OUTRAGES COMMITTED UNDER THE PRETEXT OF MARTIAL LAW.

DURING the absence of Mr. Dorr, after the 18th of May, and while he was supposed to be residing under the protection of his friend Chauncy F. Cleveland, then governor of the State of Connecticut, Gov. King issued the following proclamation : —

By His Excellency SAMUEL WARD KING, Governor, Captain General, and Commander-in-Chief of the State of Rhode Island and Providence Plantations.

Whereas THOMAS WILSON DORR, of Providence, in the county of Providence, charged with treason against the said State of Rhode Island and Providence Plantations, is a fugitive from justice, and supposed to be now within the limits of our sister State of Connecticut; and from credible information, is still pursuing his nefarious enterprise, against the peace and dignity of said State of Rhode Island and Providence Plantations; and whereas I made a requisition, on the 25th day of May last, addressed to his excellency Chauncy F. Cleveland, governor of said State of Connecticut, for the apprehension and delivery of the said Thomas Wilson Dorr, according to the constitution and laws of the United States in such case made and provided; which requisition his excellency Chauncy F. Cleveland, governor of said state, has hitherto declined to comply with; —

I do, therefore, pursuant to authority in me vested, and by advice of the Council, hereby offer a reward of one thousand dollars for the delivery of the said Thomas Wilson Dorr to the proper civil authority of this state, within one year from the date hereof, that he may be dealt with as to law and justice shall appertain.

Given under my hand and the seal of said state at the city of Providence, this eighth day of June, [L. S.] in the year of our Lord one thousand eight hundred and forty-two, and of the Independence of the United States of America the sixty-sixth.

SAMUEL WARD KING.

By his Excellency's command:
HENRY BOWEN, *Sec'y of State.*

But this proclamation had no effect, and Mr. Dorr fearlessly returned to the state on the 25th of June, and issued the following proclamation: —

STATE OF RHODE ISLAND AND PROVIDENCE PLANTATIONS.

A Proclamation, by the Governor of the same.

By virtue of the authority vested in me by the constitution, I hereby convene the General Assembly which was adjourned to meet at Providence on Monday, the 4th of July next, at the town of Glocester, on the same day, for the transaction of such business as may come before them.

And I hereby request the towns and districts, in which vacancies may have occurred by the resignation of representatives or senators, to proceed forthwith to supply the same by new elections, according to the provisions of the constitution.

Given under my hand and seal of state, at Glocester, the 25th day of June, A. D. 1842.

Thomas W. Dorr.

On the same day, June 25, 1842, the charter General Assembly, then in session at Newport, passed the following act declaring the state under martial law: —

An Act establishing Martial Law in this State.

Be it enacted by the General Assembly, as follows: —

Section 1. The State of Rhode Island and Providence Plantations is hereby placed under martial law; and the same is declared to be in full force until otherwise ordered by the General Assembly, or suspended by proclamation of his excellency the governor of the state.

In testimony whereof, I have hereunto set my hand, [L. S.] and affixed the seal of said state, at Providence, the day and year above written.

Samuel Ward King.

By his Excellency's command:
Henry Bowen, *Sec'y of State.*

And about the same time Mr. Dorr issued the following proclamation: —

General Orders.

Head Quarters, Glocester, R. I.,
June 25, 1842.

I hereby direct the military of this state who are in favor of the People's Constitution, to repair forthwith to head quarters, there to await further orders; and I request all volunteers and volunteer companies so disposed to do the same.

It has become the duty of all citizens who believe that the people are sovereign, and have a right to make and alter their forms of government, now to sustain, by all necessary means, the constitution adopted and established by the people of this state, and the government elected under the same.

The only alternative is an abject submission to a despotism, in its various practical effects, without a parallel in the history of the American states. I call upon the people of Rhode Island to assert their rights, and to vindicate the freedom which they are qualified to enjoy in common with the other citizens of the American republics.

I cannot doubt that they will cheerfully and promptly respond to this appeal to their patriotism and to their sense of justice; and that they will show themselves in this exigency to be the worthy descendants of those ancestors who aided in achieving our National Independence.
THOMAS W. DORR,
Governor and Commander-in-Chief.
By order of the Commander-in-Chief.
WM. H. POTTER, *Adjutant General.*

Before this time, troops, with an additional supply of arms and ammunition, had been sent forward by President Tyler, and were stationed in the forts on Rhode Island, ready to obey the requisition of the charter government. When martial law was announced, a wild consternation spread over the whole state; business became in a measure suspended; a thrill of horror seemed to touch all hearts, and men looked aghast upon each other. This act was passed on Saturday, and early on Sunday morning, June 26, a band of armed and unarmed men of the "law and order" party entered the office of the Daily Express, in the city of Providence searched the office throughout, and commanded the publishers to evacuate the building immediately. A fearful mob collected in the street, and threatened to destroy the building. Under these circumstances the publishers were compelled to give notice that their paper would be discontinued. This was the only office which had up to that time continued to advocate the people's cause. As soon as martial law was made known, every law and order man and every heartless ruffian appeared to suppose himself licensed to commit all such depredations as he might choose, and armed bands soon sallied forth in various directions, and commenced their outrages. The following depositions will give the reader a few samples of their proceedings.

Deposition of Leonard Wakefield.

I, Leonard Wakefield, of Cumberland, in the State of Rhode Island, forty years of age, depose and say: That I am, and have been for about fourteen years, a minister of the Methodist Episcopal church. I have resided in Rhode Island, and been a local preacher there for about fourteen years. On the 13th of June, 1842, I was at home in my office; I acted at that time as assistant to the postmaster at Cumberland. The state troops were returning from Woonsocket to Providence — about three hundred. Two of the soldiers came into the office where I was then engaged, and inquired if I had any fire-arms, and demanded the same. I delivered to them a small birding gun, which I had had for many years, and they went away with it. I then went into my house to dinner; my wife was tending a sick infant child, which was not expected to live, and which died in a few weeks after. As I sat eating my dinner, three soldiers came into the room, and two of them were stationed over me as a guard; they were armed wit' muskets; the other searched every part of the house, from the garret to the cellar, not excepting the lodging room. They found nothing, and I was then ordered to go with them; was not told where, nor for what. Two of the soldiers took me by the arms, one on each side, and marched me across the street to the tavern. I was carried into the hall of the tavern, and from thence, without any examination or inquiry, put into a wagon with other prisoners; there were twenty-one prisoners in wagons. We were then conveyed to Providence, a distance of twelve miles. The wagons containing the prisoners were in front of the body of the troops, who followed them. In each wagon there were soldiers guarding the prisoners; two on each side of me with muskets; and, so far as I could see, that was the mode each prisoner was guarded; none of them were bound. When we reached the precincts of Providence, we were taken from the wagons; the prisoners ranged two and two in file, flanked with soldiers on each side — the body of the troops in the rear; and in this order we were marched through the principal streets to one of the armories. While we were passing through the streets, garlands were thrown from windows to the soldiers; and there were shouts, and jeering, and insults heaped upon the prisoners. I heard, repeatedly, exclamations, "There goes the minister!" and in one instance, "D—n him, the next time he preaches, it will be in the state prison!" I was generally known in Providence as a clergyman. We remained at the armory about half an hour. There was no examination or inquiry of the prisoners. Some one of the officers, as I supposed, asked what should be done with the prisoners. General Edward Carrington (who, I understood, was one of the governor's council) said, "God d—n them, take them off to the state prison." The City Guards then took us in custody, having first been ordered to load with ball cartridge; which they did. We were then placed between two files of soldiers, the remaining troops in the rear, and were marched to the state prison. There were twenty-one prisoners, and the company of soldiers was a full one. We were put into the cells in the state prison. The cell that I was in had sixteen persons in it. Its dimensions were about twelve feet by nine. Under the edge of the roof there was a loophole, and in the door a hole about seven inches by five. A pipe for ventilating led from the floor through the outer wall.

We were put into the cell about sunset, and the sixteen continued confined there from Thursday evening until Sunday about noon — being let out once a day in the yard, under a guard. We slept on the floor — lying in a heap together, as we best could. The suffering from want of air and space was severe. On Sunday the prisoners were separated; and, after that, there were eight in the cell I was put in. I was confined six days, in all. I was taken before the commissioners in one of the rooms in the jail building. Stephen Branch was the chairman, and there were three others. No charges whatever were brought against me. I was asked my name, age, and residence; if I had been at Chepatchet; if I had run bullets for Dorr's men; to which last question I answered no. I was also asked about a discourse I had preached on the Sabbath at the Albion village. Mr. Branch made the inquiry. I asked him if he wanted a synopsis of the discourse, which I was ready to give. He said he only wanted what I had said about fighting. I replied that I had exhorted the people not to fight at all on either side. He asked no further question. Christopher Rhodes, who was present, but not one of the commissioners, said he knew nothing about it; but his agent at the Albion village had told him something about it. He did not state what. In answer to the question whether I had been at Chepatchet while Dorr was

12 *

there, I answered that I had; that I went at the request of a number of my neighbors, to induce the Cumberland men, who were there on the suffrage side, to come home; that I had no arms. It was true that I had gone to Chepatchet, and had an interview with the Cumberland company on the suffrage side; and, in consequence of my representations, as I believe, they left the ground and returned home.

After these inquiries were made by the commissioners, the chairman asked if any person appeared for or against me. There was none on either side. I had four of my neighbors present, to testify in my favor if necessary; but there being no charges against me, I did not call on them. I was then remanded to prison, no reason being given for that course, and remained in confinement till the next day in the afternoon, when I was again carried before the commissioners, with some fifteen others, to whom an address was made, and we were discharged. From the time I was arrested, and until discharged, nor ever after, did I hear or learn from the authorities the grounds, or charges, or suspicions, upon which I was arrested. During my imprisonment, our fare was two rations a day of stale bread and meat, and nothing else but water. I had done nothing on the suffrage side, except to express my opinions freely and fearlessly, with a temperate zeal. I had done nothing to induce, but all I could to prevent violence. The sermon alluded to, which I preached at Mr. Rhodes's village, (the Albion,) was decidedly pacific, and discouraged any attempt to take up arms.

LEONARD WAKEFIELD.

COMMONWEALTH OF MASSACHUSETTS, *Bristol, ss.*
PAWTUCKET, *May* 4, 1844.

Personally appeared the above named Leonard Wakefield, and made oath to and subscribed the forego-

ing, reduced to writing by me in his presence. Before me, B. F. HALLETT,
Commissioner, and Justice of the Peace through the Commonwealth.

Deposition of Eliab Whipple.

I, Eliab Whipple, of Cumberland, in the State of Rhode Island, farmer, thirty-six years of age, depose and say: On the 6th of July, 1842, I was arrested by Samuel Currey and two others, on a warrant of the governor and Council, on a charge of treason. I was brought to Providence, and put into prison. At the end of eight days I was examined by the commissioners and remanded — nothing appearing against me. After I had been in prison twenty-four days, I was told I was discharged; but, before I left the prison, I was arrested again by the civil authorities, and the next day sent to the jail at Newport. At the end of six days I was allowed bail in ten thousand dollars, with sureties, which I procured. At the next term of the court, the grand jury found no bill; but my recognizance was not discharged until the next term, when I was informed that the grand jury had found no bill, and the recognizance was discharged. This information I had from the attorney general. I was imprisoned thirty-one days, and under recognizance for ten thousand dollars from August, 1842, to March, 1843. The only reason for my arrest, that I ever knew of, was, that I had voted for the people's constitution and for Governor Dorr. I had never taken up arms, nor taken any part in the conflict. I went to Chepatchet solely from curiosity on Friday, the 24th of June, and returned home the next day; was unarmed, and took no part. I continued at home about my ordinary business until I was arrested.

ELIAB WHIPPLE.

COMMONWEALTH OF MASSACHUSETTS, *Bristol, ss.*
PAWTUCKET, *May* 9, 1844.

Personally appeared the above named Eliab Whipple, and made oath to and subscribed the foregoing, reduced to writing by me in his presence. Before me,
B. F. HALLETT,
*Commissioner, and Justice of the Peace
through the Commonwealth.*

Deposition of Henry Lord.

I, Henry Lord, of Providence, in the State of Rhode Island, depose and say: That I am nearly sixty years of age. I was taken by the charter troops at Acote's Hill on the morning of June 29, 1842, and was unarmed. I was the only person on the hill when the advance of the troops came up; I saw no other; this was about eight o'clock, I should judge; it might have been seven. When I saw a horseman coming, I went down the hill and met him. It was Colonel George Rivers. He asked me, (pointing to the hill,) " Will they fire?" I answered no; that there were no troops there. He then went up, two soldiers following, and gave three cheers when he took possession of the fort. There was no resistance made, for there was no one there to make it. I went down into the road, and there encountered the main body of the troops, and was taken prisoner. They then had in charge over a hundred prisoners; none were tied. The troops did not go up the hill, but marched to Sprague's hotel with the prisoners. The next morning we were mustered, and tied together with large bed-cords. The rope was passed in a close hitch around each man's arm, passing behind his back, and fastening him close up to his neighbor, there being eight thus tied together in each platoon; we had no use of the arm above the elbow. In this way we were marched on foot to Providence, sixteen miles, threatened and pricked by the bayonet if we lagged from fatigue, the ropes severely chafing the arms; the skin was off of mine. In two instances, when the soldiers were halted to refresh, we were refused the use of their cups to get water from the brook which passed the road, and had no water till we reached Greenville, about eight miles. It was a very hot day; I had had no water or breakfast that morning, and I received no food until the next day in Providence. We were marched thus tied through the streets, and, after being exhibited, were put into the state prison. Fourteen were put into my cell, which was seven feet by ten. After remaining in prison twenty-four days, I was released on parole.

HENRY LORD.

COMMONWEALTH OF MASSACHUSETTS, *Bristol, ss.*
PAWTUCKET, *May* 10, 1844.

Personally appeared the above-named Henry Lord, and made oath to and subscribed the foregoing, reduced to writing by me in his presence. Before me,

B. F. HALLETT,
*Commissioner, and Justice of the Peace
through the Commonwealth.*

Deposition of Mehitable Howard.

I, Mehitable Howard, of Cumberland, in the State of Rhode Island, wife of Joseph Howard, of said Cumberland, depose and say: That on the 29th of June, 1842, in the morning, between five and six o'clock, Alfred Ballou, with seven other men, all armed with guns, came to my house and entered it — I forbidding them to enter. Myself and grandchildren were the only ones in the house; he broke the door open, and drove it off the hinges. As Ballou came in, he seized me by the shoulders, and shook me hard, leaving prints where he took hold of me. He then pushed me, and pushed me against a post about three or four feet from where I was standing, which bruised my shoulder very much. He came up to me again, seized me, and pushed me again towards the window, saying, "Get out of the way," in a loud voice. He then gave me a shake, and left me, saying, "Where is Liberty?" meaning my son, and "where is the gun?" He went up stairs, and searched the chambers, turning the beds over in which the little children were. He then came down, and went into my lodging room, and took a gun and carried it off. I was much overcome; but when he came out, I said, "I don't fear you, Mr. Ballou." He then came up to me, laid his hands on me, and shook me, and said, in a very loud voice, "Do you know that you are under martial law?" He then took his bayonet, and put the point of the bayonet against the pit of my stomach; he pressed the bayonet against me, and said, "I will run you through," looking very angry and spiteful. The point of the bayonet went through my clothes and fractured the skin, but did not break it, but caused the blood to settle the size of a ninepence, or larger. I verily believed at the time that he intended to run me through. With my hand I knocked the bayonet away, and he stepped back, and stood and looked at me with a stern look, and then went out of the house. Ballou appeared to be the leader of the band. Some of his men were in the house; I saw two in the house with him, armed. He said nothing to me about his authority, or why he treated me so. My husband was a suffrage man, which is the only reason I know for this treatment. Ballou had been a neighbor of ours for near forty years; he was a charter man. I was hurt very bad, and unable to do my work for several days after, and have never recovered from the effects of the shock upon my system. I am sixty-two years of age. The gun has not been returned.

MEHITABLE HOWARD.

COMMONWEALTH OF MASSACHUSETTS, *Bristol, ss.*
PAWTUCKET, *May* 4, 1844.

Personally appeared the above-named Mehitable Howard, and made oath to and subscribed the foregoing, reduced to writing in her presence by me. Before me,
B. F. HALLETT,
*Commissioner, and Justice of the Peace
through the Commonwealth.*

Deposition of Otis Holmes.

I, Otis Holmes, of Providence, in the State of Rhode Island, brewer, fifty years of age, depose and say: That on Sunday, the 26th of June, 1842, my house in Providence was entered by a body of armed men. They searched the house, breaking the locks, though I offered to give them the keys. I was lying on the bed, and was taken by two men, who seized me by the collar. One was named Samuel Thomas; the other I did not know. Charles Harris, at the same time, put a pistol to my breast. They found nothing at my house but my training musket, which I had had many years; they took it, and have never returned it. They carried me to my brewery, and broke in there; I had previously offered them the keys of my premises. In the brewery they found two old ducking guns, without locks, and one old musket with a shattered lock and no ramrod. They took these, and they have never been returned. There was also a hunting powder-horn, with about half a pound of powder, and a canister of about a pound of powder, which belonged to another man who left it there. They also broke into my store and counting room, and ransacked that, my private papers, and then marched me to the office of Henry L. Bowen, Esq., justice of the peace. I was carried through the streets by two men having hold of my collar, and another in front with a pistol. There were about thirty men with muskets ; I made no resistance. The course lay through the principal street of the city. I heard no charges, and was not examined before Mr. Justice Bowen, but was marched to jail, with a file of soldiers, in company with ten others. I was put in a room in the jail, and remained there seven days, and then, without examination, put into one of the cells of the state prison, with seven others. It was large enough for us to lie down, by lying heads and points. I remained there twenty-one days. The suffering was extreme, from heat and want of air, with plenty of vermin. The health of the prisoners suffered materially. During this time I was examined by the commissioners. They charged me with keeping arms to aid the suffrage cause. No proof was shown. I was remanded. I then got a writ of habeas corpus before Judge Staples, of the Supreme Court, and went before him in a room in the jail, and, upon a hearing, was discharged. I was then immediately committed by the deputy sheriff, on a warrant from Henry L. Bowen, on a charge of treason. I then applied for another writ of habeas corpus, which Judge Staples ordered to be heard before the whole court at Newport. I was there heard, and allowed bail in the sum of twelve thousand dollars, with sureties. At the next sitting of the court in the county of Providence, the grand jury found no bill against me, and I was discharged. I was in close prison fifty-nine days.

OTIS HOLMES.

COMMONWEALTH OF MASSACHUSETTS, *Bristol, ss.*
PAWTUCKET, *May* 9, 1844.

Personally appeared the above-named Otis Holmes, and made oath to and subscribed the foregoing, reduced to writing by me in his presence. Before me,

B. F. HALLETT,
Commissioner, and Justice of the Peace through the Commonwealth.

These minions of law and order appeared to believe that they might deal as they chose with the person and property of any individual who had been known to express himself in favor of Mr. Dorr or the people's constitution; and many appeared to glory in their ruthless exploits. Commissioned and non-commissioned officers and private soldiers vied with each other in their lawless enterprises. All the streets in Providence were placed under guards of armed men, and sentinels were stationed at every corner. The faculty of Brown University dismissed the students, and gave the college buildings to the soldiers for barracks.

The jails of Providence, Newport, and Bristol were soon filled with men who had been arrested, and bound, and brought to prison by armed freebooters. And even the cells of the state prison, designed only for convicts for capital offences, were jammed as full of innocent victims as ever was the Black Hole of Calcutta. If we had not witnessed these scenes we could never have believed that men could be so instantly converted into demons; men, who but yesterday enjoyed a neighborly intercourse, by the first touch of martial law fell upon each other like angry tigers. No one who had ever been known to be in favor of suffrage was safe in his own house, and no sick room or female retreat was protected from violation. Ministers and deacons of the "law and order party" advised and assisted in arresting members of their own churches; neighbors turned against neighbors, and Christians against Christians. The Sabbath was profaned and the church desecrated; priests and deacons readily surrendered the temple of the Most High to bands of rapacious men, and brutish soldiers took up their abode in the holy tabernacle. The stillness of the sanctuary was broken with the loud clanks of armor and the rude trampings of an infidel soldiery. The church was converted into an arsenal, weapons of death were piled in the chancel, and men thirsting for blood surrounded the altar. Instead of anthems of praise and orisons of peace, the sacred choir resounded with beastly orgies, and the house of prayer became a den of thieves. Gangs of armed men, as ruthless as ever sacked a conquered city, patrolled the state; dismay went before them, and shame followed after.

Men acting under the supposed authority of martial law appeared to think that their jurisdiction was as boundless as their power. They were not satisfied to confine their operations to the narrow precincts of Rhode Island, but broke over its boundaries into Massachusetts, as the following testimony will show : —

Deposition of Draper Carpenter.

I, Draper Carpenter, of Pawtucket, in the State of Massachusetts, physician, fifty years of age and upwards, depose and say: That on the day on which Alexander Kelby was shot, I was in Pawtucket, on the Massachusetts side. In the evening there were a number of discharges of muskets from the bridge, which is the dividing line between Massachusetts and Rhode Island. The firing appeared to be in volleys. There were troops stationed on the bridge, said to be the Kentish Guards — Rhode Island troops. I did not see a suffrage man in arms that day or evening; and I have no doubt these troops were the Rhode Island charter troops. Soon after the firing commenced, a woman was brought into my office, supposed to be wounded; but it appeared that she had fainted from fright. At that time the firing ceased, but soon after commenced again, after an interval of about ten or fifteen minutes. Soon after the firing began the second time, a man came into my office, slightly wounded in the knee from a musket shot; but it was a slight wound, and I did not dress it. I did not know the person, and cannot name him; I was standing at the front window of my office, with a view to see or hear what was transpiring at the bridge. The distance from the bridge was about twenty rods, on Main Street, leading from the bridge. While standing in this position, a musket ball passed through two panes of glass in the two sashes forming the show window of the shop, passing near my head, and lodging in the shelf, which it penetrated about four inches from the edge where it entered. [The witness produces the ball, which he says he took from its lodgment, and it appears to be a musket ball of the size used for United States muskets, and not a rifle ball.] A few minutes after this, I was called on to go and see a man, Alexander Kelby, who was reported to have been shot. I directed them to bring him directly to the office, as it was no place for an examination there. They went away for that purpose; but immediately information came that he was dead. I was well acquainted with Alexander Kelby, and had generally been his family physician. He had a wife and five or six children, and had resided in Pawtucket, on the Massachusetts side, for some nine or ten years. He worked in the factory, and was rather an intellectual man, and read a great deal. I often loaned him books. He was a man of good character, and always peaceable and inoffensive. Other buildings, not in the direction of my office, on another street leading from the bridge, were fired into, as appears from the marks of the balls lodged therein, or having bounded from the brick walls. The bridge is the most central part of the village, and the two streets leading from it the most populous on this side.

DRAPER CARPENTER.

COMMONWEALTH OF MASSACHUSETTS, *Bristol, ss.*
PAWTUCKET, *May* 2, 1844.

Then the said Draper Carpenter, being duly cautioned and sworn, made and subscribed the foregoing, reduced to writing in his presence, by and before me,

B. F. HALLETT,
*Commissioner, and Justice of the Peace
through the Commonwealth.*

It appears from the testimony of the widow of Alexander Kelby that her murdered husband was a dresser tender, was about forty years of age, and worked in a manufactory on the Massachusetts side, and that by his death she was left a widow with eight small children, and without sufficient means for their support. It should be recollected that all the wicked and revolting deeds which have been mentioned, and hundreds more of the same kind, were committed under the banner of "law and order," and under the direction and in open view of a class of men professedly scrupulous about nice points of law — a class of men who claimed nearly all the piety, talent, and morality in the state, in which were found most of the public officers and a large number of the clergy; and yet this same party, with shameless impunity, trampled upon all laws, human and divine. By turning to the constitution of the United States it will be seen that Article I. of the Amendments was violated and broken by "abridging the freedom of speech and the press;" Article II. by "infringing the right of the people to keep and bear arms;" Article III. by " quartering soldiers in houses without the consent of the owners;" and Article IV., which declares that " the right of the people to be secure in their persons, houses, papers, and effects, against unreasonable searches and seizures, shall not be violated," was wholly disregarded. If the president of the United States had been as desirous to guard its constitution from violation as he was to protect a repudiated charter aristocracy, instead of aiding and abetting in these nefarious violations, he would have hindered and suppressed them.

If the height to which he had been, by accident, so suddenly raised had not made him giddy, and if he had not forgotten his own official oath, he would not at the same time have violated the rights of the people of a sovereign state and the constitution of the nation.

It is impossible to describe the scenes of more than savage barbarity which were of almost daily occurrence during this reign of terror. When the whole community is given up to the tender mercies of a lawless soldiery, no bounds can be set to their criminalities. When the father of a family finds that his house is no longer his castle, that his own sacred fireside is no protection against the violent encroachments of armed men — when he sees his home desecrated and plundered, his property destroyed, and his books and papers scattered in the street — when his wife and daughters are dragged from their beds or closets, with scarcely a garment upon them, submitted to the taunts and jeers of vile men, driven about their own house with the muzzle of the musket or pistol, and the merciless bayonet is made to penetrate the bosom of the innocent female — when the husband and father is plunged into the dungeon or driven into exile, and his home and his family left without support or protection — when the young mother, as she clasps the tender infant to her bosom, trembles lest some brutish soldier should violate her sacred retirement — when the chamber of the sick or dying is no security against sacrilegious intrusion, and when magistrates and clergymen justify and approve of all these things, — a tragedy is enacted which no language can describe or pencil paint. It crushes the resolutions of the brave and the hopes of the true. We stand aghast at the spectacle; it is the triumph of malice, and carnival of devils.

CHAPTER X.

MR. DORR'S RETURN. PROCLAMATION. DISMISSES HIS MEN, AND LEAVES THE STATE. PROCEEDINGS OF CHARTER TROOPS. ARRESTS AND IMPRISONMENT OF SUFFRAGE MEN.

LEAVING, for the present, this part of the history, we return to Mr. Dorr. His proclamation for convening the people's legislature at Chepatchet on the ensuing 4th of July was issued on the 25th of June. He had been absent from the state since the 18th instant, and had given no orders or advice concerning the fortifications at Acote's Hill; and before he decided that it was his duty to give the people another opportunity to rally in support of their constitution, he was assured, by a deputation sent him, that a large number of people had already collected at that place, who were determined, notwithstanding all their reverses, and all that threatened them at home and abroad, to persist in support of their own constitutional government. With these renewed assurances of fidelity, Mr. Dorr came to the conclusion that it was his duty to aid them in a further effort to accomplish that object, and therefore issued the afore-mentioned proclamation. It was evident that the people's legislature could not now be convened in Providence. Chepatchet was a quiet country village, situated sixteen or seventeen miles from Providence, where it was thought that Mr. Dorr's legislature might convene, and, unmolested, proceed to pass such orders and acts as might be deemed expedient. No possible harm could arise from such a meeting; but it soon became apparent that no such session could be held even there, unless the place was defended by a strong military force. It was known that, on the 23d of June, whilst Mr. Dorr was absent from the state, and nothing was doing any where by the friends of the constitution, except the small collection at Chepatchet, Governor King issued his orders as commander-in-chief to all the military of the state to put themselves in readiness for immediate service, and on the 24th of June a steamboat was ordered from Providence to bring up all the military forces from Newport, Warren, and Bristol. The boat returned the same evening, bringing several companies of artillery and seven or eight pieces of field ordnance. This boat was again ordered back the next day, and returned with several companies of infantry, numbering, in all, three or four hundred men. In the mean time orders were given to all the military forces of the state to repair forthwith to Providence. The state troops were soon brought in from all the neighboring towns, and on the next day, which was Sunday, the entire Washington brigade, five or six hundred strong, came in over the Stonington Railroad.

A company of Carbineers from New York city was brought in, each man being armed with one of Colt's six-barrelled rifles. A company of Sea Fencibles, having in charge a long Paixhan gun, (a thirty-two pounder,) arrived from Newport. By Sunday evening, June 26, the forces collected at Providence amounted to from three to four thousand men, with fifteen or twenty pieces of artillery. The city of Providence was filled with soldiers and their appliances, and nothing was heard or seen on either side but the dread array and din of war. Now, what had caused all this terrific display of hostile preparations? Was there any formidable foe in sight, any abroad or at home, to warrant these warlike preparations? Might it not have arisen from a constitutional cowardice in some, or a fear that arises from conscious guilt in others, urged on by powers behind the throne, compared with which the chief magistrate was himself a mere cipher? or had the charter authorities actually become alarmed by the falsehoods and bugbears which they had themselves conjured up and put into circulation?

Where was the foe with which this formidable charter army was to contend? Mr. Dorr was at Chepatchet, where he had attempted to convene his legislature. Some of his abiding friends had gathered around him, and a few were provided with arms. The neighboring citizens visited the place out of curiosity, and went and returned as they chose; but it has been shown, by good testimony, that only about two or three hundred men were under arms at that place at any one time. Mr. Dorr very soon became satisfied that the people's cause had become prostrated and their rights crushed by the iron heel of despotism. He saw that further efforts would be useless and improper, although the little band of brave men under arms manifested a desire to dispute the ground to the last, and, if necessary, to pour out their blood as a libation to freedom; yet Mr. Dorr believed that no such sacrifice was required of them or him, and therefore, on Monday, the 27th of June, he issued the following order: —

GLOCESTER, *June* 27, 1842.

Believing that a majority of the people who voted for the constitution are opposed to its further support by military means, I have directed that the military here assembled be dismissed.

I trust that no impediments will be thrown in the way of the return of our men to their homes.

Yours T. W. DORR.

This order was issued about four o'clock in the afternoon, and forthwith communicated to the men under arms by Gen. DeWolf and Col. Comstock, who commanded the station. Immediately on receiving the order, the military dispersed. Let not this little band of brave men be disparaged because they were few in numbers. Theirs was not the empty daring that goes with the multitude and boasts loudest when no enemy is near. Their courage arose from an abiding sense of right. The spirit of 1776 glowed in their bosoms and nerved their arms; they were true men, whom no bribes could purchase, nor threats terrify. Mr. Dorr remained at his quarters until about seven o'clock that afternoon, when he left the place. But no language can describe his heart-rending emotions when he found himself obliged to abandon a cause in which he had labored so long and sacrificed so much — a cause so big with momentous consequences to himself, to his state, to the American people, and to the world. On that eventful night a lurid halo seemed to surround the sun as he sunk beneath the horizon. A star in the American constellation, once bright and shining, now became darkened as with an eclipse : patriots wept, and strong men looked dismayed. We will now return to the royal charter army at Providence, and take a brief notice of their movements. As soon as Mr. Dorr had given orders for the dismission of the men under arms at Chepatchet, he sent a copy of that order to Providence for immediate publication in the New Age; but that communication was intercepted, the seal broken, and the paper passed over to the governor and Council. They kept it in their possession until the next day, when they gave it up to those to whom it belonged. But the New Age, in which Mr. Dorr designed the order to be published the day before, had been suppressed, and the proprietors durst not now publish any thing without a permit from the governor or his Council. At length a written permit was obtained, and the order was published in an extra from that office. But the governor and his councillors had taken advantage of the information which they obtained by the seizure of the letter the day before, which contained the order, and had hastily and slyly despatched several military squadrons, which were directed to take separate routes and proceed to Chepatchet with all possible haste, in order to capture as many men as possible before they could get home to their families. These "law and order" troops had now become very courageous — men who, the day before, were frightened at their own shadows, now became bold as lions, and on they rushed towards Chepatchet; but when they arrived there, they found nothing but an empty breastwork. Not a man remained to oppose them: therefore this heroic army marched boldly up, and took possession, and immediately despatched the following bulletin to the commander-in-chief at Providence.

Orders, No. 54.

HEAD QUARTERS, &c., }
June 28, 1842. }

The village of Chepatchet and fort of the insurgents were STORMED at a quarter before eight o'clock this morning, and *taken*, with about *one hundred prisoners*, by Colonel William W. Brown. *None killed — none wounded!*

The one hundred men, more or less, mentioned in that bulletin, were none of them found at the fortification, or any where else, under arms, but were such men as their scouts and marauding parties had picked up and taken prisoners on the route. The village of Chepatchet was situated on a public mail route between Providence and Norwich in Connecticut; and Jedediah Sprague, a very respectable man, kept a large stage hotel in the village. Knowing that Mr. Dorr had been entertained there, these rapacious " law and order " troops proceeded to take possession of and plunder the premises. The following is the deposition of Mr. Sprague: —

Deposition of Jedediah Sprague.

I, Jedediah Sprague, of Glocester, in the county of Providence, State of Rhode Island and Providence

Plantations, aged forty years, do depose and say : That
I now am, and have, for the space of about four and a
half years past, been the innholder of the Chepatchet
hotel in said town of Glocester ; that I was the keeper
of said hotel in June, A. D. 1842, at the time of the
encampment of the suffrage party, or a portion thereof,
on Acote's Hill, near said village of Chepatchet. On
Thursday, June 23, 1842, late in the afternoon, the
suffrage people aforementioned commenced encamping
on said hill ; early Saturday morning following, (to wit,
the 25th of June,) Governor Dorr arrived and took rooms
in my house. Two or three days previous to said 25th
of June, persons known to be in the interest of the
charter party, (so called,) and hostile to the suffrage
party, were reconnoitring this section of the state, both
in the day and night time. Tuesday and Wednesday
evenings, the 21st and 22d of June, 1842, expresses
arrived from Providence, bringing the intelligence that
armed companies were forming in Providence for the
purpose of making an attack on the village of Chepatchet ; in consequence of this information, a portion
of the citizens of said village, together with a few persons from other towns, formed a patrol to watch and
protect the place. On Wednesday night aforesaid,
(which was the first night of the streets being generally
guarded,) information was received that large numbers
of persons had passed the turnpike gate, about four
miles east of this village, on the direct road to Providence, who were approaching the village at about twelve
o'clock at night, which is an unusual time for travellers
to be on the roads in this part of the country. About
one o'clock on the morning of Thursday, the 23d of June
aforesaid, Messrs. Shelley, Keep, Harris, and Peckham
were apprehended, all armed with pistols ; about which
time, several carriages, apparently approaching from towards Providence, hastily turned off from the main or
turnpike road, some eighty or one hundred rods below.

The persons taken by the patrol aforesaid were supposed to be an advanced guard of the company, which, from the intelligence received, it was expected would attack the village; and it was supposed that the discharge of cannon, which took place in the village immediately after the arrest of said persons, deterred others from entering the village. It being believed that the village of Chepatchet would not be strong enough to hold out against any considerable number of armed men or strong force, the persons apprehended were marched, with said company of patrol, to Woonsocket, where said Shelley, Keep, Harris, and Peckham were discharged. On Thursday, the 23d aforesaid, said patrol returned, accompanied by a part of two military companies from Woonsocket, and commenced the encampment on Acote's Hill, as before stated. Said Acote's Hill was in possession of the suffrage party, as aforesaid, until the afternoon of Monday, June 27th. During the occupancy of said hill and the village, the suffrage people were quiet, orderly, and peaceable, and the personal rights of the citizens were respected. On Saturday morning, the 25th of June, the bar of my house, where liquors were sold, was by me, at the request of Governor Dorr, closed, and remained so until Tuesday morning, the 28th. On the afternoon of Monday, the 27th, the military on Acote's Hill disbanded, and nearly all of them quietly retired from the village. An express started from my house on Monday afternoon, bearing a communication from Governor Dorr to Walter S. Burges, Esq., of Providence, acquainting said Burges with the fact that the forces on Acote's Hill were to be disbanded, and requesting said communication to be published in the Express, the organ of the suffrage party, published in Providence.

About seven o'clock, (according to the best of my recollection,) on the morning of Tuesday, June 28, the advance guard of Colonel Brown's regiment arrived at my house in carriages, under the command, as I understood at the time, of Lieutenant John T. Pitman, (clerk of the United States Court for the district of Rhode Island,) who was well known to me at that time, and for several years previous. There were in my house, at the time said advance guard arrived, only eight male persons, besides my own family and domestics, three of whom were gentlemen from Boston, who had arrived that morning; one gentleman from Long Island, and three persons with him, who had stopped with me over night as travellers, and who had not, to my knowledge, had any thing to do with the matters at that time agitating the state; and a Mr. Lyman Cooley, who had left the village the night before, and had returned that morning to my house, through fear, as he stated, that he could not make his escape. Said Cooley was from New York city; was taken prisoner in my house that morning; imprisoned in the county jail and state's prison in Providence in a state of insanity, and soon after died an inmate of the asylum for the poor in said Providence. Mr. Cooley was formerly a Providence man. I considered him to be in a state of insanity from his appearance and conversation on the morning of the 28th, before he was taken prisoner. None of the persons in my house, at the time of the arrival of the advance guard as aforesaid, were, to my knowledge, in any way armed; there was no such instrument as a musket, gun, pistol, sword, or the like, to be seen in said house. As said advance guard drove up in front of my house in carriages, the citizens of the village soon collected in the front piazza, and about the doors, to the number of ten or a dozen, which number gradually increased for a few minutes; none of whom were, to my knowledge, armed. I was standing on the piazza in front of the entry door leading to the bar room; the persons comprising said advance guard, having alighted from their carriages, came along scatteringly, and advancing towards me. I observed one shaking hands with Mr. Alexander Eddy, a citizen of this place; heard them in conversation while approaching the spot where I was standing. As they came on to the piazza, I, turning partly around, invited them to walk in; they not heeding my invitation, I repeated it. At this juncture they all stood apparently hesitating what course to take. I stepped over the threshold of the door, and again invited them to walk in. At the last invitation, one of the advance guard placed his musket across the door afore alluded to, in the act of guarding it. Mr. Alexander Eddy at that moment attempted to pass in at the door, and the guard dropped the muzzle of his gun to prevent him from passing in; the guard then turned his left eye over his left shoulder to the street, and whilst he was looking to the street, Eddy raised the muzzle of said guard's musket, and passed into the entry. When said person who was guarding the door as aforesaid turned his face fronting the house, and saw Eddy in the entry, he brought his musket to bear upon him, (said Eddy,) and, calling him a God damned rascal, told him to come out, or he would shoot him down. At this time there was a general cry amongst the persons of the advance guard — "God damn 'em, shoot 'em down," and simultaneously a rush for the doorway. I was standing near the person who first brought his piece to bear upon Eddy, and raised the muzzle above the head of any one in the entry, by putting my hand under his gun.

There was a general rush at this time of the armed soldiers and unarmed citizens and spectators for the doorway, and the entry was immediately filled with both classes — the armed soldiers attempting to shoot the unarmed, and continually keeping up the cry of "*God damn 'em, shoot 'em down.*" I was in the midst of the scene, and was continually raising and brushing off the muskets, pistols, carbines, &c., with which they were armed; commanding them not to shoot; telling them they were not resisted by any armed force; stating to them that they produced the whole confusion and disorder, and that if they would be quiet, order would be restored; that I could and would maintain order in my house. I should think that, during this confusion, I brushed from my own person, and other unarmed persons, muskets, guns, pistols, and the like, as much as a dozen times. During the squabble aforementioned, I was pushed some seven or eight feet from the doorway into the entry, into about the midst of the crowd. In the mean time the door was pushed to, and locked by an unarmed man, and held by unarmed persons; the armed persons on the outside attempted to break said door down. Knowing that the unarmed persons in the entry could at that time protect themselves against those that were armed, I passed through the bar room from said entry, and went on to the piazza outside of the house, through one of the bar room windows, thinking I might be serviceable in preventing mischief on the outside. As I passed the first bar room window from the entry, in my attempt to get outside, some one of the soldiers thrust a pistol through a pane of glass in said window, directed or aimed at me. I passed to the next window, raised it, and went out. Being outside, and on the piazza aforesaid, the first thing that attracted my attention was said John T. Pitman with the muzzle of his musket or carbine at the key-hole of said entry door, and attempting to get it off. I was within about fifteen feet of said Pitman when I alighted from the window, and immediately approached him, and ordered him not to fire; my language was, "*For God's sake, don't you fire in there.*" This expression I think I made directly as I alighted from the window as aforesaid. I intended, if I could, to prevent said Pitman from firing in, and approached him for that purpose; but his piece was discharged when I was within about three feet of him. I recollect said Pitman's language at the time of firing was, "*I don't care a God damn; I mean to kill somebody.*" After said Pitman had discharged his piece as aforesaid, he rushed a few steps to the north, on the piazza, and then back towards the door, rapidly, appearing perfectly frantic, infuriated, and fiendish. About this time the main body of Colonel Brown's regiment were in sight, and such as had arrived proceeded to surround the house. I entered the front door, which is about twenty feet north of the one aforementioned, passed through one of the front rooms into the aforementioned entry, and unlocked the door through which said Pitman had discharged his piece. The ball which was fired through the key-hole as aforesaid, passed through the thigh of Mr. George H. N. Bardine, making a deep and severe flesh wound. Said Bardine was at the time in said entry, and near the door. Up to this time I heard no other discharge of fire-arms near or about my house, and am very positive there had been none; had there been any, I must have heard and known it. In a very few minutes my house was completely filled with armed men, and was entirely in their possession — every door guarded by soldiers. Soon after, or about the time the matters just spoken of were transpiring, I retired into the back part of the house, and discovered a soldier standing at one of the back doors with his musket cocked and bayonet fixed, and aimed into the house, and ordering the males and females to march into the back yard, one at a time. This, however, was abandoned by my assuring them that the ladies were unarmed, and would most certainly do no harm to any of them. The soldiers who took possession of my house were abusive and rough in their language and behavior, from the time they entered as aforesaid, during my continuance on the premises, which was up to four o'clock, P. M., of Wednesday the 29th. This I do not mean to apply to all of them; but it was the fact with very many. They took possession of every room in the house, and of all my effects, and ransacked from garret to cellar. There were neither arms nor munitions of war in the house, to my knowledge, at the time, except a small bird gun or fowling-piece, which was taken and carried off. Soon after the main body of Colonel Brown's regiment arrived, about half a dozen pieces of cannon were planted on the south and west sides of my house, and aimed towards it. They (that is, the soldiers) swore they would "blow us all to hell." They were prevailed upon not to fire into the house, by the interposition of two of the citizens of the village, who informed them that they were for "*law and order,*" but disapproved of their firing into the house. The guns were afterwards wheeled about, and fired a number of times, to the great destruction of windows in my house and of other houses in the immediate vicinity. There are sidelights to the door, (through the key-hole of which said Pitman discharged his piece,) with glass nine by twelve, through which he might easily see every thing which was going on in the entry aforesaid, there being four lights on each side of said door, of the aforementioned size; and the aforementioned front door, about twenty feet further north on said piazza, was open during the aforementioned squabble in the entry. Nothing prevented any one, if he chose, from passing through said last-mentioned door.

About sunrise on the morning of Tuesday, the 28th, I directed my domestics to set the table the whole length of the dining room, (one range of tables in said room will accommodate about sixty persons at a time,) and to put upon it all the victuals it would hold, and to be prepared to supply it as soon as need might require it; all of which was accordingly done. Immediately after the arrival of the troops, as aforesaid, the table aforesaid was filled, and continued to be filled from the time of their arrival in the morning, until between four and five o'clock in the afternoon : as fast as one got up another would supply the vacant place. In addition to those seated at the table eating, others were standing and eating victuals, which they took and had reached to them from the table.

There were also persons in the kitchen when the cooking was going on, who were taking victuals as the same were cooked, and others helping themselves from the closets and cellar. The table was also set for them again that evening, and a great many were victualled as aforesaid on the two succeeding days.

In taking possession of my barns, stables, and granary, they took possession of about twenty tons of hay, between eight hundred and one thousand bushels of oats, and from fifty to seventy-five bushels of corn, and between one and two tons of rye straw, — all of which was used and destroyed, with the exception of something less than one ton of hay. They also took possession of six horses at that time in the stable, five or six carriages, and as many harnesses, buffalo robes, and whips ; five of the horses were used, and I believe the other one, by the charter party, (so called ;) two of said harnesses have never been returned; four of the buffalo robes, and some half dozen or more of whips which were taken, have not, as yet, been recovered. During the Tuesday and Wednesday aforementioned, up to the time of my departure from the village, my house, barns, &c., were constantly guarded, and I was denied access to my barns and stables, and to many of the rooms in my house.

The troops of the charter party (so called) also had full possession of my liquor bar and cellar, and helped themselves to cigars, wines, and ardent spirits, according to their pleasure ; several hundred dollars worth of property was consumed or destroyed in liquors and cigars. I was generally a spectator to the scenes before described, after they had taken possession of my house; but was occasionally ordered about, at the muzzle of a presented musket or pistol, to perform some service about the house or bar. One man, in two instances, ordered me, in an authoritative tone, with a pistol presented at me, " to feed his horses ; " previous to this, all of the white males in my employ had been taken prisoners, and put under guard.

On Wednesday morning, the 29th, my wife and the females in the kitchen were put under guard, and set to work cooking; said guard was armed. Immediately after this, I was taken prisoner, but was released on parole, with my promise to be in Providence at six o'clock, P. M., of that day. I was arrested by Colonel W. W. Brown aforementioned, soon after which he left the village with between one and two hundred prisoners who had been taken at Chepatchet and the country round about. I saw said prisoners tied together in front of my house, with ropes, previous to their departure for Providence. An hour or two after my arrest, and after the departure of Colonel Brown with the prisoners, Ex-Governor William C. Gibbs sent for me to come to his room, which was in my house, when he gave me an examination as to my participation in the Rhode Island affairs ; and the following is a true copy of an instrument thereupon given to me, which was in my presence written by the Rev. Francis Vinton, of Newport, and in my presence signed by said Gibbs; which instrument is now in my possession, and at this time before me, and is exactly in the following letters, words, and figures: —

Jedediah Sprague (after due examination) is hereby released from arrest.

Wm. C. Gibbs, *General of Staff.*

June 29, 1842.

Having pledged myself to Colonel Brown to be in Providence at six o'clock in the afternoon, I, notwithstanding the release from Governor Gibbs, went into Providence to report myself according to promise, having with me said discharge from Governor Gibbs. I understood, after I arrived at Providence, that there was talk of having me again arrested. On inquiry by me, Who is going to have me arrested? the reply was, Henry L. Bowen. I exhibited my discharge or release to Governor Samuel Ward King, stating to him that I was threatened with another arrest. His reply was, in regard to the release which I had exhibited to him, *"I don't know but what it is sufficient — don't know about it — don't know."* I then went to the office of Henry L. Bowen, Esq., a justice of the peace in and for the city of Providence. I went voluntarily, not having been arrested or apprehended, saving by Colonel Brown, as aforestated. I understood that said Bowen was acting as a commissioner under martial law. He asked me a number of questions, which I answered; no witnesses were examined. Mr. Bowen finally ordered a constable in attendance to take me to prison; which was accordingly done. Said Bowen stated to me, at the time, upon my inquiring what the charge was against me, that "it was treason," and that "the evidence was, that I had entertained at my house Thomas W. Dorr, and the persons associated with him." I remained in prison twenty-two days, and suffered much from indisposition; I was in feeble health when committed — was just recovering from a long period of illness. After I had been in prison about two weeks, I was taken before a court of commissioners, as it was styled, and examined by interrogatories directed to me only. I was not confronted by witnesses, nor were any examined on the occasion, to my knowledge. After the examination as aforesaid, I was remanded to prison.

The following is a true copy of certain papers now before me, which I procured this spring from the keeper of the county jail and warden of the state's prison, and are exactly in the following words, letters, figures, and characters, to wit: —

To the Keeper of the Providence County Jail:

You are hereby required to receive, and safely keep, until further orders, Jedediah Sprague, in the debtor's apartment.

By order of the Commander-in-Chief.
        HENRY L. BOWEN.

June 29, 1842.
PROVIDENCE, *ss.*

Committed the *bodies* of the within-named Jedediah Sprague to the Providence county jail, as within commanded.

Fees, 74 cts. PELEG JOHNSON, *Constable.*

June 29, 1842.
PROVIDENCE, *ss.*

Committed the bodies of Jedediah Sprague and Joseph Hogans to the Providence county jail, by order of the governor and council, and have made my return on the mittimus, and left it with the jailer, together with the prisoner.

 Fees — 2 commitments, . . $1 48
 Carriage, ... 1 00
           ———
           2 48

    PELEG JOHNSON, *Constable.*

PROVIDENCE, *July* 21, 1842.

Jedediah Sprague, named opposite, was discharged on an order from the governor and council.

    THOMAS CLEVELAND, *Jailer.*

HEAD QUARTERS, COUNCIL CHAMBER,
PROVIDENCE, *July* 21, 1842.

SIR: You are ordered to discharge Jedediah Sprague, prisoner of war, and allow him to go at liberty.

By order of his Excellency, Samuel W. King.
L. H. ARNOLD, *one of his Council.*
To THOS. CLEVELAND, Esq.,
Keeper of the State Jail, Providence.

The above is a true copy of the original order on file.
THOS. CLEVELAND, *Jailer.*
PROVIDENCE, *April* 6, 1844.

April 6, 1844.
The above are correct copies of the original order of commitment, officer's return thereon, commitment and discharge of Jedediah Sprague.
THOMAS CLEVELAND, *Jailer.*

This deposition was sworn to before Jesse S. Tourtellot, justice of the peace.

In 1844, Mr. Sprague applied to the legislature for a remuneration for the property which the state troops had so taken, used, and destroyed. This application was rejected in the House of Representatives by a vote of 35 to 17, and in reply to his demand Mr. Sprague was told that "he had been taken and imprisoned as an insurgent, and had been let out of jail on sufferance, and ought to be thankful for being let off so easily."

The brave Colonel Brown, with the band of lawless robbers under his command, returned to Providence on the 29th of June, bringing with him one hundred and thirty prisoners, every man with his hands pinioned behind him, and all tied together with coarse ropes. In that condition they were marched, and driven, and urged on by the bayonet from Chepatchet to Providence, a distance of sixteen miles, without any refreshment. Here, fatigued and faint, — their spirits broken, their arms chafed and bleeding from the ropes, and their feet bruised and sore, — they were halted in front of the "Hoyle Tavern," so called, and were there publicly submitted to all the insults and reproaches that a profane and lawless multitude could heap upon them. After this barbarous infernalia, the prisoners were again moved along in front of Colonel Brown's own house for further insult : here they were mocked, hissed at, and spit upon, and Algerine ladies waved their handkerchiefs and threw a profusion of flowers, from their windows upon the brave conquerors. In this manner one hundred and thirty innocent citizens of Rhode Island were led through the principal streets in the city of Roger Williams, amid the loud taunts and jeers of a ruthless mob. But all this was not enough. The prisoners were next given to understand that they were to be taken back of College Hill, and there to be shot. No tongue can tell the feelings of indignation and horror which thrilled the bosoms of these innocent victims of political malice, nor shall we attempt to describe the deep anguish which often broke out in loud screeches from the children and friends of some of the prisoners. But they were not shot; their captors called themselves merciful men, and therefore marched the prisoners to the jail, and crowded them into the cells. In some cells only seven feet by nine, with a single aperture, seven inches by four, for the admission of air, fourteen prisoners were confined. When it is recollected that this was the 29th of June, and the hottest part of the season, we wonder that any ever escaped alive from those dungeons. If a single negro, who had escaped from his master in South Carolina, had been treated with half that indignity and cruelty in the city of Providence, the whole population would have rushed to his rescue.

By this time, the cells of the state prison and the filthy, dark receptacles and other apartments of nearly all the jails in the state were densely crowded with men who had been captured and made prisoners by bands of land pirates. The most heinous crime which any of the prisoners had committed was to vote for the people's constitution and for officers under it, and many of their captors and the principal leaders of these banditti were men who had also voted for that same constitution, and solemnly engaged to support it, but who had since forfeited their own engagements, and become traitors to a righteous cause. The victims were true men, their captors were false.

On the 28th of June, whilst Colonel Brown was earning such laurels at Chepatchet, Governor King gave orders to Colonel Hodges to proceed immediately to Pawtucket, and *blow up the bridge at that place.* This bridge is situated near the centre of a village, which probably contained at that time about ten thousand inhabitants. The Pawtucket River, which this bridge crosses, separates the State of Massachusetts from Rhode Island, and of course is one half in each state. This bridge is constantly occupied by passers, and is the only direct connecting medium between the separate parts of this large village. It was opposite this bridge, on the Massachusetts side, that Alexander Kelby had been shot by the "law and order" forces the day before. The following is the deposition of Harvey Chafee, who was a lieutenant in the company which was sent on that expedition.

Deposition of Harvey Chafee.

I, Harvey Chafee, of Providence, in the State of Rhode Island, forty years of age, depose and say: That, on the 28th day of June, 1842, I was first lieutenant of the united company, Train Artillery of Providence. I had formerly held the commission of lieutenant colonel in the same company, and resigned in 1833, and continued an honorary member. On the 27th of June I was elected lieutenant, and, understanding the company was only to be used as an unarmed patrol, I accepted the commission, and was qualified. The company then had no arms; Colonel Bradford Hodges was the commander. Tuesday morning, the 28th, after it was known that a man had been shot at Pawtucket, we paraded at the armory. As one of the officers, I was there shown an order from Governor King to Colonel Bradford Hodges, to this effect: "You are commanded to proceed forthwith to Pawtucket, and blow up Pawtucket bridge." The order was signed by Samuel W. King, commander-in-chief. I have a distinct recollection that such was the substance of the order, and am certain that it was an order to blow up the bridge. There were two cannon mounted, with ammunition; but we had no muskets. We were expecting every moment muskets from Massachusetts. Shortly after, the muskets did arrive at the railroad depot, from Boston, and were brought to the armory in boxes. The muskets were there taken out of the boxes, and were the United States Massachusetts muskets. They were in very bad condition; the bayonets would not fit, and could not be made to fit. They were afterwards tried, and many of them could not be got off, and the charges had to be drawn. After the muskets were distributed, we proceeded to Pawtucket with the two cannon, and, when half the distance, halted and charged the cannon with canister and grape, and the small arms with ball; then proceeded to Pawtucket bridge, and drew up the cannon so as to command the bridge and the Massachusetts side. We saw no armed persons, nor any disturbance, nor indication of an invasion of Rhode Island from Massachusetts. There was excitement growing out of what had happened the night previous, but no direct interference with us. Colonel Hodges communicated to one of the officers of one of the companies which were at Pawtucket when we arrived, that his orders were to blow up the bridge, and he took the command of the forces. During some parts of the time we were stationed there, there were as many as four hundred troops, I should judge. It was understood that Captain Olney, who commanded one of the companies, (the carbineers,) was a New York man, and not a citizen of Rhode Island. The artillery company occupied this post till Thursday noon, when we took up our line of march for Providence. While we were in Pawtucket, I could not see the least occasion for the company being stationed there. HARVEY CHAFEE.

COMMONWEALTH OF MASSACHUSETTS, *Bristol, ss.*
PAWTUCKET, *May* 10, 1844.

Personally appeared the above-named Harvey Chafee, and, being duly cautioned and sworn, made and subscribed the foregoing, reduced to writing by me in his presence. Before me, B. F. HALLETT,
Commissioner, and Justice of the Peace through the Commonwealth.

We have seen that on the 27th of June, Mr. Dorr

caused all the men who had taken up arms in support of the people's constitution to be dismissed, and the charter authorities declared, that by that act, the " war was ended ; " but their own wicked outrages did not end here. The charter troops, anxious to gain new laurels, went forward with less fear, when they found that all opposition was withdrawn. Revenge was the watchword, and although their victims were often found among their own quiet neighbors, they still " cried havoc and let slip the dogs of war " upon them. On the night of the 30th of June, 1842, after every indication of opposition to the charter government had been put to silence, Colonel Blodget, who commanded a small detachment of " law and order " troops, marched his forces into the town of Bellingham, in the State of Massachusetts, and a little past midnight, forcibly broke open and entered a public house, and proceeded to search it, and when the keeper demanded of the commanding officer his authority, Colonel Blodget replied, *By the authority of the bayonet!* At this place the party succeeded in arresting several inoffensive men, whom they marched to Rhode Island to be imprisoned, because they had been known to be in favor of the people's constitution. At the same time similar operations were going on in different parts of the state, as the following deposition will show.

Deposition of Stafford Healy.

I, Stafford Healy, of Rehoboth, in the county of Bristol, in the Commonwealth of Massachusetts, yeoman, of lawful age, testify and say: That on the twenty-ninth day of June, in the year one thousand eight hundred and forty-two, when at work for Martin Luther, in the town of Warren, in the State of Rhode Island, and being myself at that time a citizen of said Warren, I was forcibly taken by a number of armed men early in the morning, some time before sunrise, who broke into the house and took me therefrom, and carried me to a hotel, when, after making some inquiries of me, I was again removed to the jail of Bristol county, and there confined for the space of seven or eight days, when I was examined by Joseph M. Blake, and discharged in the course of three days — nothing being, as he said, found against me; and all by no authority, to my knowledge, except that of force.

STAFFORD HEALY.

Many of the principal leaders in these outrages were men, who all their lives, had either sought or held office, and who were guided on all occasions by motives of self-aggrandizement, and though professedly friendly to the dear people, always sought to crush them, as the following deposition will show.

Deposition of Albion N. Olney.

I, Albion N. Olney, of Providence, in the State of Rhode Island, attorney at law, depose and say : That on Sunday, the 26th day of June, 1842, I was on the premises of Otis Holmes, in said Providence, but not in his house, when he was forcibly dragged from it by a number of armed men, who had broken into his house. I also saw him carried through the streets, with a person holding him on each side by the collar, and armed men in front and rear. He was marched to the office of Henry L. Bowen. There were from twenty to thirty armed men, and many who were not armed. I saw among the leaders Sylvester Hartshorn, the United

States marshal for the district. He was not armed, having only a cane, but appeared to take an active part in the proceedings. I saw Mr. Holmes's brewery broken open, and also his store and counting room, and another store adjoining. Mr. Holmes, in the house and at the brewery, begged them not to break in, and he would furnish the keys; but no attention was paid to his request. While the soldiers were marching Mr. Holmes through Westminster Street, I heard Joseph F. Arnold, who was an inspector in the custom house, say to his son, (who, armed with a musket and fixed bayonet, marched directly in the rear of Mr. Holmes,) "Prick him, Frank; prick the d——d scoundrel." Mr. Arnold was standing in front of his house as the men passed, and said this in an audible voice. I heard and remember the words distinctly. On several days after, I saw Sylvester Hartshorn, the United States marshal, equipped with a musket and accoutrements, drilling and doing duty with a volunteer company of citizens. On the 18th of May I saw Hon. John Pitman, judge of the United States District Court, in the ranks of the charter troops, armed with a musket. During the period of martial law, I saw Edward J. Mallett, the Providence postmaster, doing duty as guard in College Street. At the same time that I saw Judge Pitman in the ranks, I also saw Richard W. Greene, United States district attorney, marching as one of the soldiers to go on Federal Hill, and William R. Watson, collector. ALBION N. OLNEY.

COMMONWEALTH OF MASSACHUSETTS, *Bristol, ss.*
PAWTUCKET, *May* 9, 1844.

Personally appeared the above-named Albion N. Olney, and made oath to and subscribed the foregoing, reduced to writing in his presence by me. Before me,
B. F. HALLETT,
Commissioner, and Justice of the Peace through the Commonwealth.

CHAPTER XI.

MARTIAL LAW.

Hitherto, in describing and commenting upon the outrages committed upon the persons and property of the people of Rhode Island under the pretext of martial law, we have viewed them as acts of flagrant injustice, unnecessary, and before unknown in this country, without instituting any inquiry into the validity of the act under which they were committed. But the justification set up by the authors and perpetrators of those acts deserves a further and more definite consideration. Every wrong doer in that ruthless tragedy pleads martial law in full justification of all his acts. It is believed that, in this country, martial law is but vaguely understood by the great mass of the people. We have only learned, from history, that this terrible engine was sometimes put in operation in the earlier history of some of the European nations; that it was seldom or never resorted to except in actual warfare, and then proclaimed by a military chieftain. But it is well ascertained that no civil government in the known world, except Rhode Island, has attempted to establish it over a whole empire or single state for the last two hundred years. Its consequences were found to be so abhorrent to every sentiment of humanity, that the whole civilized world united to abolish it. Now, it is evident that the Rhode Island General Assembly neither in 1842 nor at any other time before or since possessed any legal or constitutional power to place the state under martial law. The act was not authorized by any precedent in this country or in any other recently. The charter, under which that body acted, gave them no such authority, but impliedly, at least, forbade it; and by the ratification of the constitution of the United States all such power had been delegated to the General Government. The state authorities might call upon the *posse comitatus*, or the military, if necessary, to enforce their own statute laws; but this was the extent of their power. They could never authorize any functionary, civil or military, to overstep the provisions of the constitution of the United States. In short, the state had no right whatever to make or exercise any but civil laws. It may be presumed that the legislature, which passed that act in Rhode Island, did not fully realize the dangerous step they were taking; but, relying upon their own omnipotence, they assumed the tremendous responsibility of surrendering the lives and interests of the whole people to the mercy of the bayonet. At the time martial law was declared in Rhode Island, the judicial tribunals of the state were open for the trial of all offences, and their proceedings in no way interfered with or molested. Under the double rule of both civil and martial law, the state presented the strange anomaly of two separate and distinct systems of government in full operation in the same state and over the same people at the same time. But, in operating these different political engines, the acts of each were not always kept distinct from the other, but men were arrested and imprisoned under martial law, and afterwards brought to trial before a civil tribunal. All such proceedings were evidently arbitrary and illegal; they tended to break up all the foundations of social order, overturn all civil and political institutions, restore the reign of force, and make might the test of right. Martial law has never been justified except from dire necessity; it is governed by no rules, and knows no limits; it overrides and suspends all other laws during its continuance. According to the principles held in countries where martial law has been resorted to, the right to employ it arises solely from imperious necessity, and ceases the instant the necessity that called it forth has passed by; and all acts committed under any such pretext, after that necessity has ceased, have ever been held criminal. Therefore, if, on the 24th of June, 1842, such necessity had existed, and the legislature of Rhode Island had possessed the constitutional power to set up martial law, in a momentary crisis, it is obvious that on the 28th of that month the cause had entirely ceased, as the government well knew; and therefore every act of violence committed after that time, under that pretext, was just as much a crime as if no such law had ever existed. It is apparent that no such necessity ever existed at any moment during the Rhode Island controversy. The government should first have resisted the supposed rebellion by its civil officers; and if they were found unable of themselves to enforce the laws and bring delinquents to justice, they should next have called on the civil posse; and if, with that assistance, the government still found itself unable to compel obedience to its institutions, the whole military power of the state might have been called in aid of the government. But, without taking any of these steps, immediate resort was had to martial law, and all the men and munitions of war that the government could command at home or procure from abroad were forthwith turned out to prey upon all such as were supposed to entertain political principles adverse to the charter government. But even martial law, with all its summary claims, does not, as was supposed in Rhode Island, instantly convert the whole military into a band of lawless freebooters; but as soon as that law is suspended, every one who has overstepped its necessary limits is liable to be brought to trial before a civil tribunal; and, if the view which has been taken of the subject be correct, then all the acts of violence and villany committed in Rhode Island in 1842, under pretext of martial law, constitute a fearful catalogue of crimes, which never have been, and never can be, fully atoned for in this world. But we are asked, Why have not the perpetrators of these deeds been brought to trial before courts of justice? To this we answer, they could not be proceeded against out of the state for offences committed within its jurisdiction, and the highest tribunals within the state allow all such defendants to justify themselves by pleading martial law.

When we consider that nearly all the most outrageous and wicked acts of violence were committed after all opposition had ceased, and that hundreds of men were taken by violent hands from their homes, their fields, or their workshops, surrounded with muskets and bayonets, bound with ropes, and, without any kind of precept, driven to prison amid the loud taunts and insults of savage men and heartless women, crowded like sheep into dark, narrow, and filthy cells, nearly suffocated for want of air, without water sufficient to quench their thirst, fed like pigs upon two wretched and scanty meals a day, denied all intercourse with their friends, and kept in this painful condition, in some instances, for several weeks, and when at last they were brought forth from their dungeons for examination, were told that nothing was found against them; when we recollect also that the victors and their victims were, in many instances, neighbors and acquaintances; when we see bands of armed men firing at random into a crowd of innocent spectators; when we behold a defenceless individual coolly shot down, whilst without the jurisdiction of the state, and the next day, when it is known that all opposition has ceased, we see the chief magistrate of the state, without any cause whatever, send an armed squadron to blow up a bridge in the very midst of a populous city, a portion of which was beyond his jurisdiction, — when we reflect upon these and hundreds of other transactions of a like nature, we sicken at the thought of that deep depravity which breaks out in such a malicious persecution of men for opinion's sake, which has no parallel in modern times.

This terrible scourge held the whole people of Rhode Island in its paralyzing grasp from June till September, and was in full force and operation for more than half of that time. A fearful espionage watched over the whole community. Men rose, and labored, and slept, made their vows and said their prayers, nursed their sick and buried their dead, amid its impending terrors, and whilst the bloody mantle of martial law, like a funeral pall thrown over the tomb of liberty, cast its dark fold over every corner of the State of Rhode Island.

CHAPTER XII.

COMMISSIONERS APPOINTED TO EXAMINE THE PRISONERS. PROCEEDINGS. MEASURES TAKEN TO FORM ANOTHER CONSTITUTION. CONDITION OF THE PEOPLE AT THE TIME. CONSTITUTION DECLARED ADOPTED.

AT an adjourned session of the General Assembly, held at Newport in June, 1842, commissioners, as they were called, were appointed, whose duty was to hold courts of inquisition upon the prisoners, with whom the jails were crowded. It will be recollected that these prisoners had not been committed upon warrants, but by virtue of the bayonet, and they were not informed of the charges to which they would be required to answer. Each commissioner, like some grand inquisitor, possessed almost absolute power over every prisoner brought before him. The prisoners were not allowed counsel or witnesses, but each man was adjured, by the terrors of the bayonet and the dungeon, to confess his guilt and testify against himself. Some of the men, who now sat as judges in these dread tribunals, had, less than one year before, recorded their own names in favor of that constitution which they now declared illegal, and its support treason. A large number of prisoners, after having been kept in close confinement from five or six days to as many weeks, were discharged, because their judges said nothing was found against them. Yet it is believed that in most instances, as a condition of their release, the prisoners were required to engage to support the charter government. Some complied with these humiliating terms, and others spurned them; and a large number of prisoners were retained in close jail, to be tried for treason. Some were tried, found guilty, and recommended to *mercy* by the jury. Martin Luther, a respectable farmer in Warren, in the county of Bristol, was arrested some time afterwards, and found guilty of acting as moderator of a town meeting held under the people's constitution, and sentenced to pay a fine of five hundred dollars, to be imprisoned in close jail six months, and to pay all costs of prosecution. This sentence was carried into execution.

Whoever candidly reflects upon the history which has been given of the Rhode Island controversy, must, we think, be satisfied of the following facts: First, that absolute political sovereignty is always inherent in the great body of the people, and that this prerogative is before and paramount to all constitutions and civil compacts, and that the right to its exercise can never be suspended by any means whatever; and, secondly, that the great body of the people of Rhode Island, in the exercise of that right, did, in the month of December, 1841, ratify and adopt a democratic constitution for the government of the state, and that also, in accordance with that constitution, a majority of the people of the state did, in 1842, organize and set up such a government as the constitution of the United

States guarantees to every state in the Union; and, lastly, it has been shown that the government so organized and set up, and so guaranteed by the constitution of the United States, was crushed out and suppressed by the combined forces of the State of Rhode Island and the United States.

In the month of June, 1842, while martial law was in full operation, the prisons filled with its victims, and the whole population of the state shook as with an ague, while the adjacent states were thronged with exiles who had fled from the fiery indignation of their barbarous pursuers, and while any one who should declare himself in favor of the people's constitution would be immediately consigned to a dungeon, the General Assembly issued a call for a convention to form a constitution. It has already been shown that the General Assembly could not, by force of law, take any initiatory steps towards forming a constitution, and also that that body solemnly declared, by the mouth of their committee, in 1829, that the legislature could not, and would not, do any thing in the premises, and that no constitution before or since the revolution had been formed, or could be formed, more free and popular than that under which the people then lived.

Notwithstanding all this, the General Assembly now, for the first time, ascertained that the State of Rhode Island and Providence Plantations had no constitution, and therefore thought proper that immediate steps should be taken to establish one. They considered it expedient that the work should be commenced forthwith; they believed that to be a favorable time for the undertaking, when their own sabres gleamed and their own cannon roared in unison with those of the national executive. Now, when they had their iron heels upon the necks of the people, they deemed it a most favorable time to induce them humbly to accept a constitution as a special boon from the General Assembly, fearing that when they came to be released from duress, they might revive again their own constitution, which lay crushed beneath the weight of arms. Therefore the General Assembly proceeded to *request* all such of the people as possessed certain qualifications to meet in their respective towns on the 8th day of August, and vote for delegates to meet in convention and form a constitution. Pursuant to that *request*, meetings were held and delegates elected, who afterwards met in convention, and drew up a constitution, which was submitted to such of the people as were permitted to vote under its provisions. The voting took place on the 21st, 22d, and 23d days of November, 1842. The act of the General Assembly placing the state under martial law had not been repealed, and proceedings under it had only been suspended by proclamation of the governor, who might also, at any moment by proclamation, give it vitality. The people were not released from duress; they durst not speak freely their own sentiments. Many suffrage men were still in exile, and others were in prison. Large rewards were offered for Mr. Dorr, and requisitions were continually made upon the governors of the neighboring states for the flying fugitives. Under such circumstances, the voting upon the proposed constitution took place, and the most strenuous exertions were made to bring out a large vote in its favor. On counting the votes, it was found that 7024 had voted in favor of it, and 51 against it. The legislature therefore proceeded to declare the constitution adopted by a majority of 6973 votes.

Now, it will be recollected, that although the people's constitution received 13,944 votes, the charter government repeatedly declared in their General Assembly, and by their delegates in Congress, that it had not received a majority of the votes of such as had a right to vote for it, and therefore it could not be considered as an expression of the wishes of a majority of the whole people; but now, when their own constitution had received but one half that number of votes, the General Assembly proceeded without hesitation to declare it legally adopted. And yet, at the very first session of the legislature, under that constitution, it was found that 16,520 votes had been polled for general officers. This shows as plainly as figures can show, that the last constitution received only the votes of a minority.

Without taking into consideration the comparative merits of the two constitutions, we will barely remark that the people's constitution received the votes of full two thirds of all who had a right to vote upon that occasion, and the present constitution received only the votes of one third of such as were qualified to vote for it; and with these observations we leave the public to decide which of the two constitutions in question was the free and voluntary choice of the people.

The following table shows the number of votes polled in each town in the State of Rhode Island, on the 27th, 28th, and 29th of December, 1841, for the people's constitution.

Votes in the City of Providence.

	Qualified.	Not qualified.	Against.	Total.
Ward 1,	162	362		
Ward 2,	88	384		
Ward 3,	165	472		
Ward 4,	142	357		
Ward 5,	248	515		
Ward 6,	255	306		3556
Smithfield,	381	336	1	1338
Cumberland,	293	599		892
Burrillville,	134	149		283
Glocester,	192	210		402
Foster,	124	113	1	238
Scituate,	208	316		524
Johnson,	136	210		346
North Providence,	221	472	13	706
Cranston,	159	241		400
Warwick,	308	587		895
Coventry,	157	249		406
East Greenwich,	50	85	6	141
West Greenwich,	17	45		62
North Kingstown,	84	169		253
South Kingstown,	138	137	10	285
Exeter,	52	82		134
Richmond,	44	88		132
Charlestown,	64	36		100
Hopkinton,	81	81	13	175
Westerly,	107	144	1	252
Newport,	317	890		1207
Middletown,	8	22		30
Portsmouth,	67	59		126
Jamestown,	18	13		31

	Qualified.	Not qualified.	Against.	Total.
New Shoreham,	102	30		132
Tiverton,	102	172	3	277
Little Compton,	19	25	17	61
Bristol,	151	218		369
Warren,	103	106	1	210
Barrington,	28	24		52
		Total,		13,944

CHAPTER XIII.

MR. DORR'S RETURN. HIS ARREST AND IMPRISONMENT. TRIAL. CONVICTION. SPEECH. SENTENCE. REMOVAL TO STATE PRISON.

LEAVING for a time the desultory history of affairs in Rhode Island, we will return to Mr. Dorr. As has been shown, he left Chepatchet in the evening of the 27th of June, 1842. He well knew that a spirit of deadly hostility had been excited against him, and supposed that his enemies, emboldened by his flight, would cry aloud for blood. In this he was not mistaken. As soon as it was ascertained that he had left the state, Governor King issued his proclamation, offering a reward of five thousand dollars for his apprehension; but the chief magistrates of the neighboring states protected him from the fury of his mercenary pursuers. The Hon. Henry Hubbard, then governor of the State of New Hampshire, gave the exiled patriot a cordial welcome. Here Mr. Dorr found a safe asylum from the fury of his mad pursuers. The bosom of that illustrious chief magistrate glowed with true patriotic fire — his purpose was firm as his own granite hills, and his heart as pure as the snowy mantle which covered their sides — unborn generations will bless his memory for the noble deed.

Democracy had fallen in Rhode Island; the fundamental principles upon which the American governments are based had been publicly violated, and the power of an oligarchy established by the bayonet. Mr. Dorr remained a voluntary exile, hoping that the camp fires of his exulting enemies would at length be extinguished, and peace and quiet be so far restored as to allow him to return unmolested to his native state, and the bosom of his anxious friends. Confiding too much in the honor and magnanimity of his conquerors, after an absence of nearly one and a half years, he concluded to return to his native city. Accordingly, on the last day of October, 1843, in the capacity of a quiet citizen, he arrived in Providence, and entered his name at the City Hotel. Soon after this, Mr. Dorr was arrested by an officer upon the charge of treason against the State of Rhode Island and Providence Plantations, and thrust into jail in Providence, where he was kept in close confinement until Thursday, the 29th of February, 1844, when he was removed to the jail at Newport, in which county it had been decided that his trial should take place. Contrary to the common law of England and the United States, and in violation of every principle of justice and humanity, the Supreme Court of the State of Rhode Island decreed that the prisoner should be tried in a county in which he was a stranger, where it was known that almost every man was his avowed enemy, away from all his friends and his witnesses, and contrary to the earnest solicitation of the prisoner and his counsel.

We would not rashly impugn the motives of a high

judicial tribunal, or seek to strip its incumbents of their consecrated ermine; yet experience has taught us that the frailties and passions common to all men — the same love and the same hate — the same motives of interest and the same feelings of revenge — may find their way to the forum, and sit ensconced beneath the judicial robe. We would not be too uncharitable, but leave every reader to form his own opinion of the justice of the proceedings against Mr. Dorr.

On the 26th of April, 1844, nearly two years after the alleged offence was committed — after a written constitution had been adopted, and a government quietly organized under it — when nothing at home or abroad threatened to disturb the peace of the state — Mr. Dorr was taken from the prison at Newport, and brought before the Supreme Court to be tried for treason. He pleaded not guilty to the charge, and Samuel Y. Atwell and George Turner, Esqrs., were engaged as his counsel. The first motion which his counsel made to the court was for a compulsory process for witnesses for the respondent, as Mr. Dorr had already exhausted all his own means, and was unable to pay the witnesses he wished to summon. But the court refused to grant the application in the following words: "The accused possesses the means to employ counsel; it is to be presumed that he is also able to pay his witnesses for their attendance; the motion therefore cannot be granted."

Mr. Dorr stood before the court penniless and a stranger, his friends and witnesses were far away, and yet the court refused to grant him a privilege that is always allowed to the vilest malefactor.

At the time that the court removed Mr. Dorr from Providence to Newport for trial, it was well known to every one that the inhabitants of that county entertained the most violent prejudices against him. Under the charter the town of Newport had six representatives in the General Assembly, and Providence four, so that in 1840 Newport had one representative for every thousand of her population, and Providence one representative for every ten thousand. Newport was jealous of Providence, and always opposed every effort which was made to break up the old order of things, and deprive the inhabitants of that section of their prescriptive rights. Such were the feelings of the people from which a jury was to be taken to try Mr. Dorr. All were strangers to him, and if there were any unprejudiced men among them, Mr. Dorr had no means of knowing it. We shall not attempt to give a history of the empanelling of the jury; it is sufficient to say that twelve men were found who solemnly declared that they had formed no opinion as to the guilt or innocence of the prisoner; and the reader can believe them if he choose. When we consider that this exciting question had been before the people of the whole state for two years, and had been repeatedly and warmly discussed in every neighborhood and in every family, is it possible to suppose that any sane man had not formed any opinion in the matter? After the verdict was rendered, Mr. Dorr's counsel offered to prove to the court that three or four of the jurors composing the panel which convicted him, had expressed their opinions in strong terms against the prisoner previous to the trial; yet the court refused to go into the investigation, since the trial was finished, and the verdict was satisfactory to the court.

In the commencement of the trial, the points offered for the defence were the following: —

1. That, in this country, treason is an offence against the United States only, and cannot be committed against an individual State.

2. That the 4th section of the act of Rhode Island of March, 1842, entitled "An act relating to offences against the sovereign power of the state," is unconstitutional and void, as destructive of the common-law right of trial by jury, which was a fundamental part of the English constitution at the declaration of independence, and has ever since been a fundamental law in Rhode Island.

3. That that act, if constitutional, gives this court no jurisdiction to try this indictment in the county of Newport — all the overt acts being therein charged as committed in the county of Providence.

4. That the defendant acted justifiably, as governor of the state, under a valid constitution rightfully adopted, which he was sworn to support.

5. That the evidence does not support the charge of treasonable and criminal intent in the defendant.

The fourth was that upon which the defendant chiefly relied; but the court decided that proof upon that point was inadmissible, and ruled the other points against the prisoner. The whole trial, from its beginning to its termination, lasted nearly four weeks, and the defence was ably conducted by Mr. Dorr himself, and his counsel, George Turner and Samuel Y. Atwell, Esqrs.

Throughout this trial the court appears to have had

only one single object in view, and that was the conviction of Mr. Dorr. They not only refused to allow him to introduce testimony to show that he acted under the authority of a valid constitution, and without any criminal intentions, but they also refused to hear the motion argued to the court, and positively decided that the jury had nothing to do but find that the prisoner had committed the acts charged against him, and could not inquire into his motives. Now, we have been taught that a *wicked intention* was necessary to constitute crime, and that bare *acts*, without any wrong *intent*, were not in themselves criminal; but the court appear to have adopted a different rule for that special occasion, because it is easy to show that the same court, both before and since that trial, have uniformly held, that " *actus non facit reum, nisi mens sit rea* " should be regarded as an established principle in American jurisprudence, and have always allowed the accused to show, if they could, that, in doing the acts charged against them, they did not *intend* to commit a felony. But if the rule adopted in the trial of Mr. Dorr should be observed in other criminal prosecutions, no one would be safe. The man who should ignorantly and innocently pass a spurious bill, believing it to be genuine, would be liable to be punished as a counterfeiter; and any one who should have the misfortune to kill another by accident, or in self-defence, would be liable to suffer like the most atrocious murderer.

Whilst the motion of the prisoner's counsel to be heard by the court was pending, the following dialogue took place : —

Judge Staples. — I am opposed to a re-argument of this question at the present time, in the course of a jury trial. I am willing to hear it re-argued when the court are at leisure.

Judge Haile. — Nor am I disposed to hear a re-argument during the trial, when this question has once been solemnly settled. At a proper time, it can be heard. But it ought not to be heard in the hurry of a jury trial.

Mr. Dorr. — It falls strangely upon the ear of a man in my position, when I hear the judge of a court, in a case of this kind, and involving principles of such moment, make use of an expression like this — the "hurry" of this trial. I must be hurried through to judgment, then, without a hearing; and after conviction I may be heard! Is the liberty or the life of a man to be disposed of in this way? If there are any reasons why a conviction should not take place, why should they not be heard now? What reparation is it, after conviction, to hear the reasons why it was unjust? This is, literally, according to a common observation, hanging a man first, and trying him afterwards.

We are surprised, also, when, in the midst of a trial which was to consign an individual to a dungeon for life, or pronounce him innocent, a judge of that court, sitting under the solemnity of his oath, declares, "*I have no doubt of the purity of the motives of the defendant. This is the view I have always taken,*" and yet refuses to allow the defendant to introduce testimony to satisfy the jury of the same fact. The court are satisfied that the defendant was not guilty of any criminal intentions, but they will not allow him to submit the proof of his innocence to the jury. When we consider the character of the jury and the extraordinary rulings of the court in this extraordinary case, the whole transaction appears to us like a solemn farce — a mere mockery, very similar to hundreds of others which history informs us have heretofore taken place in Europe.

The following is a brief extract from the closing address of Mr. Dorr to the jury. He gave a frank and manly history of the suffrage party, and of his own conduct in connection with it, and made no attempt to disguise or deny any thing, but freely and boldly confessed much more than the government had been able to prove.

Closing Remarks of Mr. Dorr.

After Mr. Turner had concluded his summing up upon the evidence, Mr. Dorr addressed the jury for three hours in the close of the defence. The following is a summary of his remarks: —

Having addressed to the court all he had to say on the subject of treason, (which he had contended was an offence against the United States, without admitting that any such offence had, in this instance, been committed,) he now turned to the jury, and thanked them for the patience which they had thus far manifested in attending to the proceedings of a trial necessarily protracted beyond the usual length. Although the duration of the trial had been more than once alluded to by one of the honorable court, he desired to assure them that he had not intentionally trespassed on their time. Much of it had unavoidably been spent in empanelling the jury, which, in a case of this moment, could not be hastily done. The defendant had a right by law to twenty peremptory challenges; and a large number of those who had been called as jurors had disqualified themselves as they were called, by replying to the questions proposed to them, that they had formed and expressed an opinion upon the charges laid in the indictment, rendering it necessary to issue new process for summoning an additional number. It would also be recollected that the defendant had been brought here from the county to which he belonged, professedly for a more impartial trial, and among those with whom he was but little acquainted, and whose qualifications and opinions could not be investigated and ascertained without special inquiry, which it had been sometimes necessary to make through witnesses, to whom the jurors were better known than to himself. The jurors now empanelled had severally responded, under their oaths, that they had neither formed nor expressed an opinion upon the matters now in issue; and only through their avowed impartiality could the object be obtained for which the case had been, in this unusual manner, removed from the county where the offence was charged to have been committed, into another, which had been equally pervaded by the political feelings and discussions which had pervaded the whole state in the eventful period of 1842.

As so much had been said about foreign notions and foreign interference, it was proper for him to remind them that he was no stranger in their midst. He had not come here from abroad to proclaim new and strange words, at war with the original doctrines upon which our government was established. He was a native citizen of Rhode Island; and a portion of those from whom he claimed descent had been among the earlier settlers of the state. He was by birth, and still more, he trusted, in principle and feeling, a Rhode Island man. He did not stand before them as an alien to the common inheritance; and he was ready to meet his opponents in any attempt they might make to show that his efforts had been directed to any other object than the reassertion of the ancient liberties of the state, and the inherent rights of the people.

The case now presented to the jury is one of no

ordinary importance, and is not lightly to be disposed of by a hasty and inconsiderate judgment. It is not a matter of dollars and cents, to be decided by an average of opinions, but a question affecting the rights and freedom, and, to all intents, the life, of the accused. The sentence consequent upon conviction is perpetual imprisonment, with the attending deprivation of the social and political privileges of a man and a citizen — an infliction which might induce some minds to prefer the more friendly missive of the military tribunal. It is the duty of the jury to contemplate the results of their verdict. For though they are not directly responsible for the law, and sit here not to make, but to administer it, they may well be inspired, when they regard the personal rights which are now put in issue, with a solemn caution, with a spirit of sincere and earnest inquiry; fearful themselves of doing a greater wrong than that which is alleged against the individual they are called upon to try, and bearing in mind that the justice of the law is not revenge, and insists upon no doubtful constructions of the acts of the accused. The jury must be satisfied beyond a reasonable doubt, not only of the facts, but of the legal meaning and purport of the facts; and they are not called upon to offer sacrifices to state policy, or to the dignity of the law. At this distance of time from the date of the transactions in controversy, a more dispassionate and candid investigation was to be expected and demanded.

The offence charged is *political* — not against individuals, but against the state, under a system now no longer existing. The defendant necessarily does not stand alone. He acted for others. In trying him, you try also the fourteen thousand citizens who voted for the people's constitution in 1841, and who, if there be any guilt in the doctrines of '76, are equally guilty with him. Nay, more : you will try the principles of the American government and the rights of the American people; and you yourselves will in turn be tried for any wounds you may inflict upon American liberty. You are not sitting here in one corner of a small state, out of the reach of observation; and beware that no political bias incline you to do any injustice to the defendant, by way of retribution to the party with which he is connected; or how you permit yourselves to defeat the ostensible object of a fairer trial in the removal of this case; and let the public have reason to believe that it has been more fair than was intended.

The opening counsel for the state (Bosworth) had not been satisfied with the customary epithets which the forms of indictment bestow on those who are brought within the pale of the courts; but he had launched out into the language of vituperation and calumny, the not uncommon substitutes for reasoning and argument. These ebullitions of malignity do not so much indicate the character of the object upon which they are poured, as the condition of the source from which they spring. Real valor never seeks to magnify itself by depreciating the character of those who have been overcome by the fortune of the day, and avoids all questionable exultation. An honorable mind, in a great political controversy like this between the two parties of the state, conscious itself of good motives, will be slow to impute the reverse to a fair and open political opponent. The coarse remarks of the assistant to the prosecutor are left to you, with all the weight to which they are entitled. If he be not ashamed of them, they may cause some of his friends to be ashamed of him.

Without any proof that it was known at the time to the defendant, the aid of the prosecutor has laid much stress on the fact that some of his relatives, by law or blood, were found in array against him on the 17th of May, 1842; and it is insinuated, by way of arousing the prejudices of the jury, that the object of the defendant was the destruction of his own relatives and friends. In reply to this false and malicious charge, Mr. Dorr said, that, in periods of excitement, it might happen, and sometimes did happen, to those who were near, and painfully to those who are also dear to each other, to be widely separated, even to the conflict of war. He stood almost alone in his political opinions among those who were connected with him by blood. Without consulting interests, he had asked for himself what was right, and pursued it. If his views of the sovereignty and action of the people were correct, then they who placed themselves in opposition to the government, and attempted to prevent the recovery of the public property, whether strangers or relations, did so in their own wrong, and might with equal propriety be said to have been bent upon his own particular destruction. He left them to their motives, and claimed respect for his own. There are obligations of duty from which no interest or consanguinity can furnish a discharge. Mr. Dorr said that he was not aware at the time that any person related to him was engaged in the defence of the arsenal; but, from what had fallen from one of them, he had supposed that he intended to be. This person was not his brother, (now absent from the country,) whose name had been forced in here with a very apparent object, and who, though opposed in politics, was entirely capable of appreciating his motives, as he was of making the same estimate in return. But, if he had been aware that all his clan were enlisted against the law and constitution of the state, he should not have been deterred from discharging the oath of duty which rested upon him.

The offence charged is somewhat of a vague nature. What is levying war? It is not a gathering of men merely with arms in their hands. This is the description of every military training or review. Against whom is it levied? The state. Who represented the state at the time in Rhode Island? Which was the true government? or, more properly, which was the government? And, again, for what object was war levied, if at all? Was it for any lawless, unjustifiable purpose, or in defence of government, and the most valued rights of the citizen? Here we have, in addition to the mere question of fact, Were certain things done, or not? the much larger and more important questions of rights, of motives, and intentions. The indictment charges that the acts laid in it were maliciously and traitorously done. To constitute a levying of war, as it was held in 4 Cranch, 75, &c., there must be an assemblage of persons for the purpose of effecting by force a treasonable purpose. Enlistment of men to serve against government is not sufficient. It is not treason, it thus seems, to enlist men for service, even against a lawful government; much less is it to enlist them and to bring them into service against an unlawful one, existing by usurpation, and contending with force against that by which it has been rightfully supplanted. You will also bear in mind the admission of the attorney general, who properly stated, in the outset of the case, that if the defendant were the governor of the state, he had a right to do what he did. It is thus perfectly evident that the true question essential to a fair trial is that of *rights* and *motives*. There must be a treasonable intent in the levying of war, to constitute any treason at all; not a mere knowledge of what one is about, but a deliberate, set purpose and treason of the mind; as in cases of homicide, the act may be murder, or manslaughter, or no offence at all, according to circumstances and intentions.

Mr. Dorr said that, in the argument of this case, he had the disadvantage of appearing before the jury without the aid of his principal counsel, Mr. Atwell, upon whom he had relied for all the closing arguments, who had been overtaken and disabled by a severe illness just before the commencement of the case, when it was too late for the defendant to make any preparation. While he desired to acknowledge the zeal, fidelity, ability, and industry of the gentleman who assisted him, he could not but feel the absence of a counsellor whose legal eminence and eloquence, practical experience, and just weight as a lawyer in this court, were of so much importance to his clients. If the defendant have any thing to advance in his own favor, it will be said to come from a too partial source, and it weighs nothing. What he admits, is taken strongly against him; and what he may say concerning himself, may be, for the most part, better said by another.

The defence, as well as the prosecution, has drawn out upon the examination of witnesses a long detail of facts. "My great object," said Mr. Dorr, "has been to have all the facts of the case correctly ascertained; to disabuse it of all the falsehoods and calumnies with which it has been invested by the malignant ingenuity of political enemies; and to disprove all the pretended charges that have been so often repeated against myself, my political associates, and the political party with whom we have acted. I have aided by questions and by witnesses in bringing all the facts to light. There are, and have been, no secrets in the cause in which I have been engaged; there is nothing, so far as I am aware, that might not safely be brought to the light of day. In August last, I published, over my own name, a statement of all the transactions now in controversy, from beginning to end, which was generally circulated in this state. It does not differ perceptibly from the present testimony. I am willing to put it into the case, as a part of it, if the prosecutor do not object. I should have been willing to save this investigation by so doing; but it was not for the defendant to prescribe the mode of proceeding by the prosecutor, who, of course, would not have admitted the account of the defendant to be correct, and expected to make a case much more favorable to his own side of the question."

And here, let it be asked of common candor and fairness, after listening to the testimony, What has become of the shameful and groundless imputation conveyed in the fabricated watchword of "beauty and the banks;" of the "foreign desperadoes," who were to plunder and burn the city of Providence, and to invade the domestic purity of its homes; of the intervention of citizens abroad for any other object than to arrest the unjustifiable interference of the president with state rights; of the general appropriation of private property to military uses; of "the lawless and intemperate character" of those engaged in the people's cause; of the "forcible enlistments;" of the "state scrip;" of the "sword dyed in blood;" of the "waving of the torch and the firing of the gun;" and the hundred other stories and inventions that were got up by political managers and editors for effect, and have had their day, and have answered all that was expected of them? They were, no doubt, believed by some, with that credulity which alarm creates. And there were others who availed themselves of this slight pretence to go over, and basely and treacherously abandon the cause of the people to the enemy. Henceforth, let the retailers of these calumnies, which have been put down in and out of court, hold their peace.

The alleged invasion of private property by the suffrage men at Chepatchet, of which so much had been attempted at the time to be made by their opponents, was reduced to three instances: a horse borrowed, used, and returned; a cow taken and paid for; and a few boards burned on the hill!

The question was asked, whether the village of Chepatchet, the day after it was left by the suffrage men, was not sacked by the charter troops. But this, we were told, had nothing to do with the issue, and could not be gone into. It was irrelevant! There was a contrast to be disclosed.

"Of all that was really done by me," said Mr. Dorr, (aside from the fabrications alluded to,) "or that I had a part in doing, I deny nothing. I should disdain to make such a denial here or elsewhere, to preserve either liberty or life." Defendant said that if any fact had not been brought out in the testimony, which the jury were desirous of knowing, and which was within his knowledge, he was ready to state it.

"My defence before you," said Mr. Dorr, "is a justification throughout. What I did I had a right to do; having been duly elected governor of this state under a rightfully adopted and valid republican state constitution, which I took an oath to support, and did support to the best of the means placed within my power."

He then alluded to the extraordinary embarrassment in which he was placed in this portion of the defence, by the refusal of the court to permit him to make good his justification, by exhibiting the proofs of his election as governor, and the proofs of the adoption of the people's constitution, under which he had been elected; the votes given upon it having been brought here for the express purpose of authenticating it to the jury. Nor was he permitted, directly or otherwise, than in incidental remarks, to maintain, either to the court or jury, the right of the people of Rhode Island, upon American principles, to form and adopt this constitution; nor to argue any other question of law to the court or jury, than whether treason be an offence against a state or against the United States; nor to introduce proofs of his election, and of the constitution, to repel the charge of malicious and traitorous motives; nor to show by authorities that the jury are, in capital cases, the judges both of the law and of the fact.

It was with extreme surprise and regret that he thus found himself debarred from his true defence. The facts being thus plain before the jury, — that the defendant had, on several occasions, attempted to carry into effect, by military force, the constitution and government of the people, and as the chief magistrate of the state, — the jury will very naturally ask, How did all this come to pass? By what authority did the defendant these things? The reply to your very natural inquiry is a blank. The defendant is most anxious to proceed before you, and to establish all these rights; but he is not permitted. He must look to you to take care of them. He is in the condition of the mariner whose bark has been stripped by an adverse gale, and who, in directing his course to the land, can expect to reach it only with the aid of a jury mast.

The votes that were cast for the people's constitution are at hand. They who gave them are not far off. The acts of the people's legislature, under this constitution, can be proved in a moment. These and the unanswerable proofs that popular sovereignty is the just source of government, were what it was desired to lay directly before you. By the refusal of the court, the defendant feels that he has been deprived of a great right, and that justice has been denied him. Whether the doctrines on which the republic rests be admitted here or not, they are unchangeably the same. The defendant has no desire to retract his subscription to them.

Some ages ago, a natural philosopher was accused and silenced before the inquisition for teaching that the earth turned on its axis. As he retired, after his forced confession to the contrary, from the presence of the officers of the justice of that day, he exclaimed, "Still it turns!" and, in spite of all opposition of false philosophy, it has turned ever since. There are other immutable doctrines, and other honest convictions, which cannot be forced out of a man by any human process.

"The sun will not rise," said Mr. Dorr, "upon any recantation by me of the truths of '76, or of any one of the sound principles of American freedom.

"The servants of a righteous cause may fail or fall in the defence of it. It may go down; but all the truth that it contains is indestructible, and will be treasured up by the great mass of our countrymen.

"If I have erred in this Rhode Island question," said Mr. Dorr, "I have the satisfaction of having erred with the greatest statesmen and the highest authorities, and with the great majority of the people of the United States; and I have the satisfaction also of reflecting that all errors of judgment here will be corrected by the great tribunal of public opinion, which assures to all ultimate and impartial justice."

The following is an extract from the closing argument of Mr. Turner: —

After all, gentlemen, who is the prisoner at the bar? and how came he now before you for trial? Mr. Dorr is an educated gentleman, of the most respectable family and connections. It is also in evidence that he, personally, has stood high in the confidence and esteem of his fellow-citizens. He has represented the city of Providence in the General Assembly. At the time he is charged with having levied war against the state, he was the treasurer of the Rhode Island Historical Society, and had in his hands the funds of that institution to a large amount. He was a commissioner of the Scituate Bank, having control of its funds and securities, under an appointment of the legislature; and he was president of the school committee of the city of Providence. It appears also, that, as administrator or trustee, he had in his hands large amounts of the property of private individuals. During the troubles that followed the affair at the arsenal — the destitution of men, arms, ammunition, provisions, and money of the Chepatchet campaign — during his protracted exile from the state — did Governor Dorr embezzle, divert, or misapply these funds, or a farthing of them? No, gentlemen; as is shown by the testimony of Mr. Burgess, he guarded the whole with the most scrupulous care, guided by the highest sense of honor, and placed them, undiminished, beyond the reach of the perils which environed his own position. With this evidence before you, does he carry about with him any of the marks of that *rowdyism* of which we have heard so much? Have not his whole course of life, his sentiments, and his actions, been such as to free him from the imputation of having, in any thing, been governed by other motives than a desire and a zeal for the best interests of his fellow-citizens and of the state?

It has been urged by the opening counsel for the state, that the prisoner, taking counsel from his fears at Chepatchet, *ran away* from the state. It would have been an act, not of wisdom or courage, but of the wildest folly, for Mr. Dorr to have bared his devoted head to the whirlwind of popular fury that then swept over the state; or, under *legislative* martial law, to have confided his fate to the tender mercies of a drum head court martial. But when the tempest had apparently passed over — when the excitement had become somewhat allayed by time — when martial law no longer fettered the legal tribunals of the state — he came voluntarily back to the state, and submitted himself to its tribunals. He came, (when large rewards failed to bring him,) because this was his native state — his home — and because he expected, and had a right to expect, that he should be tried by a jury of his peers of the vicinages amongst whom he had always lived, and for whose benefit alone he had acted. He is now in *your hands;* and I repeat, gentlemen, that, in deciding on his case, you *may* decide upon your own fate and that of your posterity; your decision *may* involve the fate of American freedom — nay, of civil liberty itself.

Finally, gentlemen, if the evidence to which I have directed your attention should fail to satisfy your minds fully as to the purity of the prisoner's intentions, and the absence of treasonable design on his part, and doubts remain on the subject, you are bound (and will be so instructed by the court) to throw those doubts into the scale of the prisoner, and return a verdict of acquittal. I now leave him with you, under the conviction that the moment you take his life and liberty into your hands, you, at the same time, commit your characters through life, and your memories after death, to the award and decision of the great tribunal of public opinion; and I hope and trust that at its hands you may *receive* that justice which, in behalf of the prisoner, I *claim* at your hands.

When all the arguments for and against the prisoner were finished, Chief Justice Durfee delivered a lengthy charge to the jury, after which they retired, and soon returned and pronounced their verdict of guilty.

On the 25th of June, Mr. Dorr was brought into court for sentence, and when he was asked by the court if he had any thing to say why sentence should not be pronounced against him, replied as follows: —

The court have, through their officer, addressed to the defendant the usual question, whether he have any thing to say why sentence should not now be pronounced upon him. I have something to say, which shall be brief and intelligible to the court, though it must be necessarily unavailing. Without seeking to bring myself in controversy with the court, I am desirous to declare to you the plain truth.

I am bound, in duty to myself, to express to you my

deep and solemn conviction that I have not received at your hands the fair trial by an impartial jury, to which, by law and justice, I was entitled.

The trial has been permitted to take place in a county where, to say the least, it was doubtful whether the defendant could be tried according to the law of the state; and in a case of doubt like this, he ought to have had the benefit of it, especially as the trial here must be in a county to which the defendant was a stranger, in the midst of his most excited political opponents.

All but one of those freeholders, (one hundred and eight in number,) who were summoned here for the purpose of selecting a jury to try the defendant, were of the opposite party in the state, and were deliberately set against the defendant with the feelings of partisan hostility. The single democratic juror was set aside for having expressed an opinion. Of the drawn jurors, sixteen in number, two only were members of the democratic party; and one of them for cause, and the other for alleged cause, was removed.

Every one of the jury finally selected to try the defendant was, of course, a political opponent. And even as so constituted, the jury were not permitted to have the whole case presented to their consideration. They were not — as in capital, if not in all criminal, cases they are entitled to be — permitted to judge of the law and of the fact. The defendant and his counsel were not permitted to argue to the jury any matter of law.

The court refused to hear the law argued to themselves, except on the question whether treason be an offence against a state or against the United States.

The court refused to permit the defendant to justify himself by proving the constitution, the election, and the authority under which he acted; or to permit him to produce the same proofs, in order to repel the charges of malicious and traitorous motives made in the indictment, and zealously urged against him by the counsel for the state.

By the charge of the judge, the jury were instructed that the only question which they had to try was, whether the defendant intended to do the acts which he performed — a question of capacity rather than of motives and intentions.

It is true that the jury were absent more than two hours; but not for deliberation. One of them was asked, immediately after the verdict was delivered and the jury was discharged, whether they had been detained by any disagreement. He replied, "We had nothing to do. The court had made every thing plain for us."

On hearing a bill of exceptions to the verdict thus rendered, the court promptly overruled all the points of law.

The court also denied to the defendant an opportunity of showing to them that three of the jurors, before they were empanelled, manifested strong feelings, and had made use of vindictive and hostile expressions against him personally, after the defendant had established by his affidavit the fact that he was not informed of this hostility of feeling and expression before they were empanelled, and, with regard to two of them, before the verdict was rendered. The defendant expected to prove, by twelve witnesses, that one of these jurors had expressed a wish to have the defendant put to death, and had declared, shortly after the verdict, to a person inquiring the result, that "he had convicted the defendant, and that this was what he intended to do;" that another juror had also declared that the defendant ought to be executed; and that the third had frequently made the same declaration, with a wish that he might be permitted to do the work of an executioner, or to shoot him as he would a serpent, and put him to death.

Nor would the court permit the defendant to show, by proofs, which he declared on oath to have been unknown to him at the time of the empanelling of the jury, that an array of twelve men, summoned on *venire* by a deputy sheriff, were (or a considerable part of them at least) the same persons who had been selected by an attorney of this court, who assisted the officer in the service of the summons.

These and other matters, which I will not stop to enumerate, show that this trial, which has been carried through the forms of law, was destitute of the reality of justice, and was but a ceremony preceding conviction. That there is any precedent for it, in the most acrimonious period of the most excited party times in this country, I am not aware from any examination or recollection of its political history.

In a trial of an alleged political offence, involving the feelings of the whole community, and growing out of a condition of affairs which placed the whole people of the state on one side or the other of an exasperated controversy, the strictest and most sacred impartiality should have been observed in the most careful investigation both of law and fact by the jury, and in all the decisions and directions of the court. In what case should they have been more distrustful of the political bias of their own minds, more careful in all their deliberations, more earnest in the invocation of a strength above their own, that they might not only appear to be just, but do justice in a manner so above all suspicion, that the defendant, and all those with whom he is associated, might be satisfied that he had had his day in court, and that every requisition of the law had been observed and fulfilled. In how different a spirit were the proceedings of this trial conducted! And with what emotions must the defendant have listened to the declaration of one of your honors, that "in the hurry of this trial" they could not attend to the questions of law, which he so earnestly pressed upon their immediate consideration, as vitally important to the righteous determination of his case!

The result of this trial, which your sentence is about to proclaim, is the perpetual imprisonment of the defendant, and his seclusion from the face of society, and from all communication with his fellow-men.

Is it too much to say that the object of his political opponents is the gratification of an insatiable spirit of revenge, rather than the attainment of legal justice? They are also bent upon his political destruction, which results from the sentence of the court, in the deprivation of his political and civil rights. They aim also at a social annihilation, by his commitment to that tomb of the living, from which, in ordinary cases, those who emerge are looked upon as marked and doomed men, to be excluded from the reputable walks of life. But there my opponents and persecutors are destined to disappointment. The court may, through the consequences of their sentence, abridge the term of his existence here; they can annihilate his political rights; but more than this they cannot accomplish. The honest judgment of his friends and fellow-citizens, resting upon the truth of his cause, and faithful to the dictates of humanity and justice, will not so much regard the place to which he is consigned, as the causes which have led to his incarceration within its walls.

Better men have been worse treated than I have been, though not often in a better cause. In the service of that cause I have no right to complain that I am called upon to suffer hardships, whatever may be the estimate of the injustice which inflicts them.

All these proceedings will be reconsidered by that ultimate tribunal of public opinion, whose righteous decision will reverse all the wrongs which may be now committed, and place that estimate upon my actions to which they may be fairly entitled.

The process of this court does not reach the man within. The court cannot shake the convictions of the mind, nor the fixed purpose which is sustained by integrity of heart.

Claiming no exemptions from the infirmities which beset us all, and which may attend us in the prosecution of the most important enterprises, and, at the same time, conscious of the rectitude of my intentions, and of having acted from good motives in an attempt to promote the equality, and to establish the just freedom and interest of my fellow-citizens, I can regard with equanimity this last infliction of the court; nor would I, even at this extremity of the law, in view of the opinions which you entertain, and of the sentiments by which you are animated, exchange the place of a prisoner at the bar for a seat by your side upon the bench.

The sentence which you will pronounce, to the extent of the power and influence which this court can exert, is a condemnation of the doctrines of '76, and a reversal of the great principles which sustain and give vitality to our democratic republic, and which are regarded by the great body of our fellow-citizens as a portion of the birthright of a free people.

From this sentence of the court I appeal to the people of our state and of our country. They shall decide between us. I commit myself, without distrust, to their final award. I have nothing more to say.

When Mr. Dorr had finished his remarks, Chief Justice Durfee arose, and pronounced his sentence in the following words: —

Listen, Thomas Wilson Dorr, to the sentence of the court; which is, that the said Thomas W. Dorr be imprisoned in the state prison at Providence, in the county of Providence, for the term of his natural life, and there kept at hard labor in separate confinement.

The court had now gone to the extent of their province, and hurled their last bolt against their defenceless victim; and on the 27th of June, 1844, just two years after Mr. Dorr dismissed his forces at Chepatchet, he was removed to the state prison in Providence, and incarcerated in a cell, where, according to the sentence of the court, he was to remain during his natural life.

So far as we are acquainted with the history of criminal treason, it has been contrived and conducted with more or less secrecy — it has consisted of clandestine attempts to surprise and overthrow the government by force. Mr. Dorr's case was the very reverse of this. Every thing had been done in the most public manner possible, and the whole proceedings consisted of a series of steps which followed each other at intervals which gave all parties ample time to consider them. If Mr. Dorr was guilty of the highest crime known to any law because he labored to sustain a democratic government which the people had ordained, then hundreds of others were guilty of the same crime; and why should he be made a scapegoat for the sins of the whole party? Why pursue him alone with such unrelenting hostility, when there were so many others who had with him actually taken up arms?

CHAPTER XIV.

REFLECTIONS

THE history of treason shows that it has been chiefly confined to arbitrary and unjust governments, and that far the largest number of those who have suffered for that crime have been good men, who sought to relieve their own people from the oppressive measures of their rulers. If Great Britain had succeeded in overcoming the rebellion, as she called it, in her American colonies, in 1776, then George Washington and Nathaniel Greene, with all their compatriots, would have been held guilty of treason. The essential characteristics of this crime are said to consist in levying war against the sovereign power of the state to which the offender owes allegiance. In a monarchical government the sovereign power is supposed to belong to a single individual. In Russia the will of the czar is the sovereign power; therefore to resist that will is treason, because that people suppose that by divine appointment the right to rule runs forever in the blood of a certain family; and similar sentiments prevail in all countries governed by hereditary monarchs. The government of Great Britain, from which we have obtained many of our ideas of jurisprudence, is a mixture of monarchy, aristocracy, and democracy;

but the supreme or highest power is supposed to be vested forever in the crown. Therefore treason in Great Britain does not consist in levying war against Parliament, or any other special department of the government, but in levying war against the crown itself. But our government is the very reverse of monarchy; in theory it is a democracy. We hold that in the United States absolute sovereignty is vested in the people, and in them alone; and that state constitutions are the acts of the people in their absolute sovereign capacity, and at all times under their immediate control; and if this theory of our government be correct, then the will of the people is the sovereign power, and it follows, of course, that to levy war against that declared will is virtual if not legal treason. The American governments are supposed to exist by the consent of a majority of the people until the contrary is shown; but when that majority freely and publicly declare their dissent to it, and withdraw their support from it, then it cannot be treason to levy war against such minority government; but to levy war against the known and expressed will of a decided majority of the people can be nothing better than treason. It is highly important that every American citizen should fully understand the genius and principles of his own government, and know for a certainty where the sovereign power is vested. Is the question of political sovereignty yet to to be settled in this country? Have not the people of the United States yet ascertained where the supreme power may ultimately be found? Then we say that it is high time that the inquiry was made, and the question fully and permanently settled. If it is not in the whole people, then all our political teachings have been false. If it is not, as we have supposed, in the people at large, then we are no better off than the inhabitants of the old countries, and our democracy is an unmeaning term. When, hereafter, an American shall go abroad to some foreign country, and boast of the popular sovereignty of his own, may not the subjects of despotism, in derision and reproach, point him to Rhode Island? And what reply can he make to such a withering rebuke? The charter party in Rhode Island gained their ascendency, not by the free will of the people, but by force alone. Now, if the whole people had been left free from coercion at home, and threats and force from abroad, the people's government, with Mr. Dorr at its head, would doubtlessly have gone quietly into operation; and if any of the supporters of the exploded charter government had rebelled and taken up arms against the government which the sovereign people had set up, such insurgents might, with much more justice, have been brought to trial for treason before a court appointed by Mr. Dorr and his legislature. We have only to put the physical weight into the other scale, and the judicial power passes over to the other side; and if such had been the case, we have every reason to believe that the rights of men would have been better guarded and more respected, and justice better administered.

If we take a plain, common-sense view of the conduct of the parties in the Rhode Island controversy, we cannot fail to observe a striking contrast between them. Mr. Dorr and his party paid a scrupulous regard to private rights, and no individual was robbed or injured by his order; and when it was ascertained that a single beast had been killed by his men, full satisfaction was immediately made to the owner; and it has been shown by the testimony of Jedediah Sprague that when Mr. Dorr and his men quartered at his house in Chepatchet, at the request of Mr. Dorr Mr. Sprague closed his bar, and dealt out no liquor during their sta with him. But the conduct of the party professedl governed by "law and order" exhibits a striking contrast with this. They paid little or no respect to either person or property; but in open violation of law, and without shame or remorse, they assaulted, abused, robbed, and imprisoned all such as they chose. Like an army of crusaders to whom full indulgence had been granted, they seemed to feel themselves under no moral restraint, but gave full scope to all their appetites and passions, as the testimony of Mr. Sprague and other innkeepers will show.

We are credibly informed that during a single night, on the 24th of June, 1842, the keeper of a public house in the town of Bristol, by official direction, furnished the "law and order" forces with victuals, liquor, cigars, &c., to the full amount of one thousand dollars, all of which, with sundry other large bills of a similar kind, were paid by the state; but we believe that no compensation has ever been made to the hundreds of individuals who were robbed and despoiled of their property by the marauding clans of law and order. The government appear to have been ever ready to assume and justify every deed perpetrated under their own banner, and to extend their protecting batoon to every desperado who claimed the immunities of a royal charter; and at last, amid all the accumulation of enormities, whilst the whole party staggered beneath the weight of their own guilt, their hands still reeking with the blood of an innocent victim, as if one more damning deed was required to cap the frightful climax, Mr. Dorr was seized and plunged into a dungeon for life. The overthrow of the people's government in Rhode Island by force, and the condemnation and imprisonment of Mr. Dorr, are acts that will ever stand condemned by all the friends of free government throughout the world. No great principle is better settled now than that the people themselves are above all constitutions, and may, in their own time and in their own way, make new constitutions, or abolish old ones. But we are asked, Why agitate the subject anew? Why call up again the angry passions which have been hushed into repose? To this we answer, The tendency of all free governments is towards aristocracy and monarchy. This is shown by all history, and is continually witnessed in the workings of our own governments. Men clothed with authority are extremely prone to overstep their constitutional limits, and to assume powers with which their constituents never intended to invest them. Wealth and professional influence are always inclined to turn away from the people at large, and unite with honor and power however acquired. Ecclesiastical influence has almost always chosen to ally itself with political power. These facts remind us of the imperious necessity of keeping the fundamental principles of our political institutions constantly before the public; and we are more than ever impressed with the truth of the maxim, that "eternal vigilance is the price of liberty." It was because this great principle had been in a manner forgotten in Rhode Island, and by the national executive, that the strong arm of power was allowed to triumph over the people, and crush their institutions in the dust. In times of political quiet, when the government runs its smooth, monotonous course for many years, the people are extremely liable to become supine and forgetful of the pillars upon which their civil and political institutions rest; and if the time shall ever come in the United States when these fundamental principles shall be disregarded or surrendered, this will no longer be a free government, but will belong to the same class of oligarchies with which the old world is filled. Therefore it can never be amiss or out of season to agitate the subject, and keep it constantly before the people. It should form an essential part of the education of our youth, and be made the basis of all our political creeds. One generation should teach it to another, and they again to theirs, so that this life blood of political liberty may ever continue to circulate through all the American institutions. This would keep the legislative powers always in check, and make them careful to learn and do the will of the people; for upon that, and that alone, depend the safety and permanency of our free institutions. The people are not likely to rebel against themselves; and wherever treason has been supposed to be committed under an established government, it has been a sure indication of some great wrong in the ruling power. The freest governments are always safe and stable when they exist by the known and voluntary consent of the great body of the people, and no government is just, or can be long maintained, without force, when such consent is withheld.

This subject has been so thoroughly investigated, and its principles so well settled now, that it would not be advisable for any other state or any other chief magistrate to attempt to try the experiment over again. If any should, they might find themselves overwhelmed in a resistless tide of public opinion, before which their combined forces would be no more than chaff before a driving gale.

In a little more than half a century from the time when the American governments were founded upon the principle of popular sovereignty, as set forth in the Declaration of Independence, that great truth which forms the palladium of all our political institutions was denied and set at nought in a sovereign state, and its everlasting truths declared to be nothing but "rhetorical flourishes" and "glittering generalities," of no lasting import. And all this transpired in a state which was the foremost of all the sisterhood in establishing both religious and political liberty, and most careful to guard her free institutions against the encroachments of arbitrary power; a state which according to her ability, did more than any other to establish and maintain the true principles of American democracy; a state illustrious alike for her heroes and her statesmen. But alas! the fascinations of power at length ripened into tyranny, and in an unfortunate hour freedom was overthrown! If there be one thing in the history of the Rhode Island controversy more humiliating than another, it is the extraordinary obsequious sycophancy of a large class of citizens. They yielded too readily to the siren pleadings of the parasites of power, or shrank ingloriously from the threats of tyrants.

In times of religious or political quiet, men live and die without exhibiting to the world their mental or moral powers, or even knowing them themselves. But when society becomes unsettled, and its elements thrown into commotion, and shaken and tossed as with a mighty tempest, it requires a higher degree of moral integrity than falls to the lot of the mass of mankind to withstand the fury of opposing forces; and when great truths are to be set up or sustained, those who take the lead in such movements must possess a degree of firmness and decision unknown to mankind in general. Such have been the lights of the world in all religious, political, and social reformations; their iron wills were incapable of bending; to them fear was unknown; and regardless of all consequences to themselves, they have ever struggled with invincible perseverance in the paths which their consciences pointed out. Whilst thousands upon thousands have fallen out by the way, a few master spirits have reached the destined goal. Such men may be overcome or cast down by the power of tyrants, but the truths which they sought to establish, though "crushed to earth, will rise again." When such men fall, their enemies are confounded, the pillars of bigotry and error are shaken, light flashes upon the paths of truth and reason, and the final triumph of the great principles for which they contended is shadowed forth. And when all the petty tyrants who triumphed over Mr. Dorr shall be wholly forgotten, his name shall occupy a conspicuous place in the temple of political liberty, never to be effaced or destroyed until the whole structure falls. When we review the numerous tragical scenes enacted in Rhode Island in that memorable controversy, we can hardly believe them ever to have been realities; they look more like the distorted visions of a morbid imagination than sober truths; they stand without a parallel in the United States, and it is confidently hoped they will ever remain so. Nor is there much danger that similar proceedings will ever transpire in any other state. Can it be supposed that if two thirds of the people of any one of the large states had, in a regular manner, deliberately formed and adopted a democratic constitution, the menaces of any national executive would have frightened them from their purpose? or that the friends of such a constitution could have been subdued by a petty tyranny under the pretext of martial law? If it had been New York, Pennsylvania, or Ohio, instead of the small State of Rhode Island, neither John Tyler nor any other chief magistrate would have rashly dashed his military forces against the people.

CHAPTER XV.

RESOLUTIONS OF NEW HAMPSHIRE AND MAINE CONCERNING MR. DORR.

Resolutions from the Legislature of New Hampshire, communicated to the Senate of the General Assembly of Rhode Island, Jan. 8, 1845.

WHEREAS it is provided by the sixth article of the amendments of the constitution of the United States, "That in all criminal prosecutions the accused shall enjoy the right to a speedy and public trial by an impartial jury of the state and district wherein the crime shall have been committed, — which district shall have been previously ascertained by law ; and to be informed of the nature and cause of the accusation ; to be confronted with the witnesses against him ; to have compulsory process for obtaining witnesses in his favor, and to have the assistance of counsel for his defence ;" —

And whereas a citizen of one of the states of this republic (Thomas Wilson Dorr) has, by the constituted authorities of that state, been charged with the crime of treason, arraigned before its court, pronounced guilty of the offence charged, and by that court sentenced to hard labor in the state prison during his natural life ; —

And whereas, in the opinion of this legislature, all the substantial forms of justice, required to be observed in criminal cases, were during his trial for the offence disregarded, his rights grossly violated and denied to him by his removal for trial from the *vicinage* in which the crime was alleged to have been committed ; by the selection of a packed jury, all of whom were his political enemies ; and by the refusal, on the part of the judges of the court before whom he was tried, to permit him, by the strongest evidence which it was possible to offer, to establish his innocence, and to prove that the acts for which he was charged with the crime of treason were only in obedience to the constitution of the state, whose chief magistrate he was, and as such was bound to support that constitution which the people of Rhode Island had adopted ; and which evidence of adoption he offered to lay before the court, by presenting to them the votes of the people themselves, on which votes were the names of the voters, so that if fraud or illegal voting had been resorted to in the adoption of the constitution, the court would be enabled to detect the same — all of which evidence was rejected, and the decision of his guilt or innocence, in which was involved the great and important question of the right of the people to establish a constitution or form of government suited to their own wants and convenience, was referred to a jury packed for the occasion, and three of them, he offered to prove to the court, had, in violation of their oath, prejudged his case : —

Therefore, *Resolved by the Senate and House of Representatives in General Court convened,* That in the person of Thomas Wilson Dorr, now confined in the state prison of Rhode Island, the authorities of that state have trampled upon the constitution of the United States, by denying to him the right to be tried by an *impartial jury,* in the vicinage in which the crime was alleged to have been committed, and by refusing to him the right of introducing testimony tending to establish his innocence of the offence charged ; and that it is the duty of Congress to restore to the said Thomas Wilson Dorr those sacred rights guaranteed to him by the constitution, as a man and a citizen of this republic; and to wipe out the *deep* and *damning* stain stamped upon the national escutcheon by the *mock trial* and condemnation of this individual, guilty of no offence but that of maintaining the sovereignty of the people, and of obeying their sovereign will.

And whereas it is provided by the eighth article of the amendments to the constitution of the United States, that "excessive bail shall not be required, nor excessive fines imposed, nor cruel and unusual punishments inflicted," and whereas the punishment imposed upon the said Thomas Wilson Dorr is, in the opinion of this legislature, both "cruel and unusual," — unusual, as being, it is believed, the first offence of a strictly political character which has been punished by a state since the declaration of American independence — unusual when the nature of the offence is considered in connection with the plain principles upon which the government of the United States is founded, the principle of the sovereignty of the people; and whereas it is the manifest duty of the general government to protect and guard the rights of individuals so far as those rights are guaranteed by the constitution, — therefore *Resolved*, That the imprisonment of Thomas Wilson Dorr by the authorities of Rhode Island presents to the Congress of the United States a case of " cruel and unusual punishment" inflicted upon that individual for exercising, in a constitutional manner, the duties imposed upon him as chief magistrate of that state, to which office he was duly elected under a constitution adopted by a large majority of its citizens, and as such calls loudly upon the general government to extend to him, the said Thomas Wilson Dorr, that protection against tyranny and oppression which the government of these United States are bound in good faith to extend to all and every one of its citizens.

Resolved, That while we disclaim all right to interference with the internal police and regulations of our sister states, leaving to them the full exercise of sovereign power, (so far as it has not been delegated to the United States,) yet we cannot but protest against the wanton exercise of this power by the State of Rhode Island, in the case of Thomas Wilson Dorr, who, as a citizen of the United States, has rights which should be regarded as sacred, and which the general government is bound to maintain and defend.

Resolved, That we regard the doctrine of the sovereignty of the people as of vital importance to the stability and permanency of our republic, and that the people of Rhode Island, in common with the people of the other states composing this Union, possess this right — that when they speak, " *Full faith and credit shall be given in each state to their 'public acts,'* " one of which was the establishment of a constitution, adopted by a majority of her people, and another the election of officers under that constitution, of which Thomas Wilson Dorr was the chief magistrate, and as such should have been recognized by the several states composing this Union, and by the United States government itself.

Resolved, That our senators and representatives in Congress be requested to lay this preamble and resolutions before both Houses of Congress, and that the secretary of state be directed to furnish each of them with a copy of the same, and also to furnish a copy to the governors of the several states and territories.

The resolutions were signed by Governor Steele, " approved — heartily approved."

Maine legislative Resolutions in Relation to the Imprisonment of Thomas Wilson Dorr.

Whereas, we hold that " all men are born equally free and independent, have certain natural and inalienable rights, among which are those of enjoying and defending life and liberty, acquiring, possessing, and protecting property, and of pursuing and obtaining safety and happiness;" that the people are the source of all legitimate power; that all governments derive their just powers from the consent of the governed; and in the people resides full and plenary power to institute government, "to alter, reform, or totally change the same, whenever their safety and happiness require it;" and whereas the constitution of the United States guarantees to every state in this Union "a republican form of government," and provides that "in all criminal prosecutions the accused shall enjoy the right to a speedy and public trial, by an impartial jury of the state and district wherein the crime shall have been committed;" and that "no person shall be deprived of life, liberty, or property, without due process of law," — therefore,

Resolved, That the sovereign power of a state is inherent in the people, and all free governments are founded on their authority and instituted for their benefit; and that no man or set of men is entitled to supreme or exclusive privileges in the institution and support of government.

Resolved, That the sovereign power of the State of Rhode Island is inherent in the people thereof, and to them belongs the right to institute government, to change or abolish the same, as they may deem wise and proper for their safety and happiness.

Resolved, That the constitution of Rhode Island, adopted by the people in December, eighteen hundred and forty one, is republican in its form, and was rightfully adopted by a majority of the people thereof, and thereby became the permanent law of the state, and as such was entitled to the guarantee of the United States.

Resolved, That the interference of John Tyler, President of the United States, in behalf of the late charter government of Rhode Island, with the military power of the Union, by which the popular government of that state, under the constitution adopted in December, eighteen hundred and forty-one, was suppressed, was unauthorized by the constitution and laws of the United States, in derogation of both a dangerous usurpation of power and a wanton violation of the rights of the people of Rhode Island.

Resolved, That in the recent popular movement in the State of Rhode Island, we recognize in the person of Thomas Wilson Dorr a bold and uncompromising champion of the great American doctrines of the revolution, the able and stern defender of popular sovereignty, a noble son of a degenerate state, now the victim of vindictively corrupt judges, and a packed and partial jury.

Resolved, That the State of Maine, by her legislature, hereby enters her *solemn protest* against the imprisonment of Thomas W. Dorr in the state prison in the State of Rhode Island, by the authorities thereof, as unjust, illegal, malignant, and tyrannical, unbecoming the age in which we live, and deserving the marked disapprobation of the American people; and in the opinion of this legislature it is the imperative duty of the general government to adopt any and all legal and constitutional measures for his immediate release.

Resolved, That the governor be requested to cause a copy of these resolves to be transmitted to the president of the United States, to the governors of the several states, and to each of our senators and representatives in Congress. (Approved April 4, 1845.)

CHAPTER XVI.

REPORT OF A COMMITTEE OF THE HOUSE OF REPRESENTATIVES IN THE CONGRESS OF THE UNITED STATES. ALSO, SPEECH OF HON. MR. ALLEN, OF OHIO.

At the January session of the Rhode Island legislature, in 1844, a portion of the members of both Houses, twenty-six in number, signed and forwarded a memorial to Congress, setting forth the political grievances to which the people of that state had been subjected, and requesting the House of Representatives to "institute an inquiry into the facts" set forth in that memorial. That memorial, with other documents, was referred to a select committee of the House of Representatives, consisting of the following gentlemen, viz.: Messrs. Burke, Rathbun, Causin, McClernand, and Preston, who were empowered to send for persons and papers. They commenced their investigation on the 29th of February, 1844, and continued it until the 3d day of June following. In the commencement of their proceedings, they caused notice to be given to the governor of the State of Rhode Island, and also to the memorialists, of their appointment, and of the course which they intended to pursue in the investigation, in order that either party might appear, if they chose, and be heard. The committee also passed the following resolution : —

Resolved, That the president of the United States be requested to lay before this House the authority, and true copies of all requests and applications, upon which he deemed it his duty to interfere with the naval and military forces of the United States, on the occasion of the recent attempt of the people of Rhode Island to establish a free constitution in the place of the old charter government of that state; also, copies of the instructions to, and statements of, the charter commissioners, sent to him by the then existing authorities of the State of Rhode Island; also, copies of the correspondence between the executive of the United States and the charter government of the State of Rhode Island, and all the papers and documents connected with the same; also, copies of the correspondence, if any, between the heads of departments and said charter government, or any person or persons connected with said government, and of any accompanying papers and documents; also, copies of all orders issued by the executive of the United States, or any of the departments, to military officers, for the movement or employment of troops to or in Rhode Island; also, copies of all orders to naval officers to prepare steam or other vessels of the United States for service in the waters of Rhode Island; also, copies of all orders to the officers of revenue cutters for the same service; also, copies of any instructions borne by the secretary of war to Rhode Island, on his visit in 1842 to review the troops of the charter government; also, copies of any order or orders to any officer or officers of the army or navy, to report themselves to the charter government; and that he be further requested to lay before this House copies of any other paper or document in the possession of the executive, connected with this subject, not above specially enumerated.

A petition signed by General Samuel Milroy and a large number of the citizens of the State of Indiana, praying Congress to inquire into alleged abuses practised by the charter party of the State of Rhode Island, was also referred to the same committee.

The committee also notified the Rhode Island representatives in Congress to appear before them, and be heard if they thought proper. After these preliminary steps had been taken, the committee proceeded to summon witnesses and provide for taking depositions, and no deposition was taken except when both parties had been notified of the caption, and a full opportunity was given all concerned to appear and be heard. And after collecting a large amount of documentary and parol testimony, and carefully examining and considering the whole subject in all its bearings, the committee proceeded to make a long and very able report. Its great length prevents us from giving it in full. The following is an extract from that report : —

It is also worthy of remark that, in the difficulties which occurred in Rhode Island, during the attempt to establish the people's constitution, the committee have not yet learned that a single life was taken, or private property violated, by the suffrage party or any individual attached to it. This fact speaks volumes in favor of the moderation of its course, and shows conclusively that none of its members could have been actuated by criminal intentions.

It is also due to truth to remark, that the committee have reason to believe that the nineteen cases described above fall very far short of the whole number of prosecutions for similar offences. It is a fact notorious to the country, that several others have been indicted for treason, among whom is the Hon. Dutee J. Pearce, of Newport, formerly a distinguished member of Congress from the State of Rhode Island, who was a member of the House of Representatives under the people's constitution.

Another case is that of Thomas W. Dorr, who was elected to the office of governor under the people's constitution, and who has recently been tried for the crime of *treason*. He is known personally to one of the members of this committee to be a gentleman of high character, and very superior talents and accomplishments — a man whose good name would never intentionally be stained with the perpetration of crime. His native state has seldom produced a man favored with brighter faculties, or adorned with purer virtues. What could such a man care about the honor of being at the head of the government of Rhode Island, except it was to assert and vindicate what he believed to be a great principle of right, on which he believed the liberties of the people depended? He is connected by relationship with the most respectable and wealthy families belonging to the ruling party of the state; he has talents of a high order, and an education finished and complete. And if he had continued to support the interests of the charter government, his pathway to the highest honors within its gift was open and unimpeded, and his success not to be doubted. For what could such a man abandon such prospects, for the purpose of leading the people in a hazardous and perilous enterprise, if it were not to assert and vindicate a great principle? Could he be charged with a desire for the honors and emoluments of office? The office of governor of Rhode Island, with its salary of four hundred dollars, could hardly be a prize sufficiently dazzling to win such a man from his high hopes and brilliant promises. Could it be love of plunder? His enemies have admitted that, aside from his political theories, he was honest. Who, then, will for a moment suppose that Thomas Wilson Dorr ever contemplated the crime of *treason*, which implies a wicked and corrupt attempt to overthrow a government admitted to be rightfully and legitimately existing? What other obvious intention could he have, but to assert and vindicate the great principle of popular sovereignty, involved in the contest between the two parties in Rhode Island? Yet this man has been convicted of treason by a jury of twelve men, (*every one of whom was his political opponent,*) and is now liable to be sentenced to imprisonment for life for that offence. Does justice, or the security of the State of Rhode Island, require such severity of punishment? Yet the committee deprecate no mercy for Governor Dorr. The time will come when his countrymen will appreciate the great principle for which he now suffers the vengeance of his persecutors, and do justice to his acts and his motives. The same sentence will also remove from his shoulders, to those of his pursuers, the load of stigma which they have attempted to cast upon him. After the lapse of seventy years from the revolution, the cause of liberty may require the blood of some martyrs, even in America; but from it, like armed men from the dragon's teeth, will spring up myriads of brave and fearless asserters of the rights of the people, by whose courage and efforts the principles of the Declaration of Independence may be reinstated in our institutions of government.

Miscellaneous Acts of Outrage and Oppression by Persons acting under the Authority of the Charter Government.

Under the general authority conferred upon the committee, they caused a commission to be issued to the Hon.

Benjamin F. Hallett, of Boston, to take the testimony of certain witnesses therein named, in order to prove specific acts of outrage and violence, by which the people of Rhode Island were intimidated, and their constitution suppressed.* A large mass of proof has been obtained by the commissioner, in pursuance of the authority delegated to him by the committee, an abstract of which follows : —

1. The first matters inquired into by the commissioner were the outrages of the charter troops in Pawtucket, and the murder of Alexander Kilby, the particulars of which follow : —

They first call the attention of the House to the murder of Alexander Kilby, a citizen of Pawtucket, Mass. This event occurred on the 27th day of June, 1842, being immediately after the State of Rhode Island was placed under martial law. On that day, a detachment of charter troops was sent from Providence to Pawtucket, which is a large manufacturing village, situated partly in Rhode Island and partly in Massachusetts — Pawtucket River dividing the two portions of the village, which were united by a bridge. Until the arrival of these troops, there appears to have been

* Commissions were first issued to Walter S. Burgess, George Turner, and Jesse S. Tourtellot, Esqs., who were citizens of Rhode Island. Before proceeding to execute their commissions, they were threatened with prosecution by the present government of the state, under an act of the state prohibiting the administration of extrajudicial oaths — an act originally aimed at the oaths administered at masonic lodges. These threats were thrown out to intimidate the commissioners from executing their commissions, in the vain hope of suppressing the facts which the investigation by the committee was likely to elicit. Yet, as appears by the documents accompanying the president's message, in answer to a resolution of the committee, this law was repeatedly violated by Judge Pitman, Henry L. Bowen, and Thomas M. Burgess, adherents of the charter government, who did not scruple to take depositions and administer oaths contrary to its provisions ; for which they have never been called to an account, and never will be. The committee, however, were not defeated by this paltry expedient to elude an inquiry into their acts by the existing authorities of the state.

no disturbance or particular excitement among the people on either side of the river. After their arrival, and near the evening, they commenced acts of outrage and violence which can find no excuse or palliation in the conduct of the inhabitants. They began these outrages by repeated discharges of musketry, *loaded with ball cartridges,* among the populace of the village, who had been drawn together more from curiosity than any other motive, and who had offered no resistance or violence to the military. Many of the balls thus discharged rattled upon the brick walls of the houses; others penetrated and lodged inside. Two of the citizens were hit and slightly wounded, and Alexander Kilby, a peaceable and quiet citizen, was shot dead. To show the circumstances under which he was killed more particularly, the committee extract the following statement from the deposition of Samuel W. Miller, who stood near Kilby at the time he was shot. Miller was a resident of Pawtucket, on the Rhode Island side of the river. He says, —

"On Monday evening, June 27, 1842, about dusk, I crossed over the bridge from the Rhode Island to the Massachusetts side, at Pawtucket, there being a guard of armed men stationed on the bridge at that time. I went up to Mr. Abell's hotel, and remained there until about half past eight o'clock, P. M., when a person came in and stated that a woman had been killed on the bridge. I had previously heard the discharges of musketry, but, supposing them to be blank cartridges, I did not take any notice of them. I immediately started for the bridge, to learn if the report was correct, and had proceeded as far as the corner of Mr. William Sweet's shop, within eighteen yards of the soldiers at the bridge, when I was accosted by Mr. Alexander Kilby, who put out his hand and asked when I was going down the river. At that moment I saw two of the soldiers on the bridge taking deliberate aim at us, and heard Nehemiah Potter, of Pawtucket, then in command of the soldiery, and whom I knew well, give the order to fire. I know that he was the person who gave the order to fire. I grasped Kilby's hand to pull him one side; but before I could succeed, one of the guns went off, and he fell dead at my feet; the other missed fire, which probably saved my own life. I left Kilby on the ground, and hurried back to Abell's hotel, the soldiers continuing to fire, the effects of which may be seen in a number of ball holes in the buildings in the vicinity of the bridge on the Massachusetts side. . . . Kilby, at the time he was shot, was doing nothing to assail or provoke the soldiers, nor had I seen him. . . . I never knew nor saw Kilby take any part in the suffrage cause. I saw no persons assailing or insulting the soldiers when Kilby was killed, and knew no reason why they should have fired on us."

Several other witnesses confirm the testimony of Miller in all its essential particulars, as well in respect to the killing of Kilby, and the indiscriminate firing upon the citizens of Pawtucket, as to the fact that the troops had no adequate provocation for such an unjustifiable and atrocious outrage. No coroner's inquest was held on the body of Kilby; and he was buried while the bridge was surrounded by the charter troops with cannon loaded and matches lighted, the funeral procession passing near to them in its way to and from the place of burial.

Thus was a peaceable and inoffensive man murdered in cold blood, in mere wantonness, and without a pretence of justification by the charter troops of Rhode Island. Kilby, the murdered man, left a wife and seven children in indigent circumstances. After his death, it is proved that the citizens of Pawtucket and other places contributed sums of money, amounting to about two hundred dollars, for their relief. But the authorities of Rhode Island have done nothing to mitigate the privations and sorrows of a family whose protector and father was shot down by the wanton act of troops in their own employment.

Other acts of violence were committed upon persons and property at the same time by the charter troops. Among them are the following cases : —

Daniel F. Cutting was hit in the arm with a musket ball, and slightly wounded. Another man, William R. Silloway, was slightly wounded in the knee with a musket ball. Robert Abell and Larned Scott, while passing over the bridge on to the Rhode Island side, in a covered carriage, were shot at without cause or provocation, the ball penetrating the carriage, and passing through between the two inmates, at the imminent hazard of their lives. Samuel W. Miller was arrested by the charter troops without cause, rudely treated, and finally discharged. His house was searched, his shop broken open, and his property damaged. Amos Ide was arrested by James N. Olney, a citizen of New York, and placed under a guard of four men, two of whom said they were citizens of New York, and one was a citizen of Massachusetts. He was finally discharged, nothing appearing against him.

John S. Despeau was arrested without cause, taken to Providence, and discharged. The soldiers took possession of his confectionery shop, and converted a portion of its contents to their own use, for which he never has been paid.

The witnesses all concur in the statement that the disturbances which occurred in Pawtucket were produced by the charter troops sent there from Providence. All the acts of violence and outrage detailed above were unprovoked and unjustifiable; and the discharge of loaded muskets into the centre of a populous village can be ascribed to no other motive than a wanton disposition to destroy human life. For proof of the facts above stated, the committee refer to the depositions of the witnesses.

2. The second matter inquired into by the commissioner was the detention of Governor Dorr's order to disband the suffrage forces, by which the peace of the state and the lives of its citizens were kept in peril a day longer; and the interference with the public press.

The testimony under this head shows that before seven o'clock in the afternoon of the 27th day of June, 1842, Governor King and his council had intercepted and knew Governor Dorr's order to disband his troops, which was enclosed in a letter to Walter S. Burgess, Esq., with an urgent request that the order should be forthwith published in the Express newspaper, the organ of the suffrage party, and that Governor King and his council, together with *Colonel James Bankhead, of the United States army, (who appears to have been present at the consultation,)* believed that the suffrage troops had been disbanded. It further shows that Governor King and his council intercepted and broke open Governor Dorr's letter, and detained it until nine o'clock the next morning. The depositions under this head, and that of Colonel Harvey Chaffee, taken to prove the facts hereinafter stated under the fourth head, establish the very material fact, that on Monday evening, the 27th of June, it was known to the charter authorities, civil and military, that Dorr had disbanded his men, and resistance was at an end; that they knew he only desired to have his men allowed to return peaceably to their homes; that they had the means to have published his order on Monday evening or Tuesday morning, and thus have put an end to the excitement and all the subsequent outrages; that, with this knowledge, *they suppressed the order until about Tuesday noon;* and, in the mean time, they sent their troops to Chepatchet, who captured the abandoned fort, and seized and conveyed to Providence a large number of innocent persons as prisoners, besides committing numerous other outrages upon the persons and property of suffrage men ; that, instead of sending the intelligence of the disbandment of the suffrage forces to Pawtucket, to quiet matters there, they sent two companies of troops, which led to the murder of Kilby, as has been before described. The testimony also proves that some four hours after they knew in Providence that the whole suffrage enterprise was at an end, within four miles of Providence, and after it was known that Kilby had been shot, Governor King sent a park of artillery to Pawtucket to blow up the bridge between Rhode Island and Massachusetts.

It further appears, by the deposition of Robert Abell, taken by the committee, that on the night Kilby was shot, (June 27,) at about twelve o'clock, John Whipple, Esq., of Providence, escorted by two armed men, entered Abell's house, and told him Dorr had left Chepatchet, and the war was over. This fact brings the knowledge home to the charter authorities before most of the outrages hereinafter mentioned were committed, and demonstrates, beyond the power of contradiction, *that revenge, and not defence, was the ruling motive of the charter authorities and their adherents, after the disbanding of the suffrage men.*

The testimony under this head also proves a direct interference of armed men, coupled with the menaces of the charter party to suppress the suffrage press, and by which the Express newspaper was suppressed, as is directly proved by the depositions of its proprietors and editors, whose testimony is confirmed by the fact that Governor King gave them a license to publish the order of Governor Dorr disbanding his troops.

Aaron Simons, a person attached to the office of the Herald, states that Samuel Dexter, son-in-law to the present governor of the state, (James Fenner,) came into the office, made use of abusive and violent language, saying " that the press and types ought to be thrown into the street, and that he would be one to help do it. From threats out doors, and other causes, the press was kept in awe during the continuance of martial law, and the liberty of the press was, in a great measure, suppressed."

For the threatening and abusive language, tending to excite the angry passions of the mob, indulged in by the adherents of the charter government towards the conductors of the suffrage press, the committee refer to the testimony.

3. The third branch of the testimony taken by the commissioner relates to the arrests, searches, and acts of violence committed upon the persons and property of the suffrage citizens of Rhode Island. The following are the most striking cases : —

The first is the case of Leonard Wakefield. He was a Methodist clergyman, residing in Cumberland, Rhode Island. He was arrested on the 30th day of June, 1842, (three days after all appearance of hostility on the part of Governor Dorr had ceased,) and taken, with twenty-one other prisoners, to Providence, marched through the principal streets of that city amid the jeers and insults of the mob, committed to prison, and confined in a loathsome cell twelve feet by nine, poorly ventilated, with *fifteen other persons,* and kept on an allowance of two rations of stale bread and meat per day. He was imprisoned five or six days, and, nothing appearing against him, he was discharged. He was in favor of the suffrage cause, but had always exhorted both parties not to resort to arms.

Elias Whipple was arrested on the 6th day of July, confined in prison for the space of thirty-one days, on a charge of treason, and required to find recognizance in the sum of $10,000, which he succeeded in doing. The grand jury found no bill against him. He had taken no part in the conflict, but to vote for the constitution and Governor Dorr.

Mehitable Howard, of Cumberland, a female, aged sixty-two years, was grossly assaulted and insulted. The following is her plain and simple story, exhibiting a cowardly ruffianism on the part of her assailants, as disgraceful to humanity as it was unprovoked and uncalled for. She says, —

"On the 29th of June, 1842, in the morning, between five and six o'clock, Alfred Ballou, with seven other men, all armed with guns, came to my house and entered it, I forbidding them to enter. Myself and grandchildren were the only persons in the house. He broke the door open, and drove it off the hinges. As Ballou came in, he seized me by the shoulders, and shook me hard, leaving prints where he took hold of me. He then pushed me, and pushed me against a post about three or four feet from where I was standing, which bruised my shoulder very much. He came up to me again, seized me, and pushed me again towards the window, saying, 'Get out of the way,' in a loud voice. He then gave me a shake, and left me, saying, 'Where is Liberty?' (meaning my son,) ' and where is the gun?' He went up stairs, and searched the chambers, turning the beds over in which the little children were. He then came down, went into my lodging room, and took a gun and carried it off. I was much overcome; but when he came out, I said, ' I don't fear you, Mr. Ballou.' He then came up to me, laid his hands on me, shook me, and said, in a very loud voice, 'Do you know that you are under martial law?' He then took his bayonet, and put the point of the bayonet against the pit of my stomach. He pressed the bayonet against me, and said, ' I will run you through,' looking very angry and spiteful. The point of the bayonet went through my clothes, and fractured the skin, but did not break it, but caused the blood to settle the size of a ninepence, or larger. I really believed at the time he intended to run me through. With my hand I knocked the bayonet away, and he stepped back, and stood and looked at me with a stern look, and then went out of the house. My husband was a suffrage man, which is the only reason I know for this treatment. Ballou had been a neighbor of ours for near forty years. He was a charter man. I was hurt very bad, and unable to do much work for several days after, and have never recovered from the effects of the shock upon my system. I am sixty-two years of age."

Nehemiah Knight was arrested for saying it was "a mean business to shoot Kilby." He was again arrested, and marched through the streets of Providence, to the armory, by a gang of white men and *negroes* armed, (mainly negroes,) and was guarded by negroes. He was kept in confinement two days, when, nothing appearing against him, he was discharged.

Elizabeth Nutter was assaulted and rudely treated by one of an armed band of charter men, while they were searching the house of a Mr. Haswell, where she resided.

Otis Holmes, a citizen of Providence, of great respectability, had his dwelling house, store, and brewery broken open by a band of armed charter men. He offered them his keys; but they preferred to force their way by violence. After searching his house, store, and brewery, he was marched off — two men holding him by the collar, while another walked in front, with a pistol, to the office of Henry L. Bowen. The gang consisted of thirty men with muskets. He made no resistance; he heard no charges against him, and, without examination, was committed to jail, where he remained seven days; and then, without examination, he was put into one of the cells of the state prison, with seven others. He adds, " It was large enough for us to lie down by lying heads and points. I remained there twenty-one days. The suffering was extreme from heat and want of air, with plenty of vermin. The health of the prisoners suffered materially. During the time, I was examined by the commissioners. They charged me with keeping arms to aid the suffrage cause. No proof was shown. I was remanded. I then got a writ of *habeas corpus* before Judge Staples of the Supreme Court, and went before him in a room in the jail, and, upon a hearing, was discharged. I was then immediately committed by the sheriff, on a warrant from Henry L. Bowen, on a charge of treason. I then applied for another writ of *habeas corpus*, which Judge Staples ordered to be heard before the whole court at Newport. I was there, and allowed bail in the sum of $12,000, with sureties. At the next sitting of the court in the county of Providence, the grand jury found no bill against me, and I was discharged. I was in close prison fifty-nine days."

Henry Lord, a non-combatant, was taken near Acote's Hill, marched with other prisoners, with arms pinioned, to Providence, and there confined in the state prison, with thirteen others, in a cell seven feet by ten, in which he was kept twenty-one days, and discharged on parole.

The house of Martin Luther, in the town of Warren, was broken open on the 29th of June, 1842, by nine armed charter men, and the female inmates rudely treated — their lodging rooms being broken into before they had time to put on their necessary clothing. They used violent language to the mother of Mr. Luther, pointing a weapon at her breast, and threatening to "run her through" if she did not tell where her son Martin was.

Stafford Healey, a hired man of Mr. Luther, was, at the same time the transaction last described took place, forcibly seized by the same armed men who broke into Mr. Luther's house, carried to jail, where he was confined seven days, and then discharged — nothing appearing against him.

Jedediah Sprague was arrested and confined in prison twenty-two days on a charge of treason, when, nothing appearing against him, he was discharged. His family were also grossly maltreated by the charter military at Chepatchet, and his property despoiled and forcibly taken away to a large amount, ($2546, as he alleges,) which he has never been able to recover, and for which the government of Rhode Island have, as yet, allowed him nothing. For a particular account of the gross maltreatment of the females of his family and the plunder of his property, reference is made to his testimony. (See pages 156–166.) Other depredations were also committed by the charter troops upon the property of the citizens of Chepatchet, as appears by the testimony.

4. The fourth and last matter of inquiry was the taking of Acote's Hill, Dorr's post at Chepatchet; orders to the military; interference of the United States officers, and the using of the custom house at Providence as a place of deposit for military stores belonging to the charter authorities. Without giving a digested abstract of the testimony under the last-mentioned heads, the committee will briefly refer to the facts which it establishes.

They will first give an account of the capture of Acote's Hill. It appears from the testimony that the encampment of Governor Dorr was broken up on the morning of the 27th of June, 1842. This fact the charter government had learned from the intercepted order of Governor Dorr disbanding his forces; and, of course, before a soldier was ordered by them to Chepatchet, there was no enemy to meet, no fighting to be done, and no honors to be won by the toil and blood of battle. The troops, therefore, were sent to capture a deserted fort — an achievement which they performed with a chivalrous heroism which became an enterprise so desperate, as will be seen by the following account of the incidents connected with the expedition. On the morning of the 28th, the charter troops arrived from Providence. As they approached, they discharged their pieces at persons indiscriminately, whom they happened to see, and capturing such persons as they took a fancy to capture. There was no person in the encampment of Governor Dorr, and nobody in arms in or about the hill, and no resistance whatever was offered by any one to the charter force. Having made their bloodless assault upon the dismantled fortress, they returned to a hotel near by, where several persons were captured and confined, and sundry acts of violence and insult to peaceable citizens were committed. The scene is thus described by Mr. Joseph Holbrook, a gentleman residing in Boston, who was an eye witness. He says, "An advance of from eighteen to twenty-five men, of the charter troops, (so called,) came up to the hotel; the main body of a division of about seven hundred men not being then in sight. The advance party were armed with rifles or carbines, and swords, and pistols; and as they approached at double-quick time, they fired their pieces, without any apparent cause or the least provocation, at any persons they saw indiscriminately. When this advance party came up to the hotel, I inquired of one of them who commanded the party; and he said Lieutenant Pitman, and pointed him out to me. From what I then learned and saw, I have not the least doubt that this person was Mr. Pitman, the clerk of the United States courts of Rhode Island. I said there was no need of violence. Several persons were standing in the entry of the hotel, the front door being open. There was no show of resistance, and nothing to make it with. One of the persons in the entry was recognized, by the men who came up, as Mr. Eddy, a suffrage man, as I then understood. He was called by name, and ordered to come out. He replied that he should not. Two of the armed party then rushed into the house, to force him out. A scuffle ensued between them in the entry, and the front door was accidentally shut. Lieutenant Pitman, observing this, gave the door a kick with his foot, but it did not open; he then levelled and took aim with his carbine, and appeared to be going to discharge it. Seeing this, I caught him by the shoulder, and begged of him not to fire, as he might kill some of his own men, as well as others. He replied, 'I don't care a God damn, if I can kill somebody,' and instantly fired. A ball passed through the key-hole of the front door, and took effect in the thigh of Horace Bardine; and I saw him in a few minutes coming from the house, led by two men, and shot in the thigh. Lieutenant Pitman's party charged upon them as soon as they appeared, and were forced back; and I did not see Bardine afterwards."

Another witness (Colonel Mitchell, of Boston) gives substantially the same account of the conduct of the charter troops on the occasion referred to, and states the additional fact, *that Colonel Bankhead, of the United States army, was there in company with the charter troops.*

The next day, after picking up as many stragglers as they could find to swell their triumph, the charter army returned to the city of Providence with their prisoners in charge, and the spoils and plunder of the enemy. The finale of this celebrated military enterprise is thus described by Henry Lord, a man sixty years of age, who was among the captives. The troops had in charge about one hundred prisoners, all unarmed men, whom they had picked up by the wayside in their march from Providence. He says, "The next morning, we were mustered and tied together with large bed cords. The rope was passed in a close hitch around each man's arm, passing behind his back, and fastening him close to his neighbor, there being eight thus tied together in each platoon. We had no use of the arm above the elbow. In this way we were marched on foot to Providence, sixteen miles; threatened and pricked by the bayonet if we lagged from fatigue, the ropes severely chafing our arms; the skin was off of mine. In two instances, when the soldiers were halted, we were refused the use of their cups to get water from the brook which passed the road, and had no water till we reached Greenville, about eight miles. It was a very hot day; I had had no water or breakfast that morning, and I received no food until the next day in Providence. We were marched thus tied through the streets, and, after being exhibited, were put into the state prison. Fourteen were put into my cell, which was seven feet by ten. After remaining in prison twenty-five days, I was released on parole." — (See Lord's testimony, page 140.)

Such was the achievement of the charter troops at Chepatchet, and such the exhibition they made in their march of triumph through the streets of Providence!

The testimony under the last-named head proves also the following important facts, namely: —

That the United States troops at Fort Adams were provided with ammunition, flints, and haversacks to carry rations. Provisions were also prepared for them for two days' service. They were daily inspected, and in every respect prepared for active service, *and were given to understand by their officers that they were to act on the charter side against the suffrage cause.*

That the magazine at Fort Adams was used as a depository for powder belonging to the charter government, which was taken away from time to time.

That cartridges for cannon, and United States muskets, were delivered to the charter troops from the United States magazine at Fort Adams.

That the United States custom house at Providence

was made a depot of arms and accoutrements by the charter authorities.

That the following officers and persons in the service of the United States took an active part on the charter side, bearing arms and serving in the military, viz.: John Pitman, United States judge for the district of Rhode Island; John S. Pitman, clerk of the United States courts; Edward J. Mallet, postmaster at Providence; William R. Watson, United States collector; Sylvester Hartshorn, United States marshal; Richard W. Greene, United States district attorney; Peleg Aborn, United States surveyor; Remington Arnold, inspector of customs; and Elisha H. Rhodes, United States boatman. All these individuals were seen in arms in the ranks of the charter troops, and Edward J. Mallet and Sylvester Hartshorn were particularly officious in heading armed men and searching the houses of citizens belonging to the suffrage party. For the details of which, the committee must refer to the testimony taken by the commissioner.

It is also proved that arms belonging to the State of Massachusetts were provided for the use of the charter troops; and it is also in proof that boxes of accoutrements marked "U. S. A.," and belts bearing the initials of the United States, were among the deposits of arms at the custom house in Providence. This, and other facts proved in the course of the investigation, leave no doubt on the minds of the committee *that both arms and ammunition were supplied to the charter troops from the stores of the United States.*

The testimony shows that, especially after the declaration of martial law, the most lawless and outrageous proceedings, on the side of the charter party, took place in reference to the persons and property of the suffrage party. Every individual of the former party seemed to imagine himself clothed with a license to invade the domiciles of the latter, seize and injure their property, and commit assaults upon their persons. Never in the history of this country were the rights of the minority, in a political quarrel, so grossly disregarded and so wantonly violated. And never in our annals were such outrages perpetrated, even under the iron rule of martial law. The committee have given but few of the instances of insult and outrage upon persons and property which have come to their knowledge in the course of their investigations; a full detail of which would require more time and space than they could devote to this portion of their report. And they are bound, in justice to the suffrage party,to say that, during all their trials, so well calculated to exhaust their forbearance, they were guilty of no bloodshed nor personal violence. Their fellow-citizens of the charter side suffered neither in person nor property by their acts.

CONCLUSION.

The committee cannot forbear, in concluding the views which they have very hastily, and therefore crudely and imperfectly, thrown together in relation to the questions of fact and of right connected with the suffrage movement in Rhode Island, to submit a few remarks designed to awaken the House, and, through the House, the American people, to the transcendent importance of the great leading question involved in this inquiry, viz.: THE INHERENT SOVEREIGN RIGHT OF THE PEOPLE TO CHANGE AND REFORM THEIR EXISTING GOVERNMENTS AT PLEASURE.

It is the solemn conviction of their minds, that upon the full, free, and universal acknowledgment of this sacred right, in this and in every other country pretending to be free, the liberties of the people depend. For if they surrender this great principle, and admit that the sovereign power of the state does not reside in them, but in the political organization, or actual existing government, and that they cannot correct the defects in the original organic forms of government, or cannot abolish them and substitute others in their places, without the consent of the existing government, what defence have they against the encroachments of those in power, either by actual and forcible usurpation, or false and insidious construction of the fundamental law? What ramparts exist against the approaches of despotic power? In what does the doctrine that the people cannot resort to their ultimate right of sovereignty, without the consent of the existing authorities of a state, as contended for by the president of the United States, differ in substance and essence from the *divine right of kings*, openly preached in the dark ages of European despotism?

The committee feel more deeply the importance of this subject of their investigation, from the great and imminent danger which now threatens the invaluable conservative principle of popular sovereignty, upon which, in their humble belief, the whole fabric of the American system of republican government is reared. They have seen, with deep regret and anxious alarm, the principle for which they are contending openly scoffed down and repudiated by one of the great political parties into which the people of this country are divided. They have seen it smothered by the leaders of that party in the Senate of the United States, who refused to listen to the complaints of the aggrieved people of Rhode Island, or to make an effort to stay the executive arm of the government, when it was unlawfully levelled against them and their cause. (See the speech of Mr. Allen, of Ohio, in the Senate of the United States, on the Rhode Island question, page 257.) And, lastly, they have seen one of the leaders of that party, now their acknowledged candidate for the highest office in the gift of the American people, arraying himself against the cause of free government, and denying and repudiating, in his open approval of the course of the president in the late difficulties in Rhode Island, the great principle upon which all free governments must be founded, VIZ., THE SOVEREIGNTY OF THE PEOPLE. When the committee witness the spectacle of a large and powerful party, individually and collectively, through its organized political bodies, and its head and leader avowing openly and undisguisedly doctrines inimical to the liberties of the people and the principles of free government, they cannot but be deeply alarmed for the safety and perpetuity of our republican institutions. Therefore it is, that they look upon the question presented to the House and the country, by the people of Rhode Island, as the most solemn and momentous in its character of any that has arisen since the American revolution. On its decision by the American people depends the ultimate fate of free governments, and the weal or woe of countless millions destined to fill the places which we fill, and in their appropriate time become the watchmen and guardians of the temple of liberty, and the venerable and sacred monuments which it contains.

The committee are aware that it is alleged against the investigation in which they have been engaged, that no good can result from it. It is urged that the events which have given rise to it are past and gone, and no practical results can be attained by agitating the matter at this day. It is urged that, even if it were to appear that the people of Rhode Island were right in the principle they contended for, no remedy could now be extended to them; and, therefore, it is best that the wrongs they have suffered should be permitted to slumber undisturbed in the dark tomb of events, which have lived their brief moment, and passed away to be buried and forgotten. But is it not of some consequence that the great principle involved in the suffrage movement should be defined and settled, even if no other benefit can result from this investigation ? Is it not of the utmost importance that the people of the several states of this Union should be apprised of the views of Congress (which has an ultimate supervision over all their constitutions) in relation to the great question of their right to change and reform them, that they may know how far they may be permitted to exercise this right, and in what mode, and under what restrictions ? It is for the want of this very knowledge that a large majority of the people of Rhode Island have been involved in all the consequences of alleged treason, and many of them actually indicted and prosecuted, with a view to subject them to its terrible penalties. It is for the want of this knowledge that they have been denounced as rebels and insurgents, and have been conquered and subdued by the government which they believed was ruling over them without right, aided by the military power of the Union.

The people of Rhode Island, in common with the whole body of the American people, confided in the assurance contained in the Declaration of Independence, that they had a right to alter or abolish existing forms of government, and institute other forms in their places. They saw this great right proclaimed in the constitutions of twenty of the sovereign states of this Union ; they saw it promulgated, in clear and emphatic terms, by all the great writers upon the subject of free government ; and they had no doubt it was their right. And is it for a moment to be supposed that the majority of the people of a state, comprising in its ranks many of its best and purest citizens, would have incurred the perils of treason, and exposed themselves to the odious charge of insurrection and rebellion, and all their train of penalties, persecutions, and disgrace, on the pretence of exercising a great right, without entertaining an honest and sincere belief that they possessed it? And, if they have not this right, is it not due to justice and humanity that these deluded people should be disabused of their delusions, and taught the unwholesome truth that they are the *subjects* of government, and not its sovereigns, and that they cannot meddle with its fundamental forms, without first obtaining the consent of those who happen to possess, for the time being, the offices and power of government? In the belief of the committee, it is due to the unfortunate people of Rhode Island, whose honest motives have led them to incur the sufferings and persecutions of which they are now the victims, as well as to the American people at large, who may, from the same view (true or mistaken) of their rights, incur the same penalties and persecutions, to settle the question of the right of the people over their governments, which hitherto they have supposed existed in their own consent, and were instituted for their own benefit. For this reason, if no other could be assigned, the committee believe the investigation with which they have been charged will be attended with beneficial results, not only to the people of Rhode Island, who are immediately interested, but to the people of the whole Union, whose rights are involved in the issue of this question.

And they exult in the belief that their views and opinions touching the important matters involved in this inquiry have been so decidedly expressed as to leave no doubt in relation to their character. They do not hesitate to avow, in the most emphatic terms, their profound and conscientious conviction that the people of Rhode Island were right in the principle on which they acted in their late effort to establish a republican constitution in place of the old charter, under which they had so long lived. They believe that the doctrines promulgated by the president, in relation to the rights of the people in such cases, and the aid given by the executive of the United States to the charter authorities, by which they were enabled to conquer the people and suppress their government, are at war with the great principle which lies at the very foundation of free government, and not warranted by the constitution. The committee believe that the president, in sustaining the pretensions of a government which had been abolished by the people of Rhode Island, and which held its power by direct and flagrant usurpation, has inflicted a blow upon the cause of popular rights, for which a long life of meritorious service cannot atone. And that the evil example set in this matter by the executive may not hereafter be regarded as a precedent for similar invasions of the rights of the people, on the part of those who may be clothed with the dignity and power of the presidential office, they recommend to the House to impress upon it the seal of its most decided and emphatic condemnation.

In accordance with the facts found in the matter submitted to the committee by the House, and the principles endeavored to be maintained by them, they report, for the consideration of the House, the accompanying resolutions.

Resolved, That all free men, when they form the social compact, are equal; and that no man, or set of men, are entitled to exclusive, separate, public emoluments or privileges from the community.

Resolved, That all power is inherent in the people, and all free governments are founded on their authority, and instituted for their peace, safety, and happiness; and for these ends they have at all times an unalienable and indefeasible right to alter, reform, or abolish their government, in such manner as they may think proper.

Resolved, That the sovereign power of the State of Rhode Island is inherent in the people thereof; and that they have at all times the unalienable and indefeasible right to alter, reform, or abolish their government, in such manner as they may think proper; and that any constitution or frame of government, republican in its form, adopted by them, is entitled to the guarantee of the United States, until abrogated by an act of said people, as solemn and authentic as that by which it was adopted.

Resolved, That the constitution adopted in December, 1841, by the people of Rhode Island, is republican in its form, and was rightfully adopted by a majority of said people, and, as such, was entitled to the guarantee of the United States until it was virtually surrendered by the assent of said people to the existing constitution of said state, as indicated by the act of registering their names and voting in the first general election under said last-mentioned constitution.

Resolved, That the government established under the constitution adopted by the people of Rhode Island in December, 1841, and duly organized according to its provisions, was, until the said constitution was surrendered by the assent of the people to the existing constitution, the legitimate constitutional government of said state; and that all acts, laws, and proceedings of said government, under said constitution of 1841, and in accordance therewith, and the records thereof, are entitled to full faith and credit in all the other states of the Union, and in the courts of the United States.

Resolved, That the interference by the president of the United States with the military power of the Union, on the side of the late charter government of Rhode Island, against the constitution adopted in 1841, and by which the same was suppressed, was unauthorized by the constitution and laws of the United States, and in derogation of the rights of the people of Rhode Island.

Resolved, That John Pitman, United States judge for the district of Rhode Island; John T. Pitman, clerk of the United States courts for the district of Rhode

Island; Edward J. Mallet, postmaster at Providence; William R. Watson, collector of customs at the port of Providence; Sylvester Hartshorn, marshal of the United States for the district of Rhode Island; Richard W. Greene, attorney of the United States for the district of Rhode Island; Peleg Aborn, surveyor at the port of Pawtuxet; Remington Arnold, inspector of customs; and Elisha H. Rhodes, United States boatman at said port of Pawtuxet, by personally interfering with arms, in a military capacity, in the late political contest of the people of Rhode Island, growing out of the attempt to establish a constitution for said state, have been guilty of conduct unauthorized by the constitution and laws of the United States, of evil example, and tending to compromit the government of the United States in its relations with the State of Rhode Island, and to produce forcible collision between the people of said state and the authorities of the United States, at the imminent hazard of involving the whole Union in the calamities and horrors of civil war.

The foregoing report was signed by Hon. Edmund Burke, chairman of the select committee.

The following speech was made in the Senate of the United States on the 17th of May, 1842, by Mr. Allen, of Ohio.

Mr. Allen said he proposed, before he sat down, to submit two other resolutions; and, in doing so, he would offer to the Senate some reasons upon which those resolutions were founded. He believed this had been the habitual practice in the Senate; and he hoped that, in this case, he would not be prevented from following the same practice. He would read, in the hearing of the Senate, the resolutions which he proposed to offer, in order that the Senate might judge of their propriety. He found upon the files of the Senate a document containing a series of resolutions passed by the legislature of the State of Rhode Island, by which the governor of that state was requested to inform the president of the United States, and the two Houses of Congress, that a new system of government had been adopted in that state, and was now in full operation. It had, therefore, been brought officially to the notice of the Senate that the people of Rhode Island had adopted a constitutional form of government, and that that government is now in full operation. This communication left the Senate no alternative; they could not close their eyes to the fact that there were, at this time, two governments in actual existence within that state — one of which must be right, and the other wrong. In this state of affairs the president of the United States had assumed to himself the power and authority of deciding this vital and momentous question, by pledging himself to support the old form of government, established under the charter granted by Charles the Second, and against that government determined upon and adopted by the people. This being the state of the facts, it was a question of propriety and of power with the Senate to take into consideration — when informed of these facts by authority, real or pretended, of the State of Rhode Island, and knowing the course which the president of the United States had taken in the matter — whether it was consistent with the duty which they owed to the constitution of the country to remain quiet spectators of a civil war, in which the powers of the federal government were to be brought to bear against the constitution which the people had formed for themselves, and in support of that charter which had been rendered null and void by the American revolution, and under which, since the period of the revolution, that state had no right to exercise the functions of an integral portion of this Union, of a sovereign state, or to send senators or representatives to this Congress. They had no more right to take part in the legislation of this Union than they had to sit and legislate in the British Parliament. Sir, said Mr. A., the question is one of serious import. More — infinitely more — important is it than any question of a bank, a tariff, or any question of national policy which can arise under our form of government. It is a question upon which rests the whole system of the civil government of this country, and of the civil liberties of its people. The president of the United States has undertaken to decide the question for the American people — and that, too, against the people themselves. Well, sir, I said, and I repeat it, and it is with no unkind feelings towards any one; for reasons for such feeling I have none, but for the contrary feeling I have many; but to illustrate the bearing of a great truth — a truth which has shaken the globe itself, and which I hope will continue to govern the world as long as it continues its revolutions upon its axis. I say again, there was no constitutional form of government in Rhode Island, by which that community could be considered to be properly a member of this Union, until the constitutional form of government was framed and established, and brought into being, May 3, 1842.

Sir, what is the state of this matter? The old thirteen states of this confederacy consisted of what were, prior to 1776, the thirteen colonies of Great Britain, of which Rhode Island and Providence Plantations was one. A revolt took place among the colonies; that revolt assumed the form and bore the aspect of a war; as such, it was prosecuted to its final, its successful, its glorious termination. This war was so begun, prosecuted, and ended, with the express view on the part of the colonists of absolving themselves, in the language of the Declaration of Independence, from all allegiance to the throne of Great Britain. The war was successful; American independence was purchased by American blood. All political connection with Great Britain ceased to exist, and it was made an essential part of that instrument by which the states were declared free, that they were to be considered also sovereign and independent. To this declaration the State of Rhode Island stands pledged, because that declaration was necessarily submitted to, and confirmed by, the legislature of that state.

Yes, sir, the legislature of Rhode Island confirmed that declaration by a solemn resolve, forever absolving themselves from all connection with, or relation to, British authority. Well, sir, after the state had thus annulled the charter of Charles II. of Great Britain, by this revolution and this declaration, where did they obtain their right to have a government independent of the people, in whom, by the new constitution of these United States, the sovereignty was vested? The charter did not provide for its own amendment or for its own modification; it was an emanation from the throne of Great Britain, and could only be modified, changed, or in any way affected by the throne itself, or by an act of the British Parliament. And it is the most extraordinary political anomaly that has characterized this extraordinary age, that, sixty years after the annulling of the charter by the revolution, the president of the American republic is called on to give life and vitality to it again. That charter was predicated upon the allegiance of that community to the British crown; and it existed with the restriction that the laws, rules, and regulations of the Governor and Company should not contravene the laws and statutes of Great Britain; and that one fifth of the precious metals to be found in the soil was the property of the British government, and to be paid into the British treasury. Well, what became of their allegiance to the British government when they lifted the sword of revolution? It was destroyed; the relation was severed, the charter was dissolved. How was this dissolution effected? By authority of the

British crown? No, sir; by the people themselves. And can the British charter be restored by American legislation? No, sir; because it was founded upon the existence of British supremacy. Can the state itself give vitality to the charter? I answer, no; because it would be inconsistent with American independence. And here let me be permitted to say that, inasmuch as it cannot be binding upon the state, it cannot upon any part of the state. If the whole cannot revive it, neither can a majority, and much less can a minority. It would be impossible for the people of Rhode Island, if they were unanimous to a man, to revive it. They are bound to treat it as a dead letter; and this obligation binds the legislature as firmly as it binds the people. If the charter still lives, it is because it is indestructible, and must live forever; and if it does not exist, as I contend, there results this appalling consequence — that the whole government of the State of Rhode Island, from the revolution up to the 3d of May, 1842, has been a sheer, a downright, a blasphemous usurpation. Yes, sir, a usurpation; for after the revolution was accomplished, the charter was dead. The declaration of American independence took place, and the revolution followed; every thing that was British — every vestige of British power and authority — perished. It was entirely cut off from the face of this continent. How, then, has this form of government continued to exist? It could only be in this way: At the time when the revolution closed, it is probable that the number of those having rights confirmed to them by the charter amounted to a majority of the population, and they were willing that the charter should stand, that they might enjoy the benefits of freeholders, and be the lords and masters of the increasing multitudes by whom the state became speedily populated. There is one peculiarity about this state of things, to which an American cannot close his eyes — that it is an exact inversion of our political institutions. It leaves it in the power of the legislature to declare who shall have the privilege of voting; and, consequently, they may pass a law excluding every one but themselves — perpetuating to themselves and to their descendants the privilege, and excluding all others. The sovereignty is thus vested in the agent, and not in the principal — in the representatives of the people, and not in the people themselves.

Well, sir, under these circumstances, what did the people of Rhode Island gain by the revolution? They thought they were struggling to exchange British authority for the rights of civil liberty. Yet we see the great body of the people — three fifths, at least, of the entire population — being disfranchised, left to the remaining two fifths the power of governing. But we have seen that the people have regenerated the government — have thrown off this usurpation under which they have so long been deprived of their rights; and I will here ask, By what authority, under this charter, (if it does exist,) do senators from that state occupy places upon this floor? Does the charter authorize the state to elect senators to the Congress of the United States? Sir, does the charter authorize a convention of the people of Rhode Island to incorporate that state into the body of the American republic? I presume not, sir. By what authority, then, did they act, when they became a constituent part of this Union? Was it under that charter, granted more than a century before the revolution — was it by virtue of that charter, under which the majority of the inhabitants were disfranchised, that that state took refuge, like a tempest-tost vessel, and became safely moored in the harbor of the republic? Do you bring the charter into the federal constitution with you? No, sir; the people of the State of Rhode Island adopted, in solemn convention assembled, the federal constitution — the vital, elementary principle of civil liberty. It was recognized by all parties. Without this, the state could not have become a member of the Union, because the constitution requires that this shall be done. This was not the work of a party; it was effected by the fathers of the revolution, who laid down the fundamental law of civil liberty — men whose veins were drained of their life-blood in procuring that independence and the enjoyment of that civil liberty for their descendants. What did that convention do? They declared "that there are certain natural rights of which men, when they form a social compact, cannot deprive or divest their posterity; among which are the enjoyment of life and liberty, with the means of acquiring, possessing, and protecting property, and pursuing and obtaining happiness and safety;" "that all power is naturally vested in, and consequently derived from, the people; that magistrates, therefore, are their trustees and agents, and at all times amenable to them;" "that the powers of government may be reassumed by the people, whensoever it shall become necessary to their happiness."

Never was there a declaration stronger or more comprehensive than this, made by the sovereign people of the State of Rhode Island. Well, sir, what have they subsequently done? Why, as soon as they got snugly established as a part of the Union, the Governor and Company of the province effected the resumption of the sovereignty, because there was not popular power enough around them to resist. They resumed the sovereignty, meting out to the people as much right and as much wrong as those sovereign legislators thought proper to mete out. Instead of having their own duties prescribed to them, they assumed the right to prescribe to the people — their lords and masters — how much liberty they should enjoy. Sir, the president of the United States, it seems, is now called upon to sustain this charter of a British monarch. John Tyler is called on to act as Charles II. of England would have done in enforcing this charter — by force of arms. Who ever before heard of an appeal to an American president to support British authority? And I say again, if he has the right to call in the aid of an armed force to sustain that authority, the independence of this country does not exist. Such a proceeding might be tolerated in Canada; but, in relation to one of the states of this Union, the supposition is as ridiculous as it is odious. The president declares that he feels himself bound, and that it is his duty, to employ an armed force, if it becomes necessary, in order to enforce obedience to this usurpation, which has been for half a century in existence in Rhode Island; he will march an armed force of American citizens into that state, in martial array, to shoot down the people, in order to sustain that charter, which it was the main object of the revolution to destroy. Let him try it! let him try it! The president is a man, and but a man; he is an officer of the government, and but an officer.

The power which constitutes the president rests neither with this body nor its friends; it possesses a moral force which is superior to either. Let the president undertake to march an army into Rhode Island, to put down the liberties of the people at the point of the bayonet, and he will have done a deed of which his posterity will be ashamed — of which the nation will be ashamed. But, though he threatens to do it, and stands officially pledged to do it, I tell him (as I have told him face to face) that the American people will not permit him to do it. Here is what will test the question, [holding up a placard.] This I look upon as the first flash of indignation from the enraged brow of an angry people; and I warn the president to take notice of the lightning's flash, as being the forerunner of a storm that will cover him with deep disgrace.

Yes, sir, this is a government of principle, sustained by the sense of the people; and the man who rashly undertakes to put down popular liberty in this country will meet with signal discomfiture. In connection with my honorable colleague, I have the honor of representing one of the great and glorious states of this Union; and, sir, I can assure you that I speak the feelings of the great body of the people, acting only under the promptings of a bold and heroic magnanimity, when I say that they would be roused — that they would rally as one man in defence of our glorious liberties, whether invaded by foreign or domestic foes.

I now offer a resolution, which will test the sense of this body upon the vitality of our whole system. I have introduced into it nothing but what has been prompted by a natural impulse of patriotism — nothing but will be responded to by the whole body of my countrymen. Had the Senate acted upon the resolution when it was first offered, the president would have retracted; he would not now have stood pledged; the government of the people would have gone on; the rights of all would have been protected by the votes of all.

CHAPTER XVII.

PROPOSITIONS FOR THE RELEASE OF MR. DORR ON CONDITION THAT HE WILL ENGAGE TO SUPPORT THE EXISTING CONSTITUTION. HE REFUSES, AND IS AFTERWARDS SET AT LIBERTY BY AN ACT OF GENERAL AMNESTY. REJOICINGS AND CONGRATULATIONS, ETC.

The leaders of the " law and order " party in Rhode Island have made repeated efforts to justify themselves in view of the people of the sister states, and various printed documents have been extensively circulated for that purpose ; and it is obvious that many of the errors and mistakes that are found abroad with regard to this matter have arisen from such sources. It has been said that Mr. Dorr would not have been sent to the state prison even after sentence if he had consented to take an oath. The circumstances upon which that report is founded are simply these : During the trial and conviction of Mr. Dorr, disinterested men of all parties, at home and abroad, regarded the proceedings as extremely unjust ; and before he was removed to the state prison, his persecutors heard with concern the loud murmurs which arose against them from all quarters. They wished to screen themselves from the threatening indignation, and therefore devised the following scheme :

Mr. Dorr's father was induced to petition the legislature for the liberation of his son, and a delegation of the "law and order" party visited Governor Dorr while he remained in prison at Newport, informed him of the said petition, and offered to advocate its passage on condition that he would engage to take an oath to support the existing constitution of that state. This overture was promptly rejected, and Mr. Dorr gave the gentlemen to understand that he would never take an oath to support a government which owed its existence to the power of the bayonet; he would not sacrifice his principles or his honor to save himself from a dungeon or a gibbet, and he desired no favors from a government the validity of which he did not acknowledge. The legislature being in session at the same time, a member of the Senate visited Mr. Dorr in prison in order to ascertain his determination with regard to the proposed overture. During that interview Mr. Dorr disclaimed all knowledge of any such petition on his part, and requested the honorable senator, in his name, "to protest against any action by the General Assembly upon said petition." That petition was, however, presented, but not acted upon. Whether those individuals who thus endeavored to operate upon Mr. Dorr could or could not have induced the General Assembly to pass the act which they proposed, it is impossible to say; but it is certain that no action was taken upon the subject at that time, and it is well known that he would never have consented to any such propositions if they had been made. The inconsistency of this manœuvre is apparent. An individual had been proved guilty, as his enemies said, of the most atrocious and abominable of all crimes, which implied a total moral depravity; and now they offer to set him at liberty if he will engage to support their cause. It was not the prisoner that these officious "law and order" men sought to relieve, but themselves and their own party. Public opinion had found them guilty of a great wrong, and they hoped to escape its impending sentence by casting away their victim.

At the January session ot the General Assembly, 1845, the subject was brought up again without the knowledge or consent of Mr. Dorr, and the following act passed.

Thomas W. Dorr liberated on Condition of his taking the Oath of Allegiance to the State. January, 1845.

Upon the petition of Sullivan Dorr and Lydia Dorr, his wife, praying for an act of amnesty, —

Voted and resolved, That the prayer thereof be so far granted as that Thomas W. Dorr be liberated from his confinement in the state prison, upon his taking the following oath or affirmation : —

" I do solemnly swear (or affirm) that I will bear true faith and allegiance to the State of Rhode Island and Providence Plantations; and that I will support the constitution and laws of this state and of the United States. So help me God. (Or, this affirmation I make and give upon the peril of the penalty of perjury.) "

Said oath or affirmation shall be administered by the clerk of the Supreme Court, sitting in any county in the state, or by one of the justices thereof in vacation, and be recorded upon the records of said court in the county in which the same is taken; and the warden of the state prison is hereby directed to furnish said Dorr with a copy of this resolution, and whenever he shall signify his desire to take said oath or affirmation, to attend said Dorr before said court or justice ; and upon his taking said oath or affirmation, to discharge him accordingly.

This act plainly showed that the same rancorous spirit with which Mr. Dorr had been persecuted still existed in all its bitterness ; and it also showed that his enemies were desirous to compromise with public opinion, and purchase a pardon for themselves by pretending to grant one to Mr. Dorr.

Every member of that legislature well knew that Mr. Dorr had once solemnly sworn to support the people's constitution ; and now that body offered to release him if he would violate that oath. Now, when the government had deprived him of all his civil and political rights, and taken away his oath, as if in mockery, they call upon him to go before the same haughty and arbitrary tribunal which had, as he knew, unjustly doomed him to a felon's cell, and there swear allegiance to a government which had been established by force, in violation of the inherent and constitutional rights of the people at large. His enemies well knew that a compliance with that act would mar his spotless reputation, and clothe him with perpetual shame. With this mark upon their victim, he might go abroad to be despised and spurned by all men. His oath could never again be taken. By law he had already been deprived of all the rights and privileges of a citizen, or even a human being, and nothing but a compliance with this act seemed necessary to complete his destruction. But those who composed that legislature were mistaken in their man. From a lofty moral eminence he looked down upon them with contempt. His conduct was governed by a high moral sense unknown to his enemies. He would not barter his conscience for his freedom or his life. He spurned the graceless overture, and, like Cato of old, gave his persecutors to understand that he disdained any boon which they had power to offer.

Every where abroad the people applauded the heroic firmness of Mr. Dorr, and condemned the shameful tyranny of his persecutors. It was evident that a storm was gathering — dark rolling clouds charged with indignant thunders appeared in the horizon and seemed to threaten with destruction the Rhode Island bastile. Under these circumstances it was thought prudent to liberate their victim, and, therefore, the General Assembly, on the 26th day of June, 1845, passed the following act : —

An Act to pardon certain Offences against the sovereign power of the State, and to quiet the Minds of the good Citizens thereof.

SECTION 1. No person shall be hereafter prosecuted for any crime or offence which may have been committed against this state, and enumerated in the act entitled "An act in relation to offences against the sovereign power of the state," passed April 2, 1842; and every person who is under recognizance, indictment, or sentence for or on account of any such offence, shall be and is hereby discharged from such recognizance, indictment or sentence, and from all the civil and penal consequences thereof.

Sec. 3. Any person who has been convicted of the crime of treason against this state, and is now in prison under the sentence of the law provided for such offence, shall be forthwith discharged from such imprisonment, and the keeper or warden of the prison where any such person may be, shall discharge such person from such imprisonment upon the production to him of a copy of this act certified by the secretary of state. (Passed June 26, 1845.)

The language of this act, together with the circumstances under which it passed, seems to deserve a passing notice. Who "had been convicted of the crime of treason against that state, and was in prison under sentence"? No one, as the legislature well knew, but Thomas Wilson Dorr; yet his name is cautiously withheld from the act, and the general reader might be led to suppose that it was an act of general amnesty designed to set at liberty many persons, without any particular reference to him. Now, when not only the slow unmoving finger of scorn, but the strong arm of power, was seen pointing towards Rhode Island, and it had become obvious that if his persecutors did not soon unloose his chains, they would be stricken off, — as if to deny their own fears and hide as much as possible their own shame, they release their victim under the disguise of an act of general amnesty.

Under this act, on the 27th of June, Mr. Dorr was discharged. It will be recollected that it was on the 27th of June, 1842, that he dismissed his forces at Chepatchet, and on the 27th of June, 1844, he was committed to the state prison in Providence, and at length, on the 27th of June, 1845, he was discharged from prison. As soon as he was restored again to light and life, he was met with the joyful greetings of thousands, at home and abroad, as the following testimonials show.

GOVERNOR DORR.—We learn that the parents of Governor Dorr, on Thursday last, availed themselves of a permission to visit their son in prison, and that they found him in a very bad state of health.

We have also learned from other sources, that the maladies with which Governor Dorr has been afflicted, since his imprisonment, have been increased of late, and little or no hope can be entertained of his long continuance in life, unless he shall be speedily relieved from prison.—*Republican Herald, Providence, May 24, 1845.*

GOVERNOR DORR LIBERATED.—We stop the press to announce the fact that the bill before the legislature for the liberation of Governor Dorr, and for a general amnesty, as given in our legislative proceedings, was passed into a law this morning. The news, together with an authenticated copy of the act, was brought to this city, yesterday, at half past two o'clock, and was immediately carried over to the prison by Walter S. Burges, who took with him a carriage to receive Governor Dorr and convey him from the loathsome scene of his wrongs and sufferings, who is now, at three and a half o'clock, making preparations to quit the prison. Hundreds of citizens are crowding the prison door, and hundreds more in carriages, on horseback, and on foot, are thronging the roads leading to that hated place, to get a glimpse at this victim of persecution, and once more welcome him on his restoration to his friends, the people, and to the world.

He comes forth, not restored to his civil rights, but he comes to receive a joyful welcome, and the deepest sympathy and the warmest reception from a people who highly appreciate his public services and noble sacrifice in their behalf. The citizens are animated by a warm and generous enthusiasm by this event, but the most commendable tranquillity prevails in the city.

The loud booming of the cannon from Smith's and Federal Hills, and the waving of the flags from the hickory poles and flag-staffs, give unequivocal token of the general and undisguised joy which pervades all ranks and sexes in the city.

Governor Dorr is now restored to his liberty, and the people are rejoicing with exceeding great joy. — *Republican Herald, June 28, 1845.*

THE FLAME IS SPREADING. — One hundred guns were fired at Cambridgeport, on Monday noon, in token of joy at the liberation of Governor Dorr; flags were waving through the day, and rockets let off at night. We have not room to copy the account of the affair given in the Boston Times. Strong manifestations of joy have been made in other places, the particulars of which we shall give as soon as we are able. The train has been laid, and the match applied, and as the news travels onward, these outbursts of enthusiasm will be heard to the utmost bounds of our land, till the whole line pours forth one grand *feu de joie.* — *Republican Herald, July 2, 1845.*

THOMAS W. DORR. — As for Governor Dorr, his reputation is safe with the people, and he will live to see the people triumphant, and their enemies overthrown. He but acted his part as the legal governor of Rhode Island, and took constitutional measures only to support the government of the people. If he failed in the main, relying too much upon the hearty support of those who had pledged themselves to do their duty, and if *they* proved recreant in the hour of trial, the people will see that *he* has stood fast by the principle of popular sovereignty, and will cherish his memory accordingly.

They know he has sacrificed the applause of many of his fellow-associates and townsmen, his early position in Rhode Island, and the smiles of fortune. In fine, he has sacrificed all but his *honor* — and the country will see that his reputation is cared for, and his course vindicated. — *Boston Times.*

RESOLUTION OF THE NEW HAMPSHIRE LEGISLATURE. — The committee of the New Hampshire legislature, to which was referred the governor's message on the late undignified answer returned by our legislature to the communication from that executive, reported the following resolution, which was adopted by that legislature : —

Resolved, by the Senate and House of Representatives in General Court convened, That the statements contained in the preamble and resolutions of the legislature of this state at its session in 1844, relating to the unjust and tyrannical treatment of Thomas Wilson Dorr by the authorities of Rhode Island are true ; that they are fully sustained by the evidence in the case, and by the records of the court before whom he was tried ; and that the Assembly of Rhode Island never can, by resolutions denunciatory of this or any other legislature, wipe out from the page of history the deep stain which must ever attach itself to that state, until full and complete justice be done to that much injured individual. — *Republican Herald, July 4,* 1845.

GOVERNOR DORR. — The friends of human rights must receive the announcement of Governor Dorr's release with unbounded joy; they must hail it as an earnest of the onward march of the spirit of Liberty, and they must continue to animate and encourage their Rhode Island friends to the achievement of a still greater victory. Let the fiat go forth, — *Governor Dorr's rights must be restored,* — and the result will not disappoint the lovers of liberty and right. Up, then, freemen! Sleep not, while a worthy and distinguished citizen is denied the privileges guaranteed to every man by the great Magna Charta of our liberties. Governor Dorr will be restored — and by an Algerine legislature, too. It were too much for these narrow-hearted and selfish men to give him his liberty and his rights together; yet, we repeat, the same power which opened his prison doors a few days ago, will at another time restore him to his civil rights. Agitate, agitate — and all will be well. The stern sentiment of the democracy must be respected. — *Wayne County (Ohio) Standard.*

A Visit to Governor Dorr.

PAWTUCKET, *July* 29, 1845.

Mr. Editor: Yesterday, for the first time since the doors of the Rhode Island bastile grated upon their hinges, to usher once more into life and liberty the patriot Dorr, I had the pleasure of grasping that hand which would sway the sceptre of justice and mercy over all. And if my heart ever had cause to overflow with gratitude to the Disposer of all events for his goodness, it was when I was permitted to greet the noble martyr in the home of his childhood, where the loved scenes of his youth had so long mourned his absence, and where for months, ay, years, his voice had not echoed in the halls of his father. I found him surrounded with all the comforts and elegances which wealth or affection could bestow; but, alas! the richest treasure, health, was wanting, and his countenance and feeble step betrayed disease and anguish of body, while his mind had been preserved in all its purity by a power higher than

that which had so long aimed to destroy the noblest work of God. And as I contemplate that lofty brow upon which the eternal principles of truth and justice were written, I thought the man who could wish or inflict punishment upon one like him must have a kindred spirit with the demons of another world.
(Signed,) A. E. H.

THOMAS W. DORR. — This persecuted patriot has received invitations from the democratic republican general committees of the cities of New York and Albany, to visit those cities, and unite with his democratic friends "in a public expression of gratitude to an overruling and all-wise Providence, for the recent triumph of the principles of our free institutions over brute force and party oppression, and of a just and irrepressible indignation in view of the abuse of political power, unparalleled in the annals of civilized nations." Unfortunately the health of Mr. Dorr is so impaired by the petty tyranny and vengeful and dastardly cruelty of the Algerines of Rhode Island, as to prevent a compliance with the invitations of his friends; but we hope that, once more enjoying liberty, and permitted to breathe the free air of heaven, he will soon be able to leave the polluted atmosphere of Rhode Island, and unite with his friends in the enjoyment of the unrestrained friendship of American democracy and the congratulations of freemen. — *Hudson Gazette.*

GOVERNOR DORR'S LIBERATION. — Every real friend of liberty must rejoice, and every real friend of liberty does rejoice, in the liberation of Governor Dorr from the prison in which he has been confined by the contemptible vindictiveness of the party which has ever been hostile to human rights. He is now that for which he ventured all to render his oppressed fellow-citizens, a *freeman*; and if we may infer the future from the popular enthusiasm which greeted his restoration to liberty, he will receive, as an appendage to his freedom, the highest honors which a grateful and intellectual people can bestow. The work of reformation, which began with the election of Governor Jackson, has been well sustained by the liberation of Governor Dorr, and will, we trust, be worthily prosecuted by the election of Governor Dorr to the executive chair. — *Philadelphia Ledger, (neutral.)*

Celebration at Philadelphia, July 4th, 1845, by the Young Men's Democratic Association.

Governor Dorr — A brave man; a patriot of the revolutionary stamp! Neither the threat of protracted imprisonment, nor the promise of liberation, could induce him to abandon the requisition of honor, or his determined adherence to equal rights. (Nine cheers.)

Among the volunteer toasts were the following : —

By E. W. C. Greene : —

The liberation of Thomas W. Dorr — We hail it as another evidence of the prevalence of democratic sentiments. (Nine cheers.)

By the committee : —

Thomas W. Dorr — A martyr to the great and incontrovertible principles so ably set forth in his sentiment, so nobly contended for in his actions, and for which he has, like an indomitable patriot, so long and magnanimously suffered. We rejoice that this day, so dear to Americans and democrats, is not still desecrated by the incarceration of one of the most devoted champions of the rights and supremacy of the people. (Nine cheers.)

The following is the letter of Governor Dorr, in reply to an invitation to attend the celebration : —

PROVIDENCE, *July* 2, 1845.

Gentlemen: It has been wholly out of my power, until the present moment, to acknowledge your friendly and gratifying letter of June 12, which conveys an invitation to take part in celebrating the anniversary of our national independence. It would give me great pleasure to join you on this occasion in renewing our accustomed tribute to the principles, the acts, and the men of the American revolution, and, in so doing, to strengthen our allegiance to the great cause of freedom, which has been bequeathed to the patriotism and vigilance of each succeeding generation. But, for reasons which you will duly appreciate, I shall not be able to avail myself of this opportunity for a social interview, and must propose the accompanying sentiment as a substitute for my personal attendance.

With the best wish for your success in advancing the objects of the association, I am very truly and respectfully your friend and fellow-citizen.

(Signed,) THOMAS W. DORR.

To Messrs. J. N. Cardozo, J. A. Stevens, and others, committee.

The Declaration of American Independence — Always true, and not merely designed for once to set forth a rhetorical enumeration of abstract, barren "belligerent" rights. The absolute supremacy of the people over their political institutions, is the primary vital doctrine of our democratic republic. It was sealed with the blood of the revolution. It was trampled upon in this state in 1842. It was avenged in the election of the present chief magistrate of the Union. It carries terror in its front only to tyrants. When it shall be obscured and lost, the people of this country will cease both to enjoy and to deserve the rights and blessings of a free government. (Thirteen cheers.)

THOMAS W. DORR. — Shouts of the democracy are

heard in every portion of our land; and for what? The friend of liberty, Thomas W. Dorr, is again free from the enclosure of the prison walls.

The good men of the revolution opposed the British charters of their own states.

Thomas W. Dorr opposed a like charter of his own state. Many of the former were imprisoned by the British; the latter was also imprisoned by the lovers of British institutions.

The names of the men of the revolution are embalmed in glory. So will be the name of Governor Dorr. His grievous wrongs will be remembered; his sufferings can never be forgotten. Honest in principle and firm in purpose, he scorned the humiliating proposition of his persecutors, and chose a prisoner's life rather than a dishonorable surrender of principle. The people admired his integrity, and came to his rescue. The spell of tyranny in Rhode Island is broken. Its remnants may be felt for a season, but they are crumbling, while the tree of liberty is growing freshly. The strength of the tyrants, in death throes, was spent upon Dorr. A stouter heart and firmer patriot could not have been selected among the sons of liberty. Most nobly has he sustained his cause, keenly has he suffered, and more proud is his triumph. He suffered for principles near and dear to the people of this land; but not for himself. A base surrender of those principles, on his part, would have saved him the pangs of a prison cell. But he was not the man to make the surrender, and happily in his case is the admirable saying of Bryant verified — "Truth, crushed to earth, shall rise again."

The people will do justice to the man and his principles. While those who have attempted to blacken his character and crush him are sinking into disgrace, Thomas W. Dorr will rise to distinction. The glad shouts of freemen, at his release are welcome to every son of liberty. — *Hartford Times.*

CHAPTER XVIII.

AN ACT OF THE RHODE ISLAND LEGISLATURE TO RE-
VERSE AND ANNUL THE JUDGMENT OF THE SUPREME
COURT AGAINST MR. DORR.

It may be presumed that the court which pronounced sentence upon Mr. Dorr seriously expected he would suffer its unmitigated rigor, and dole out the remainder of his life in that horrible sarcophagus to which that decree consigned him, and that the records of their own supreme tribunal would stand unimpeached and undisturbed to testify against him forever. A few fleeting years passed, and a mighty change came over their mad vision. Public opinion not only set their victim at liberty, but justified and applauded his conduct, and, finally, expunged the foul stain which his enemies had cast upon his name, and converted the records of that court into perpetual testimony against itself, as the following preamble and enactment of the Rhode Island legislature show.

An Act to reverse and annul the Judgment of the Supreme Court of Rhode Island for Treason, rendered against Thomas W. Dorr, June 25, A. D. 1844.

Whereas the General Assembly of this state hath from time to time exercised the powers conferred upon it by the charter of King Charles the Second, "to alter, reverse, annul, or pardon, under their common seal or otherwise, such fines, mulcts, imprisonments, sentences, judgments, and condemnations as shall be thought fit:"

And whereas the same powers were continued to the General Assembly under the existing constitution of this state by the terms thereof, which provide " that the General Assembly shall continue to exercise the powers they have heretofore exercised, unless prohibited by this constitution ;" and by the provision that "the Supreme Court established by this constitution shall have the same jurisdiction as the Supreme Judicial Court" theretofore existing :

And whereas an alleged political offence, for which a judgment hath been rendered in favor of the state, may in certain cases furnish a proper occasion for the exercise of such high powers :

And whereas upon the trial of Thomas Wilson Dorr for the alleged crime of treason, there was an improper and illegal return of jurors in this, that one hundred and seven jurors from one political party were designedly selected by the sheriff, in part with the aid and assistance of persons acting in behalf of the state, and only one juror from the other political party, and the accused was tried in a county other than that in which the alleged offence was committed and in which he resided, and he was allowed but two days with any, and but a few hours with some of the panel of jurors in which to inquire as to their disqualifications or obtain proof thereof, and was not allowed, after the peremptory challenge of several such jurors, and after obtaining proof of such disqualifications, to withdraw said peremptory challenges, and to challenge said jurors for cause, or to have a new trial in consequence thereof :

And whereas the court denied the jury the right to pass upon questions of law, though said court had previously, in accordance with the common law, held that the jury might in criminal cases "take upon themselves the responsibility of deciding questions of law;" and the accused was not allowed to show in justification or in explanation of his motives or intent, that he acted under a constitution which had been adopted by a large majority of the people of the state, and an election under the same as governor of the state, and in accordance with what he deemed to be his right and duty in consequence thereof:

And whereas the said Thomas Wilson Dorr was thereby wrongfully convicted:

And whereas it is desirable for the best interests of this state that the wrongs thereby inflicted upon said Dorr, and upon the people of the state, should be redressed, and that the animosities created by the civil commotions which preceded and accompanied said trial should cease and determine:

And whereas it has been the custom of our English forefathers, (but for which there hath been happily no occasion heretofore in the history of this country,) whenever judgments for treason have been thus illegally and wrongfully obtained, to reverse by act of Parliament such judgments, and to direct, to the end that justice be done to those who have been thus convicted, that the records thereof be cancelled or destroyed:

It is enacted by the General Assembly as follows: —

SECTION 1. The judgment of the Supreme Court, whereby Thomas Wilson Dorr, of Providence, on the twenty-fifth day of June, A. D. 1844, was sentenced to imprisonment for life, at hard labor, in separate confinement, is hereby repealed, reversed, annulled, and declared in all respects to be as if it had never been rendered.

SEC. 2. To the end that right be done to the said

Thomas Wilson Dorr, the clerk of the Supreme Court for the county of Newport is hereby directed to write across the face of the record of said judgment the words, " Reversed and annulled by order of the General Assembly, at their January session, A. D. 1854."

Sec. 3. The secretary of state is hereby directed to transmit a copy of this act to each of the governors of the several states, and to the Congress of the United States.

Sec. 4. This act shall take effect from and after its passage.

This act passed at the January session, 1854. It was evident at that time that Mr. Dorr was declining, and could not long survive, and it is not supposed that he regarded the measure with much interest. If his persecutors were disposed to acknowledge their own guilt, he could have no objection; but for himself, he humbly confided in a higher and purer tribunal. Yet he might have looked upon this legislative act as an indication of that universal condemnation which the world would pass upon his enemies.

CHAPTER XIX.

SKETCH OF MR. DORR'S LIFE.

It does not come within our province at this time to present the reader with a complete biography of Mr. Dorr, and, after the history which has already been given of that political controversy in which he so largely participated, every one must have become acquainted with the most prominent traits in his character. We have not intended unnecessarily to invade the sacred province of his private life, or to rush unbidden into the domestic circle; but we hold that the public character of every man is public property, and liable at all times to be examined and judged of. Our chief object in the present case is to place the motives and conduct of Mr. Dorr in their true light before the public, and to show that the cause in which he was engaged, and to which he sacrificed so much, was 'a just and righteous cause, and that, through all his reverses, he ever maintained his unflinching fidelity. We are aware that his memory needs no eulogium from us, and that the shafts of his enemies will finally crumble to dust beneath the immortal mound with which time will mark his history; yet, for the satisfaction of such of our readers as may be wholly unacquainted with his private life, it seems proper that we should give a brief sketch of his early history.

THOMAS WILSON DORR was born in the town of Providence and State of Rhode Island, November 5, 1805. His parents were among the most wealthy and respectable citizens, and their numerous connections comprised a very considerable portion of the prominent families of the place at that time. It does not belong to us to give a history of his early life; we will, therefore, pass it over with a single remark. The same nice sense of right and wrong, and the same scrupulous regard for truth, which marked the boyhood of George Washington, marked also the early character of Thomas Wilson Dorr; and the history of his life shows that he maintained that integrity with equal fidelity. His father being wealthy, no pains or expense was spared in his education. His preliminary studies were pursued at Exeter Academy, New Hampshire, and at the age of fourteen he entered Harvard College, where he graduated with much honor in 1823, being the second in his class.

Soon after his graduation he commenced the study of law, and spent two years in the city of New York under the tuition of Chancellor Kent and Vice Chancellor M'Coun. He afterwards returned to his native city, and made himself thoroughly acquainted with the laws of his own state, under the instruction of some of her ablest jurists. It is presumed that no young man, either before or since, ever came to the bar in Rhode Island better qualified, or with more flattering prospects. Irreproachable in morals, urbane in his manners, and mild and unassuming in all his intercourse, he deserved and received the respect and esteem of all with whom he associated; and it is said, that in his professional practice he ever maintained the same undeviating integrity which marked the character of his whole life. As an advocate he was not brilliant; yet his arguments were clear, forcible, and convincing. But we cannot give a history of his professional career, because it is with his public life that we are chiefly concerned: we wish to show that Mr. Dorr did not rashly and ignorantly rush into the political arena. Perhaps no man in Rhode Island had a more thorough or more polished education, or better understood the true principles of American jurisprudence. From 1834 to 1837 he represented the city of Providence in the General Assembly, and also at other times held many important offices; and if he had been less honest and more ambitious, he might easily have obtained the highest office in the gift of the people of that state. His family and its aristocratic connections placed him in the highest class, and posts of honor and power seemed to beckon him to their embrace. But when he looked abroad among mankind, and surveyed the great inequality which every where obtained, — when he beheld one class, by the mere accident of wealth or position, control and oppress those who were less fortunate, but not less worthy, — a spirit of philanthopy overcame all his ambitious aspirations, and he became devoted to the interests of the oppressed. He saw a large portion of the citizens of his own state actually outlawed and deprived of all their political rights by the arbitrary acts of unauthorized legislation. He resolved to forego his own individual interests, and exert himself in behalf of his disfranchised fellow-citizens. He made their cause his cause, and determined to stand or fall with it. We have given the reader the outlines of that eventful struggle which followed, and have shown that a large portion of that same oppressed people, for want of courage and fidelity, abandoned their own cause, and became leagued with their oppressors. Cowardice and treachery united with the bayonet to crush the people and overthrow their leaders; but no human power was able to subdue Mr. Dorr. He had embarked in a righteous cause, and no reverses could damp his ardor or divert him from his purpose. His enemies did, indeed, deprive him of his liberty, and consign him to a felon's cell; but in so doing they exhibited in him a most extraordinary example of magnanimous fidelity.

In his early life, Mr. Dorr manifested the most delicate sense of moral obligations; this governed all his subsequent life; he was ever the most precise and punctual of all men; there was nothing but truth in himself, and he expected to find it in all others; consequently he thought too well of the world, and confided far too much in professions and promises. To one possessed of a less degree of moral integrity the perfidy of others might have been less unexpected and less painful. But when his intercourse with the world had taught him its fickleness and its treachery, — when he saw those in whom he had reposed entire confidence become his enemies and persecutors, and came to reflect upon the injustice and infidelity with which he had been met, he became, in a measure, misanthropic; and although he still greeted his friends with as much warmth as ever, yet he became distrustful of all the world beside, and disinclined to mingle in society at large.

In all his domestic habits, Mr. Dorr was strictly and rigidly temperate, and his social intercourse was ever marked with those becoming courtesies and amenities which betoken a highly cultivated and refined taste, and before the political storm burst upon him he had few or no enemies, and it might at first appear somewhat surprising that one whose whole conduct was so respectful and courteous should so suddenly have so many and so bitter enemies; but this is readily accounted for when we consider that in political controversies there is always a large class of men who have no fixed principles of their own, but follow the lead of political weathercocks, as momentary interest or inclination may dictate. As soon as it was ascertained that the president of the United States would sustain the charter government with the national troops, hundreds upon hundreds, in quick succession, abandoned the cause of the people, and rushed boldly to the standard of law and order; and many, who but a short time before were among the most ardent supporters of the people's constitution, now became suddenly incensed against Dorr and his party, and often prided themselves upon their political prowess, and vied with each other in acts of violence and injustice. After careful inquiry and mature deliberation, Mr. Dorr adopted the course which his conscience approved, and no dangers or difficulties could turn him aside from his purpose. When the weak and irresolute had fallen by the way, and his enemies had overcome and scattered abroad nearly all those on whom he had relied for support, he remained firm and unmoved. He stood erect and alone, and defied the storms like a majestic oak in the midst of a forest which had been prostrated by some wild tornado — and there his character will stand through all coming ages, and ever grow brighter as time rolls on.

It is not pretended that Mr. Dorr was free from the errors, imperfections, and infirmities common to all men. His moral sensibilities led him into mistakes; he thought too well of the world, and his standard of ethics was fixed too high for practical purposes; he chose to consider men as they ought to be rather than as they really are. He was no shrewd calculator, and had too little selfishness to deal with mankind to his own benefit; but instead of taking advantage of the errors and mistakes of other men, he nobly sought to benefit them by correcting their own mistakes. If he had been false to his own convictions and the interests of his fellow-men, wrapped up in his own selfishness, he might have cast himself upon the swelling tide of popularity, and rode fearlessly upon its proudest crests; fanned by the breezes of popular favor, he might have basked securely in its glowing sunshine, and mocked the complaints of the people. Sitting complacently upon an eminence, where fortune had placed him, he might have beheld, with a haughty indifference, all the petty storms that should rage around him. But nothing could induce him, sacrilegiously, to violate his own conscience; his aspirations were of a higher and nobler nature; he sought not to exalt himself, but to elevate the masses, to add his strength to their weakness, and restore the down-trodden to their just position in society. By uniting with the suffrage party he had nothing to gain for himself, but every thing to lose. Wealth, with its gaudy trappings, he despised; he listened reverently to the teachings of his own conscience, and looked with contempt upon empty and transitory popularity. He offered his best services to his fellow-men, not to gain any thing for himself, but to benefit them; and in his fall he shared the fate common to men of great mental powers and moral courage.

It is worthy of remark, that the same class of men who resisted Mr. Dorr and the people of Rhode Island, in 1842, supported the notorious Hartford Convention, in 1812. His most bitter enemies belonged to that same old party, and in some instances were the very same individuals who once sat in that nocturnal conclave. And, indeed, we might go farther back, and show that men of the same political character that opposed Washington, Greene, Adams, and Jefferson, when the American people were struggling against the tyranny of Great Britain, opposed Mr. Dorr and the people of Rhode Island, when they were struggling against the tyranny of their own state, maintained under the pretext of a British charter.

The disease of which Mr. Dorr died was *Chronic Pemphigus*. This affection is not so common in this country as in some others, yet when it has made its appearance here, in adult subjects, we believe it has generally been induced or matured by confinement in damp or unwholesome situations.

Mr. Dorr was imprisoned, in all, twenty months. During his exile, and previous to his arrest in Providence, he was constantly and anxiously engaged in physical and intellectual exercises; and, again, during his long harassing trial at Newport, in consequence of the illness of his principal advocate, he was obliged to labor incessantly in conjunction with his remaining counsel, in the management of his defence. The whole case was a novel one. He was compelled to take his trial among strangers, before a court whose every word and act evinced hostility towards him, and the most implacable of his enemies stood around, thirsting for his blood — they knew not why. Under all these embarrassing and heart-rending circumstances, he labored day and night in conducting his defence, and reporting the trial; and as soon as that judicial farce was over, he was immediately thrust into a filthy dungeon, whose damp, sepulchral atmosphere was pregnant with death. As a stream suddenly dammed up soon recoils upon itself, so the confinement of Mr. Dorr shocked and deranged his system; and although he was somewhat relieved for a time, by being allowed to walk in the corridor, yet the bad air of his prison cell, and the want of cheerful exercise, continued to exert their morbid influence upon him during the whole period of his incarceration, and at the moment of his liberation it was evident that his protracted imprisonment had wrought fearful changes in his physical system. The muscles had lost their tone, the hepatic and chylopoietic viscera had become seriously deranged, and a *Chronic Pemphigus* supervened, under which he finally sank.

There are few individuals who can long endure solitary imprisonment. In general, it is equivalent to a lingering death. The stillness of the grave creeps over the isolated victim encased within cold stone walls, and life goes out by solitary extinction. Mr. Dorr's bodily organization, his social and domestic habits, were illy adapted to such a condition, and if his confinement had been continued much longer he would doubtless have expired in prison. Although he was severely indisposed at the time of his liberation, yet his friends indulged the fond hope that when he came to be released from that dark and noisome cell, and allowed to breathe pure air and take proper exercise, he might regain his health; but they were disappointed. Notwithstanding every reasonable effort was made to improve his condition, he continued steadily to decline. By confinement his system had suffered irreparable morbid changes, and no human means could stay their progress. He bore his severe sufferings with his characteristic fortitude, and at last calmly sunk beneath the weight of his infirmities. He died in the city of Providence, Dec. 27, 1854, aged forty-nine years. Being of Episcopal parentage, he was early initiated as a member of that church, and he continued steadfast in that faith to his last hour. At his request, a few days before his death, the Rev. Mr. Waterman, rector of St. Stephen's Church in Providence, gave him the sacrament. He died as he had lived, with an abiding confidence in the truths of Christianity.

Let those who are disposed to impugn his motives and asperse his character, first cleanse their own garments and cast the beams out of their own eyes, and then, if they can, they may proceed to point out the dark spots in his character. The selfish, unthinking multitude may not recognize in him any unusual degree of moral fidelity; it is by close examination and deep reflection that his character is best understood. As no one but an artist can judge so correctly of the beauty of a piece of sculpture or painting, so none but those possessed of high moral attainments themselves can fully appreciate the prominent traits in the character of Mr. Dorr. But when that time does come, as come it must, when the prejudice against him, with all its bitterness and hatred, shall have fully passed away, mankind will see in him one of the most extraordinary examples of virtuous fidelity which the history of the world affords.

APPENDIX.

CHARTER OF 1643, GRANTED UNDER THE AUTHORITY OF PARLIAMENT.

The following is the first charter to the people of Rhode Island, incorporating them "*by the name of the Incorporation of Providence Plantations in the Narragansett Bay in New England,*" granted under the authority of the Parliament of England, in 1643, giving them "*full power and authority to govern and rule themselves,*" &c.

WHEREAS by an Ordinance of ye Lords and Comons now assembled in Parliament bearing date the 2d day of November Anno Dom. 1643. Robert Earlle of Warwick is constituted & ordained Governor in Chief & Lord high Admiral of all thos Islands and other Plantations inhabited and planted by or belonging to any of his Majesties ye King of England subjects (or wch hereafter may be inhabited and planted by or belonging to them) w^{thin} ye bounds and upon ye Coasts of America, And whereas ye said Lords & Comons have thought fitt and thereby ordained, y^t Phillipp Earle of Pembroke, Edward Earle of Manchester, William Vicont Say and Seale, Phillipp Lord Whorton, John Lord Roberts, members of ye house of Peers, Sir Gilbert Garard, barrenet, Sir Arthur Helsrigge, Barrenet, Sir Henry Vaune Junior Knight, Sir Benjamin Rudyerd,

Knight, John Pim, Oliver Cromwell, Dennis Bond, Miles Corbett, Cornelius Holland, Sammuell Vassell, John Rolle and William Spurstowe, Esquirese members of ye house of Comons, should be Commissioners to joyne in aide & assistance wth ye said Earle.

And whereas for the better governing & preserving of ye said Plantations it is thereby ordained, y^t the aforesaid Govern^r and comm^{rs} or ye greater number of them shall have power and authority from time to time, to nominate, appoint, & constitute, all such subordinat Govern^{rs} Counselors, Commanders, officers, and agents, as they shall judge to be best affected, and most fitt and serviceable to govern ye said Islands & Plantations, and to provid for, ordere, & dispose all things wch they shall from time to time find most fitt and advantageouse for ye said Plantation, and for the better security of ye owners & inhabitants thereof to Assine ratify & confirme, soe much of their afore mentioned authority & power, and in such manner, & to such Parsons, as they shall Judge to be fitt, for ye better Governing & preserving of ye said Plantations & Islands from open violence, prejudice, disturbance and distractions. And whereas their is a tract of Land in ye Continent of America aforesaid called by ye name of ye Naragansett Bay, bordering North and Northest on the Patten of ye Massechusetts, East & Southeast on Plymouth Patten, south on ye oation, and on ye weast and Northweast By Indians called Nahoggansucks alias Narragansetts; ye whole tract extending about twenty and five English miles, into ye Pecut river and Country, and whereas divers well affected and industrious English Inhabitants of ye Townes of Providence, Portsmouth, and Newport, in the tract aforesaid, have adventured to make a nearer neighborhood & sosiaty to & wth ye great body of the Narragansetts wch may in time by ye blessing of GOD upon their endeavours lay a surer foundation of happiness to all America, & have also purchased, & are pur-

APPENDIX. 297

chasing of & amonst ye said Natives, some other places wch may be convenient both for plantation, and also for Building of shipps, supply of pipe staves, & other Marchandice ; And whereas ye said English have represented their desires to ye said Earle and Comm^{rs} to have their hopeful beginnings approved and confirmed by granting unto y^m a free charter of civel incorporation and Gouvornment, y^t they may order and govern their plantations, in such manner as to maintain justice, & peace both amongst themselves and towards almen, wth whom they shall have to doe ; In due consideration of ye Premises ye said Robert Earle of Warwick Gover^{nr} in Chiefe, Lord High Admirall of ye said Plantations, and ye greater Number of ye said Commissionours, whose names and seales are her under written and subjoyned out of a desire to incourage ye good beginnings of ye said Plantations, doe by ye authority of ye aforesaid ordinance of Lords & comons give grant & confirm to ye aforesaid Inhabitants of ye Towns of Providence, Portsmouth, and Newport, a free and absolute Charter, of civel incorporation, to be known, by ye name of the Incorporation of Providence Plantations, in the Narraganset bay in New England, *together wth full power and authority, to Govern and rule themselves, and such others as shall hereaftere inhabitt w^{thin} any part of ye said tract of Land by such a forme of Civel Gover^{mnt} as by voluntary consent of all or ye greatest part of th^m shall be found most serviceable in their Estates and condition* and to that end, to make and ordain such civel Laws and constitutions and to inflict such Punish^{mts} uppon transgressors and for execution thereof soe to place & displace, Officers of Justice, as they or ye greatest part of y^m shall by free consent agree unto — Provided nevertheless y^t ye said Laws, Constitutions and Punishments for ye civell Govern^{mt} of ye said Plantation be conformable to ye Lawes of England, soe farre as ye nature & Constitution of ye place will admitt ;

APPENDIX.

And always reserving to ye said Earle and Comm^{rs} and there successors power and authority soe to dispose ye General Gover^{mt} of y^t as it stands in refferance to ye rest of ye Plantations in America, as they shall commissionate from time to time most conducing to ye Generall good of ye said Plantations, ye Honour of his Magisty, & ye sarvice of this State, and ye said Earll & Comm^{rs} doe further authorice ye aforesaid Inhabitants, for ye better transacting of there Publique affaires to make and use a Publique seale as ye knowne seale of Providence Plantations in ye Narragansetts Bay in New England, in Testimony whereof ye said Robert Earle of Warwick & comm^{rs} have hereunto set there hands and seales ye seventeenth day of March ye nineteenth year of ye Raine of our Soveraine Lord King Charles and in ye yeare of our Lord GOD 1643.

ROBERT WARWICK.

Phillip Pembrook, Say & Seale, P. Whartone, Arthur Helsrige, Cor. Holland, Hen. Vane, Sam Vassell, John Rool, Miles Corbet.

CHARTER GRANTED BY KING CHARLES II.

Charles, the Second, by the grace of God, King of England, Scotland, France, and Ireland, defender of the faith, &c., to all to whom these presents shall come, greeting: Whereas we have been informed by the humble petition of our trusty and well-beloved subject, John Clarke, on the behalf of Benedict Arnold, William Brenton, William Coddington, Nicholas Easton, William Boulston, John Porter, John Smith, Samuel Gorton, John Weeks, Roger Williams, Thomas Olney, Gregory Dexter, John Coggeshall, Joseph Clarke, Randall Holden, John Greene, John Roome, Samuel

Wildbore, William Field, James Barker, Richard Tew, Thomas Harris, and William Dyre, and the rest of the purchasers and free inhabitants of our island, called Rhode Island, and the rest of the colony of Providence Plantations, in the Narragansett Bay, in New England, in America, that they, pursuing, with peaceable and loyal minds, their sober, serious, and religious intentions, of godly edifying themselves, and one another, in the holy Christian faith and worship, as they were persuaded; together with the gaining over and conversion of the poor ignorant Indian natives, in those parts of America, to the sincere profession and obedience of the same faith and worship, did, not only by the consent and good encouragement of our royal progenitors, transport themselves out of this kingdom of England into America, but also, since their arrival there, after their first settlement amongst other our subjects in those parts, for the avoiding of discord, and those many evils which were likely to ensue upon some of those our subjects not being able to bear, in these remote parts, their different apprehensions in religious concernments, and, in pursuance of the aforesaid ends, did once again leave their desirable stations and habitations, and with excessive labor and travel, hazard and charge, did transplant themselves into the midst of the Indian natives, who, as we are informed, are the most potent princes and people of all that country; where, by the good Providence of God, from whom the Plantations have taken their name, upon their labor and industry, they have not only been preserved to admiration, but have increased and prospered, and are seized and possessed, by purchase and consent of the said natives, to their full content, of such lands, islands, rivers, harbors and roads, as are very convenient, both for plantations, and also for building of ships, supply of pipe staves, and other merchandise: and which lie very commodious, in many respects, for commerce, and to accommodate our southern plantations, and may much advance the trade of this our realm, and greatly enlarge the territories thereof; they having, by near neighborhood to and friendly society with the great body of the Narragansett Indians, given them encouragement, of their own accord, to subject themselves, their people, and lands unto us; whereby, as is hoped, there may, in time, by the blessing of God upon their endeavors, be laid a sure foundation of happiness to all America: and whereas, in their humble address, they have freely declared, that it is much on their hearts (if they may be permitted) to hold forth a lively experiment, that a most flourishing civil state may stand and best be maintained, and that among our English subjects, with a full liberty in religious concernments; and that true piety, rightly grounded upon gospel principles, will give the best and greatest security to sovereignty, and will lay in the hearts of men the strongest obligations to true loyalty: Now know ye, that we, being willing to encourage the hopeful undertaking of our said loyal and loving subjects, and to secure them in the free exercise and enjoyment of all their civil and religious rights, appertaining to them as our loving subjects; and to preserve unto them that liberty, in the true Christian faith and worship of God, which they have sought with so much travail, and with peaceable minds, and loyal subjection to our royal progenitors and ourselves, to enjoy: and because some of the people and inhabitants of the same colony cannot, in their private opinions, conform to the public exercise of religion, according to the liturgy, forms, and ceremonies of the Church of England, or take or subscribe the oaths and articles made and established in that behalf; and for that the same, by reason of the remote distances of those places, will (as we hope) be no breach of the unity and uniformity established in this nation: Have therefore thought fit, and do hereby publish, grant, ordain, and declare, that our royal will and pleasure is, that no person within the said colony, at any time hereafter, shall be any wise molested, punished, disquieted, or called in question, for any differences in opinion in matters of religion, and do not actually disturb the civil peace of our said colony; but that all and every person and persons may, from time to time, and at all times hereafter, freely and fully have and enjoy his and their own judgments and consciences, in matters of religious concernments, throughout the tract of land hereafter mentioned, they behaving themselves peaceably and quietly, and not using this liberty to licentiousness and profaneness, nor to the civil injury or outward disturbance of others; any law, statute, or clause, therein contained, or to be contained, usage or custom of this realm, to the contrary hereof, in any wise, notwithstanding. And that they may be in the better capacity to defend themselves, in their just rights and liberties, against all the enemies of the Christian faith, and others, in all respects, we have further thought fit, and, at the humble petition of the persons aforesaid, are graciously pleased to declare, that they shall have and enjoy the benefit of our late act of indemnity and free pardon, as the rest of our subjects in other our dominions and territories have; and to create and make them a body politic or corporate, with the powers and privileges hereinafter mentioned. And accordingly our will and pleasure is, and of our especial grace, certain knowledge, and mere motion, we have ordained, constituted, and declared, and by these presents, for us, our heirs, and successors, do ordain, constitute, and declare, that they, the said William Brenton, William Coddington, Nicholas Easton, Benedict Arnold, William Boulston, John Porter, Samuel Gorton, John Smith, John Weeks, Roger Williams, Thomas Olney, Gregory Dexter, John Coggeshall, Joseph Clarke, Randall Holden, John Greene, John Roome, William Dyre, Samuel Wildbore, Richard Tew,

William Field, Thomas Harris, James Barker, —— Rainsborrow, —— Williams, and John Nickson, and all such others as now are, or hereafter shall be, admitted and made free of the company and society of our colony of Providence Plantations, in the Narragansett Bay, in New England, shall be, from time to time, and forever hereafter, a body corporate and politic, in fact and name, by the name of the Governor and Company of the English Colony of Rhode Island and Providence Plantations, in New England, in America; and that, by the same name, they and their successors shall and may have perpetual succession, and shall and may be persons able and capable, in the law, to sue and be sued, to plead and be impleaded, to answer and be answered unto, to defend and to be defended, in all and singular suits, causes, quarrels, matters, actions, and things, of what kind or nature soever; and also to have, take, possess, acquire, and purchase lands, tenements, or hereditaments, or any goods or chattels, and the same to lease, grant, demise, aliene, bargain, sell, and dispose of, at their own will and pleasure, as other our liege people of this our realm of England, or any corporation or body politic within the same, may lawfully do. And further, that they, the said Governor and Company, and their successors, shall and may, forever hereafter, have a common seal, to serve and use for all matters, causes, things, and affairs, whatsoever, of them and their successors; and the same seal to alter, change, break, and make new, from time to time, at their will and pleasure, as they shall think fit. And further, we will and ordain, and by these presents, for us, our heirs and successors, do declare and appoint that, for the better ordering and managing of the affairs and business of the said company, and their successors, there shall be one governor, one deputy governor, and ten assistants, to be from time to time constituted, elected, and chosen out of the freemen of the said Company for the time being, in such manner and form as is hereafter in these presents expressed; which said officers shall apply themselves to take care for the best disposing and ordering of the general business and affairs of and concerning the lands and hereditaments hereinafter mentioned to be granted, and the plantation thereof, and the government of the people there. And, for the better execution of our royal pleasure herein, we do, for us, our heirs and successors, assign, name, constitute, and appoint the aforesaid Benedict Arnold to be the first and present governor of the said Company, and the said William Brenton to be the deputy governor, and the said William Boulston, John Porter, Roger Williams, Thomas Olney, John Smith, John Greene, John Coggeshall, James Barker, William Field, and Joseph Clarke, to be the ten present assistants of the said Company, to continue in the said several offices, respectively, until the first Wednesday which shall be in the month of May now next coming. And further, we will, and by these presents, for us, our heirs and successors, do ordain and grant that the governor of the said Company for the time being, or, in his absence, by occasion of sickness, or otherwise, by his leave and permission, the deputy governor for the time being, shall and may, from time to time, upon all occasions, give order for the assembling of the said Company and calling them together, to consult and advise of the business and affairs of the said Company. And that forever hereafter, twice in every year — that is to say, on every first Wednesday in the month of May, and on every last Wednesday in October, or oftener in case it shall be requisite, — the assistants and such of the freemen of the said Company, not exceeding six persons for Newport, four persons for each of the respective towns of Providence, Portsmouth, and Warwick, and two persons for each other place, town, or city, who shall be, from time to time, thereunto elected or deputed by the major part of the freemen of the respective towns or places for which they shall be so elected or deputed, shall have a general meeting or assembly, then and there to consult, advise, and determine in and about the affairs and business of the said Company and Plantations. And further, we do, of our especial grace, certain knowledge, and mere motion, give and grant unto the said Governor and Company of the English Colony of Rhode Island and Providence Plantations, in New England, in America, and their successors, that the governor, or, in his absence, or by his permission, the deputy governor of the said Company, for the time being, the assistants, and such of the freemen of the said Company as shall be so as aforesaid elected or deputed, or so many of them as shall be present at such meeting or assembly as aforesaid, shall be called the General Assembly; and that they, or the greatest part of them present, whereof the governor, or deputy governor, and six of the assistants, at least to be seven, shall have, and have hereby given and granted unto them, full power and authority, from time to time, and at all times hereafter, to appoint, alter, and change such days, times, and places of meeting and General Assembly as they shall think fit; *and to choose, nominate, and appoint such and so many other persons as they shall think fit, and shall be willing to accept the same, to be free of the said Company and body politic, and them into the same to admit;* and to elect and constitute such offices and officers, and to grant such needful commissions, as they shall think fit and requisite for the ordering, managing, and despatching of the affairs of the said Governor and Company and their successors; *and, from time to time, to make, ordain, constitute, or repeal such laws, statutes, orders, and ordinances, forms and ceremonies of government and magistracy,* as to them shall seem meet, for the good and welfare of the said Company, and for the government and ordering of the lands and hereditaments hereinafter mentioned to be granted, and of the people that do, or at any time hereafter shall, inhabit or be within the same; so as such laws, ordinances, and constitutions so made be not contrary and repugnant unto, but as near as may be, agreeable to the laws of this our realm of England, considering the nature and constitution of the place and people there, and also to appoint, order and direct, erect and settle, such places and courts of jurisdiction, for the hearing and determining of all actions, cases, matters, and things happening within the said colony and plantation, and which shall be in dispute and depending there, as they shall think fit; and also to distinguish and set forth the several names and titles, duties, powers, and limits of each court, office, and officer, superior and inferior; and also to contrive and appoint such forms of oaths and attestations, not repugnant, but, as near as may be, agreeable, as aforesaid, to the laws and statutes of this our realm, as are convenient and requisite, with respect to the due administration of justice and due execution and discharge of all offices and places of trust by the persons that shall be therein concerned; and also to regulate and order the way and manner of all elections to offices and places of trust, and to prescribe, limit, and distinguish the numbers and bounds of all places, towns, or cities, within the limits and bounds hereinafter mentioned, and not herein particularly named, who have, or shall have, the power of electing and sending of freemen to the said General Assembly; and also to order, direct, and authorize the imposing of lawful and reasonable fines, mulcts, imprisonments, and executing other punishments, pecuniary and corporal, upon offenders and delinquents, according to the course of other corporations within this our kingdom of England; and again to alter, revoke, annul, or pardon, under their common seal, or otherwise, such fines, mulcts, imprisonments, sentences, judgments, and condemnations, as shall be thought fit; and to direct, rule, order, and dispose of all other matters and things, and particularly that which relates to the making of purchases of the native Indians, as to them shall seem meet; whereby our said people and inhabitants in the said Plantations may be so religiously, peaceably, and civilly governed, as that, by their good life and orderly conversation, they may win and invite the native Indians of the country to the knowledge and obedience of the only true God and Saviour of mankind; willing, commanding, and requiring, and by these presents, for us, our heirs, and successors, ordaining and appointing that all such laws, statutes, orders, and ordinances, instructions, impositions, and directions, as shall be so made by the governor, deputy governor, assistants, and freemen, or such number of them as aforesaid, and published in writing, under their common seal, shall be carefully and duly observed, kept, performed, and put in execution, according to the true intent and meaning of the same. And these our letters patent, or the duplicate or exemplification thereof, shall be to all and every such officer, superior or inferior, from time to time, for the putting of the same orders, laws, statutes, ordinances, instructions, and directions, in due execution, against us, our heirs and successors, a sufficient warrant and discharge. And further, our will and pleasure is, and we do hereby, for us, our heirs, and successors, establish and ordain, that yearly, once in the year, forever, hereafter, namely, the aforesaid Wednesday in May, and at the town of Newport, or elsewhere, if urgent occasion do require, the governor, deputy governor, and assistants of the said Company, and other officers of the said Company, or such of them as the General Assembly shall think fit, shall be, in the said General Court or Assembly to be held from that day or time, newly chosen for the year ensuing, by such greater part of the said Company, for the time being, as shall be then and there present; and if it shall happen that the present governor, deputy governor, and assistants, by these presents appointed, or any such as shall hereafter be newly chosen into their rooms, or any of them, or any other the officers of the said Company, shall die or be removed from his or their several offices or places, before the said general day of election, (whom we do hereby declare, for any misdemeanor or default, to be removable by the governor, assistants, and Company, or such greater part of them, in any of the said public courts, to be assembled as aforesaid,) that then, and in every such case, it shall, and may be lawful to and for the said governor, deputy governor, assistants, and Company aforesaid, or such greater part of them, so as to be assembled as is aforesaid, in any their assemblies, to proceed to a new election of one or more of their Company, in the room or place, rooms or places, of such officer or officers, so dying, removed, according to their discretions; and immediately upon and after such election or elections made of such governor, deputy governor, assistant, or assistants, or any other officer of the said Company, in manner and form aforesaid, the authority, office, and power, before given to the former governor, deputy governor, and other officer and officers, so removed, in whose stead and place new shall be chosen, shall, as to him and them, and every of them, respectively, cease and determine: *Provided always,* and our will and pleasure is, that as well such as are by these presents appointed to be the present governor, deputy governor, and assistants, of the said Company, as those that shall succeed them, and all other officers to be appointed and chosen as aforesaid, shall, before the undertaking the execution of the said offices and places respectively, give their solemn engagement, by oath, or otherwise, for the due and faithful performance of their duties in their several offices and places, before such person or persons as are by these presents hereafter appointed to take and receive the same, that is to say: the said Benedict Arnold, who is hereinbefore nominated and appointed the present governor of the said Company, shall give the aforesaid engagement before William Brenton, or any two of the said assistants of the said Company; unto whom we do by these presents give full power and authority to require and receive the same; and the said William Brenton, who is hereby before nominated and appointed the present deputy governor of the said Company, shall give the aforesaid engagement before the said Benedict Arnold, or any two of the assistants of the said Company; and unto whom we do by these presents give full power and authority to require and receive the same; and the said William Boulston, John Porter, Roger Williams, Thomas Olney, John Smith, John Greene, John Coggeshall, James Barker, William Field, and Joseph Clarke, who are hereinbefore nominated and appointed the present assistants of the said Company, shall give the said engagement to their offices and places respectively belonging, before the said Benedict Arnold and William Brenton, or one of them; to whom respectively we do hereby give full power and authority to require, administer, or receive the same: and further, our will and pleasure is, that all and every other future governor or deputy governor, to be elected and chosen by virtue of these presents, shall give the said engagement before two or more of the said assistants of the said Company for the time being; unto whom we do by these presents give full power and authority to require, administer, or receive the same: and the said assistants, and every of them, and all and every other officer or officers to be hereafter elected and chosen by virtue of these presents, from time to time, shall give the like engagements, to their offices and places respectively belonging, before the governor or deputy governor for the time being; unto which said governor, or deputy governor, we do by these presents give full power and authority to require, administer, or receive the same accordingly. And we do likewise, for us, our heirs, and successors, give and grant unto the said Governor and Company, and their successors, by these presents, that, for the more peaceable and orderly government of the said Plantations, it shall and may be lawful for the governor, deputy governor, assistants, and all other officers and ministers of the said Company, in the administration of justice, and exercise of government, in the said Plantations, to use, exercise, and put in execution, such methods, rules, orders, and directions, not being contrary or repugnant to the laws and statutes of this our realm, as have been heretofore given, used, and accustomed, in such cases, respectively, to be put in practice, until at the next, or some other General Assembly, special provision shall be made and ordained in the cases aforesaid. And we do further, for us, our heirs, and successors, give and grant unto the said Governor and Company, and their successors, by these presents, that it shall and may be lawful to and for the said governor, or in his absence, the deputy governor, and major part of the said assistants for the time being, at any time when the said General Assembly is not sitting, to nominate, appoint, and constitute such and so many commanders, governors, and military officers as to them shall seem requisite for the leading, conducting, and training up the inhabitants of the said Plantations in martial affairs, and for the defence and safeguard of the said Plantations; and that it shall and may be lawful to and for all and every such commander, governor, and military officer, that shall be so as aforesaid, or by the governor, or, in his absence, the deputy governor and six of the said assistants, and major part of the freemen of the said Company present at any General Assemblies, nominated, appointed, and constituted according to the tenor of his and their respective commissions and directions, to assemble, exercise in arms, martial array, and put in warlike posture the inhabitants of the said colony, for their special defence and safety; and to lead and conduct the said inhabitants, and to encounter, expulse, expel, and resist, by force of arms, as well by sea as by land, and also to kill, slay, and destroy, by all fitting ways, enterprises, and means whatsoever, all and every such person or persons as shall, at any time hereafter, attempt or enterprise the destruction, invasion, detriment, or annoyance of the said inhabitants or Plantations; and to use and exercise the law martial in such cases only as occasion shall necessarily require; and to take or surprise, by all ways and means whatsoever, all and every such person and persons, with their ship or ships, armor, ammunition, or other goods of such persons as shall, in hostile manner, invade or attempt the defeating of the said Plantation, or the hurt of the said Company and inhabitants; and, upon just causes, to invade and destroy the native Indians, or other enemies of the said colony. Nevertheless, our will and pleasure is, and we do hereby declare to the rest of our colonies in New England, that it shall not be lawful for this our said colony of Rhode Island and Providence Plantations, in America, in New England, to invade the natives inhabiting within the bounds and limits of their said colonies, without the knowledge and consent of the said other colonies. And it is hereby declared, that it shall not be lawful to or for the rest of the colonies to invade or molest the native Indians, or any other inhabitants, inhabiting within the bounds and limits hereafter mentioned, (they having subjected themselves unto us, and being by us taken into our special protection,) without the knowledge and consent of the Governor and Company of our Colony of Rhode Island and Providence Plantations. Also our will and pleasure is, and we do hereby declare unto all Christian kings, princes, and states, that if any person, which shall hereafter be of the said Company or Plantation, or any other, by appointment of the said Governor and Company for the time being, shall, at any time or times hereafter, rob or spoil, by sea or land, or do any hurt or unlawful hostility to any of the subjects of us, our heirs or successors, or any of the subjects of any prince or state, being then in league with us, our heirs or successors, upon complaint of such injury done to any such prince or state, or their subjects, we, our heirs and successors, will make open proclamation within any parts of our realm of England, fit for that purpose, that the person or persons committing any such robbery or spoil shall, within the time limited by such proclamation, make full restitution or satisfaction of all such injuries done or committed, so as the said prince, or others so complaining, may be fully satisfied and contented; and if the said person or persons who shall commit any such robbery or spoil, shall not make satisfaction, accordingly, within such time, so to be limited, that then we, our heirs and successors, will put such person or persons out of our allegiance and protection; and that then it shall and may be lawful and free for all princes or others to prosecute, with hostility, such offenders, and every of them, their and every of their procurers, aiders, abettors, and counsellors, in that behalf: *Provided, also,* and our express will and pleasure is, and we do, by these presents, for us, our heirs and successors, ordain and appoint, that these presents shall not, in any manner, hinder any of our loving subjects, whatsoever, from using and exercising the trade of fishing upon the coast of New England, in America; but that they, and every or any of them, shall have full and free power and liberty to continue and use the trade of fishing upon the said coast, in any of the seas thereunto adjoining, or any arms of the seas, or salt water, rivers and creeks, where they have been accustomed to fish; and to build and set upon the waste land belonging to the said colony and plantations, such wharves, stages, and work houses, as shall be necessary for the salting, drying, and keeping of their fish, to be taken or gotten upon that coast. And further, for the encouragement of the inhabitants of our said colony of Providence Plantations to set upon the business of taking whales, it shall be lawful for them, or any of them, having struck whale, dubertus, or other great fish, it or them to pursue unto any part of that coast, and into any bay, river, cove, creek, or shore, belonging thereto, and it or them, upon the said coast, or in the said bay, river, cove, creek, or shore, belonging thereto, to kill and order for the best advantage, without molestation, they making no wilful waste or spoil; any thing in these presents contained, or any other matter or thing, to the contrary notwithstanding. And further also, we are graciously pleased, and do hereby declare, that if any of the inhabitants of our said colony do set upon the planting of vineyards, (the soil and climate both seeming naturally to concur to the production of wines,) or be industrious in the discovery of fishing banks, in or about the said colony, we will, from time to time, give and allow all due and fitting encouragement therein, as to others in cases of like nature. And further, of our more ample grace, certain knowledge, and mere motion, we have given and granted, and by these presents, for us, our heirs and successors, do give and grant, unto the said Governor and Company of the English Colony of Rhode Island and Providence Plantations, in the Narragansett Bay, in New England, in America, and to every inhabitant there, and to every person and persons trading thither, and to every such person or persons as are or shall be free of the said colony, full power and authority, from time to time, and at all times hereafter, to take, ship, transport, and carry away, out of any of our realms and dominions, for and

APPENDIX. 313

towards the plantation and defence of the said colony, such and so many of our loving subjects and strangers as shall or will willingly accompany them in and to their said colony and plantation; except such person or persons as are or shall be therein restrained by us, our heirs and successors, or any law or statute of this realm; and also to ship and transport all and all manner of goods, chattels, merchandises, and other things whatsoever, that are or shall be useful or necessary for the said Plantations, and defence thereof, and usually transported, and not prohibited by any law or statute of this our realm; yielding and paying unto us, our heirs and successors, such the duties, customs, and subsidies, as are or ought to be paid or payable for the same. And further, our will and pleasure is, and we do, for us, our heirs and successors, ordain, declare, and grant, unto the said Governor and Company, and their successors, that all and every the subjects of us, our heirs and successors, which are already planted and settled within our said colony of Providence Plantations, or which shall hereafter go to inhabit within the said colony, and all and every of their children, which have been born there, or which shall happen hereafter to be born there, or on the sea, going thither, or returning from thence, shall have and enjoy all liberties and immunities of free and natural subjects within any the dominions of us, our heirs or successors, to all intents, constructions, and purposes, whatsoever, as if they, and every of them, were born within the realm of England. And further, know ye, that we, of our more abundant grace, certain knowledge, and mere motion, have given, granted, and confirmed, and, by these presents, for us, our heirs and successors, do give, grant, and confirm, unto the said Governor and Company, and their successors, all that part of our dominions in New England, in America, containing the Nahantick and Nanhyganset, alias Narragansett Bay, and countries and parts adjacent, bounded on the west, or westerly, to the middle or channel of a river there, commonly called and known by the name of Pawcatuck, alias Pawcawtuck River, and so along the said river, as the greater or middle stream thereof reacheth or lies up into the north country, northward, unto the head thereof, and from thence, by a straight line drawn due north, until it meets with the south line of the Massachusetts colony; and on the north, or northerly, by the aforesaid south or southerly line of the Massachusetts colony or plantation, and extending towards the east, or eastwardly, three English miles to the east and north-east of the most eastern and north-eastern parts of the aforesaid Narragansett Bay, as the said bay lieth or extendeth itself from the ocean on the south, or southwardly, unto the mouth of the river which runneth toward the town of Providence, and from thence along the eastwardly side or bank of the said river (higher called by the name of Seacunck River) up to the falls called Patuckett Falls, being the most westwardly line of Plymouth colony, and so from the said falls in a straight line, due north, until it meet with the aforesaid line of the Massachusetts colony, and bounded on the south by the ocean; and, in particular, the lands belonging to the towns of Providence, Pawtuxet, Warwick, Misquammacock, alias Pawcatuck, and the rest upon the main land in the tract aforesaid, together with Rhode Island, Block Island, and all the rest of the islands and banks in the Narragansett Bay, and bordering upon the coast of the tract aforesaid, (Fisher's Island only excepted,) together with all firm lands, soils, grounds, havens, ports, rivers, waters, fishings, mines royal, and all other mines, minerals, precious stones, quarries, woods, wood grounds, rocks, slates, and all and singular other commodities, jurisdictions, royalties, privileges, franchises, preëminences, and hereditaments whatsoever, within the said tract, bounds, lands, and islands aforesaid, or to them or any of them belonging, or in any wise appertaining: *To have and to hold* the same unto the said Governor and Company and their successors forever, upon trust, for the use and benefit of themselves and their associates, freemen of the said colony, their heirs and assigns, to be holden of us, our heirs and successors, as of the manor of East Greenwich, in our county of Kent, in free and common soccage, and not *in capite*, nor by knight service; yielding and paying therefor to us, our heirs and successors, only the fifth part of all the ore of gold and silver which, from time to time, and at all times hereafter, shall be there gotten, had, or obtained, in lieu and satisfaction of all services, duties, fines, forfeitures, made or to be made, claims and demands whatsoever, to be to us, our heirs or successors, therefor or thereout rendered, made, or paid; any grant, or clause in a late grant, to the Governor and Company of Connecticut Colony, in America, to the contrary thereof in any wise notwithstanding. The aforesaid Pawcatuck River having been yielded, after much debate, for the fixed and certain bounds between these our said colonies, by the agents thereof, who have also agreed that the said Pawcatuck River shall be also called alias Norrogansett or Narrogansett River; and, to prevent future disputes, that otherwise might arise thereby, forever hereafter shall be construed, deemed, and taken to be the Narrogansett River in our late grant to Connecticut colony mentioned as the easterly bounds of that colony. And further, our will and pleasure is, that, in all matters of public controversy, which may fall out between our colony of Providence Plantations and the rest of our colonies in New England, it shall and may be lawful to and for the Governor and Company of the said colony of Providence Plantations, to make their appeals therein to us, our heirs and successors, for redress in such cases, within this our realm of England; and that it shall be lawful to and for the inhabitants of the said colony of Providence Plantations, without let or molestation, to pass and repass, with freedom, into and through the rest of the English colonies, upon their lawful and civil occasions, and to converse and hold commerce and trade with such of the inhabitants of our other English colonies as shall be willing to admit them thereunto, they behaving themselves peaceably among them; any act, clause, or sentence, in any of the said colonies provided, or that shall be provided, to the contrary in any wise notwithstanding. And lastly, we do for us, our heirs and successors, ordain and grant unto the said Governor and Company, and their successors, by these presents, that these our letters patent shall be firm, good, effectual, and available in all things in the law, to all intents, constructions, and purposes whatsoever, according to our true intent and meaning hereinbefore declared; and shall be construed, reputed, and adjudged in all cases most favorably on the behalf, and for the best benefit and behoof, of the said Governor and Company, and their successors; although express mention of the true yearly value or certainty of the premises, or any of them, or of any other gifts or grants by us, or by any of our progenitors or predecessors, heretofore made to the said Governor and Company of the English colony of Rhode Island and Providence Plantations, in the Narragansett Bay, New England, in America, in these presents is not made, or any statute, act, ordinance, provision, proclamation, or restriction, heretofore had, made, enacted, ordained, or provided, or any other matter, cause, or thing whatsoever, to the contrary thereof in any wise notwithstanding. In witness whereof, we have caused these our letters to be made patent. Witness ourself at Westminster, the eighth day of July, in the fifteenth year of our reign.

By the King:

HOWARD.

CONSTITUTION OF THE STATE OF RHODE ISLAND AND PROVIDENCE PLANTATIONS,

ADOPTED BY THE PEOPLE, DEC. 27, 28, & 29, 1841.

WE, the people of the State of Rhode Island and Providence Plantations, grateful to Almighty God for his blessing vouchsafed to the "lively experiment" of religious and political freedom here "held forth" by our venerated ancestors, and earnestly imploring the favor of his gracious providence towards this our attempt to secure upon a permanent foundation the advantages of well-ordered and rational liberty, and to enlarge and transmit to our successors the inheritance that we have received, do ordain and establish the following constitution of government for this state.

ART. I. — DECLARATION OF PRINCIPLES AND RIGHTS.

1. In the spirit and in the words of Roger Williams, the illustrious founder of this state, and of his venerated associates, we declare "that this government shall be a democracy," or government of the people, "by the major consent" of the same, "only in civil things." The will of the people shall be expressed by representatives freely chosen, and returning at fixed periods to their constituents. This state shall be, and forever remain, as in the design of its founder, sacred to "soul liberty," to the rights of conscience, to freedom of thought, of expression, and of action, as hereinafter set forth and secured.

2. All men are created free and equal, and are endowed by their Creator with certain natural, inherent, and inalienable rights, among which are life, liberty, the acquisition of property, and the pursuit of happiness. Government cannot create or bestow these rights,

which are the gift of God; but it is instituted for the stronger and surer defence of the same, that men may safely enjoy the rights of life and liberty, securely possess and transmit property, and, so far as laws avail, may be successful in the pursuit of happiness.

3. All political power and sovereignty are originally vested in, and of right belong to, the people. All free governments are founded in their authority, and are established for the greatest good of the whole number. The people have, therefore, an unalienable and indefeasible right, in their original, sovereign, and unlimited capacity, to ordain and institute government, and in the same capacity to alter, reform, or totally change the same, whenever their safety or happiness requires.

4. No favor or disfavor ought to be shown, in legislation, toward any man, or party, or society, or religious denomination. The laws should be made not for the good of the few, but of the many; and the burdens of the state ought to be fairly distributed among its citizens.

5. The diffusion of useful knowledge, and the cultivation of a sound morality in the fear of God, being of the first importance in a republican state, and indispensable to the maintenance of its liberty, it shall be an imperative duty of the legislature to promote the establishment of free schools, and to assist in the support of public education.

6. Every person in this state ought to find a certain remedy, by having recourse to the laws, for all injuries or wrongs which may be done to his rights of person, property, or character. He ought to obtain right and justice freely and without purchase, completely and without denial, promptly and without delay, conformably to the laws.

7. The right of the people to be secure in their persons, houses, papers, and possessions, against unreasonable searches and seizures, shall not be violated; and no warrant shall issue but on complaint in writing upon

probable cause, supported by oath or affirmation, and describing as nearly as may be the place to be searched, and the person or things to be seized.

8. No person shall be held to answer to a capital or other infamous charge, unless on indictment by a grand jury, except in cases arising in the land or naval forces, or in the militia, when in actual service, in time of war or public danger. No person shall be tried, after an acquittal, for the same crime or offence.

9. Every man being presumed to be innocent until pronounced guilty by the law, all acts of severity, that are not necessary to secure an accused person, ought to be repressed.

10. Excessive bail shall not be required, nor excessive fines imposed, nor cruel or unusual punishments inflicted; and all punishments ought to be proportioned to the offence.

11. All prisoners shall be bailable upon sufficient surety, unless for capital offences, when the proof is evident or the presumption great. The privilege of the writ of habeas corpus shall not be suspended, unless when, in cases of rebellion or invasion, the public safety shall require it.

12. In all criminal prosecutions, the accused shall have the privilege of a speedy and public trial, by an impartial jury; be informed of the nature and cause of the accusation; be confronted with the witnesses against him; have compulsory process to obtain them in his favor, and at the public expense, when necessary; have the assistance of counsel in his defence, and be at liberty to speak for himself. Nor shall he be deprived of his life, liberty, or property, unless by the judgment of his peers, or the law of the land.

13. The right of trial by jury shall remain inviolate, and in all criminal cases the jury shall judge both of the law and of the facts.

14. Any person in this state, who may be claimed to

be held to labor or service, under the laws of any other state, territory, or district, shall be entitled to a jury trial, to ascertain the validity of such claim.

15. No man in a court of common law shall be required to criminate himself.

16. Retrospective laws, civil and criminal, are unjust and oppressive, and shall not be made.

17. The people have a right to assemble in a peaceable manner, without molestation or restraint, to consult upon the public welfare; a right to give instructions to their senators and representatives; and a right to apply to those invested with the powers of government for redress of grievances, for the repeal of injurious laws, for the correction of faults of administration, and for all other purposes.

18. The liberty of the press being essential to the security of freedom in a state, any citizen may publish his sentiments on any subject, being responsible for the abuse of that liberty; and in all trials for libel, both civil and criminal, the truth, spoken from good motives, and for justifiable ends, shall be a sufficient defence to the person charged.

19. Private property shall not be taken for public uses without just compensation, nor unless the public good require it; nor under any circumstances until compensation shall have been made, if required.

20. The military shall always be held in strict subordination to the civil authority.

21. No soldier shall, in time of peace, be quartered in any house, without the consent of the owner; nor in time of war, but in manner to be prescribed by law.

22. Whereas Almighty God hath created the mind free, and all attempts to influence it by temporal punishments, or burdens, or by civil incapacitations, tend to beget habits of hypocrisy and meanness; and whereas a principal object of our venerated ancestors in their migration to this country, and their settlement of this

state, was, as they expressed it, to hold forth a lively experiment, that a flourishing civil state may stand, and be best maintained, with full liberty in religious concernments: We therefore declare that no man shall be compelled to frequent or support any religious worship, place, or ministry whatsoever, nor be enforced, restrained, molested, or burdened in his body or goods, nor disqualified from holding any office, nor otherwise suffer, on account of his religious belief; and that all men shall be free to profess, and by argument to maintain, their opinions in matters of religion; and that the same shall in no wise diminish, enlarge, or affect their civil capacities; and that all other religious rights and privileges of the people of this state, as now enjoyed, shall remain inviolate and inviolable.

23. No witness shall be called in question before the legislature, nor in any court of this state, nor before any magistrate or other person authorized to administer an oath or affirmation, for his or her religious belief, or opinions, or any part thereof; and no objection to a witness, on the ground of his or her religious opinions, shall be entertained or received.

24. The citizens shall continue to enjoy, and freely exercise, all the rights of fishery, and privileges of the shore, to which they have been heretofore entitled under the charter and usages of this state.

25. The enumeration of the foregoing rights shall not be construed to impair nor deny others retained by the people.

ART. II. — OF ELECTORS AND THE RIGHT OF SUFFRAGE.

1. Every white male citizen of the United States, of the age of twenty-one years, who has resided in this state for one year, and in any town, city, or district of the same for six months, next preceding the election at which he offers to vote, shall be an elector of all officers

who are elected, or may hereafter be made eligible, by the people. But persons in the military, naval, or marine service of the United States, shall not be considered as having such established residence, by being stationed in any garrison, barrack, or military place in any town or city in this state.

2. Paupers and persons under guardianship, insane, or lunatic, are excluded from the electoral right; and the same shall be forfeited on conviction of bribery, forgery, perjury, theft, or other infamous crime, and shall not be restored unless by an act of the General Assembly.

3. No person who is excluded from voting, for want of the qualification first named in section first of this article, shall be taxed, or be liable to do military duty; provided that nothing in said first article shall be so construed as to exempt from taxation any property or persons now liable to be taxed.

4. No elector who is not possessed of, and assessed for, ratable property in his own right, to the amount of one hundred and fifty dollars, or who shall have neglected or refused to pay any tax assessed upon him, in any town, city, or district, for one year preceding the town, city, ward, or district meeting at which he shall offer to vote, shall be entitled to vote on any question of taxation, or the expenditure of any public moneys in such town, city, or district, until the same be paid.

5. In the city of Providence, and other cities, no person shall be eligible to the office of mayor, alderman, or common councilman, who is not taxed, or who shall have neglected or refused to pay his tax, as provided in the preceding section.

6. The voting for all officers chosen by the people, except town or city officers, shall be by ballot; that is to say, by depositing a written or printed ticket in the ballot box, without the name of the voter written thereon. Town or city officers shall be chosen by ballot,

on the demand of any two persons entitled to vote for the same.

7. There shall be a strict registration of all qualified voters in the towns and cities of the state; and no person shall be permitted to vote, whose name has not been entered upon the list of voters before the polls are opened.

8. The General Assembly shall pass all necessary laws for the prevention of fraudulent voting by persons not having an actual, permanent residence, or home, in the state, or otherwise disqualified according to this constitution; for the careful registration of all voters, previously to the time of voting; for the prevention of frauds upon the ballot box; for the preservation of the purity of elections; and for the safe-keeping and accurate counting of the votes; to the end that the will of the people may be freely and fully expressed, truly ascertained, and effectually exerted, without intimidation, suppression, or unnecessary delay.

9. The electors shall be exempted from arrest on days of election, and one day before, and one day after the same, except in cases of treason, felony, or breach of the peace.

10. No person shall be eligible to any office by the votes of the people, who does not possess the qualifications of an elector.

Art. III. — Of the Distribution of Powers.

1. The powers of the government shall be distributed into three departments — the legislative, the executive, and the judicial.

2. No person or persons connected with one of these departments shall exercise any of the powers belonging to either of the others, except in cases herein directed or permitted.

ART. IV. — OF THE LEGISLATIVE DEPARTMENT.

1. The legislative power shall be vested in two distinct Houses : the one to be called the House of Representatives, the other the Senate, and both together the General Assembly. The concurrent votes of the two Houses shall be necessary to the enactment of laws ; and the style of their laws shall be : " Be it enacted by the General Assembly, as follows."

2. No member of the General Assembly shall be eligible to any civil office under the authority of the state, during the term for which he shall have been elected.

3. If any representative, or senator, in the General Assembly of this state, shall be appointed to any office under the government of the United States, and shall accept the same, after his election as such senator or representative, his seat shall thereby become vacant.

4. Any person who holds an office under the government of the United States may be elected a member of the General Assembly, and may hold his seat therein, if, at the time of his taking his seat, he shall have resigned said office, and shall declare the same on oath, or affirmation, if required.

5. No member of the General Assembly shall take any fees, be of counsel or act as advocate in any case pending before either branch of the General Assembly, under penalty of forfeiting his seat, upon due proof thereof.

6. Each House shall judge of the election and qualifications of its members ; and a majority of all the members of each House, whom the towns and senatorial districts are entitled to elect, shall constitute a quorum to do business ; but a smaller number may adjourn from day to day, and may compel the attendance of absent members, in such manner, and under such penalties, as each House may have previously prescribed.

7. Each House may determine the rules of its proceedings, punish its members for disorderly behavior, and, with the concurrence of two thirds of the members elected, expel a member; but not a second time for the same cause.

8. Each House shall keep a journal of its proceedings, and publish the same when required by one fifth of its members. The yeas and nays of the members of either House shall, at the desire of any five members present, be entered on the journal.

9. Neither House shall, without the consent of the other, adjourn for more than two days, nor to any other place than that at which the General Assembly is holding its session.

10. The senators and representatives shall, in all cases of civil process, be privileged from arrest during the session of the General Assembly, and for two days before the commencement, and two days after the termination, of any session thereof. For any speech in debate in either House, no member shall be called in question in any other place.

11. The civil and military officers, heretofore elected in grand committee, shall hereafter be elected annually by the General Assembly, in joint committee, composed of the two Houses of the General Assembly, excepting as is otherwise provided in this constitution; and excepting the captains and subalterns of the militia, who shall be elected by the ballots of the members composing their respective companies, in such manner as the General Assembly may prescribe; and such officers, so elected, shall be approved of and commissioned by the governor, who shall determine their rank; and, if said companies shall neglect or refuse to make such elections, after being duly notified, then the governor shall appoint suitable persons to fill such offices.

12. Every bill and every resolution requiring the concurrence of the two Houses, (votes of adjournment

excepted,) which shall have passed both Houses of the General Assembly, shall be presented to the governor for his revision. If he approve of it, he shall sign and transmit the same to the secretary of state; but if not, he shall return it to the House in which it shall have originated, with his objections thereto, which shall be entered at large on their journal. The House shall then proceed to reconsider the bill; and if, after such reconsideration, that House shall pass it by a majority of all the members elected, it shall be sent, with the objections, to the other House, which shall also reconsider it; and, if approved by that House, by a majority of all the members elected, it shall become a law. If the bill shall not be returned by the governor within forty-eight hours (Sundays excepted) after it shall have been presented to him, the same shall become a law, in like manner as if he had signed it, unless the General Assembly, by their adjournment, prevent its return; in which case, it shall not be a law.

13. There shall be two sessions of the General Assembly in every year; one session to be held at Newport, on the first Tuesday of June, for the organization of the government, the election of officers, and for other business; and one other session on the first Tuesday of January, to be held at Providence, in the first year after the adoption of this constitution, and in every second year thereafter. In the intermediate years, the January session shall be forever hereafter held in the counties of Washington, Kent, or Bristol, as the General Assembly may determine before their adjournment in June.

ART. V. — OF THE HOUSE OF REPRESENTATIVES.

1. The House of Representatives shall consist of members chosen by the electors in the several towns and cities, in their respective town and ward meetings, annually.

2. The towns and cities shall severally be entitled to elect members according to the apportionment which follows, viz.: Newport to elect five; Warwick, four; Smithfield, five; Cumberland, North Providence, and Scituate, three; Portsmouth, Westerly, New Shoreham, North Kingstown, South Kingstown, East Greenwich, Glocester, West Greenwich, Coventry, Exeter, Bristol, Tiverton, Little Compton, Warren, Richmond, Cranston, Charlestown, Hopkinton, Johnston, Foster, and Burrillville, to elect two; and Jamestown, Middletown, and Barrington, to elect one.

3. In the city of Providence, there shall be six representative districts, which shall be the six wards of said city; and the electors resident in said districts, for the term of three months next preceding the election at which they offer to vote, shall be entitled to elect two representatives for each district.

4. The General Assembly, in case of great inequality in the population of the wards of the city of Providence, may cause the boundaries of the six representative districts therein to be so altered as to include in each district, as nearly as may be, an equal number of inhabitants.

5. The House of Representatives shall have authority to elect their own speaker, clerks, and other officers. The oath of office shall be administered to the speaker by the secretary of state, or, in his absence, by the attorney general.

6. Whenever the seat of a member of the House of Representatives shall be vacated by death, resignation, or otherwise, the vacancy may be filled by a new election.

ART. VI. — OF THE SENATE.

1. The state shall be divided into twelve senatorial districts; and each district shall be entitled to one senator, who shall be annually chosen by the electors in his district.

2. The first, second, and third representative districts in the city of Providence, shall constitute the first senatorial district; the fourth, fifth, and sixth representative districts in said city, the second district; the town of Smithfield, the third district; the towns of North Providence and Cumberland, the fourth district; the towns of Scituate, Glocester, Burrillville, and Johnston, the fifth district; the towns of Warwick and Cranston, the sixth district; the towns of East Greenwich, West Greenwich, Coventry, and Foster, the seventh district; the towns of Newport, Jamestown, and New Shoreham, the eighth district; the towns of Portsmouth, Middletown, Tiverton, and Little Compton, the ninth district; the towns of North Kingstown and South Kingstown, the tenth district; the towns of Westerly, Charlestown, Exeter, Richmond, and Hopkinton, the eleventh district; the towns of Bristol, Warren, and Barrington, the twelfth district.

3. The lieutenant governor shall be, by virtue of his office, president of the Senate; and shall have a right, in case of an equal division, to vote in the same; and also to vote in joint committee of the two Houses.

4. When the government shall be administered by the lieutenant governor, or he shall be unable to attend as president of the Senate, the Senate shall elect one of their own members president of the same.

5. Vacancies in the Senate, occasioned by death, resignation, or otherwise, may be filled by a new election.

6. The secretary of state shall be, by virtue of his office, secretary of the Senate.

Art. VII. — Of Impeachments.

1. The House of Representatives shall have the sole power of impeachment.

2. All impeachments shall be tried by the Senate; and when sitting for that purpose, they shall be on oath

or affirmation. No person shall be convicted, except by a vote of two thirds of the members elected. When the governor is impeached, the chief justice of the Supreme Court shall preside, with a casting vote in all preliminary questions.

3. The governor, and all other executive and judicial officers, shall be liable to impeachment; but judgment, in such cases, shall not extend further than to removal from office. The party convicted shall, nevertheless, be liable to indictment, trial, and punishment, according to law.

ART. VIII. — ON THE EXECUTIVE DEPARTMENT.

1. The chief executive power of this state shall be vested in a governor, who shall be chosen by the electors, and shall hold his office for one year, and until his successor be duly qualified.

2. No person holding any office or place under the United States, this state, any other of the United States, or any foreign power, shall exercise the office of governor.

3. He shall take care that the laws are faithfully executed.

4. He shall be commander-in-chief of the military and naval forces of the state, except when called into the actual service of the United States; but he shall not march nor convey any of the citizens out of the state, without their consent, or that of the General Assembly, unless it shall become necessary in order to march or transport them from one part of the state to another, for the defence thereof.

5. He shall appoint all civil and military officers whose appointment is not by this constitution, or shall not by law be otherwise provided for.

6. He shall, from time to time, inform the General Assembly of the condition of the state, and recommend

to their consideration such measures as he may deem expedient.

7. He may require from any military officer, or any officer in the executive department, information upon any subject relating to the duties of his office.

8. He shall have power to remit forfeitures and penalties, and to grant reprieves, commutation of punishments, and pardons after conviction, except in cases of impeachment.

9. The governor shall, at stated times, receive for his services a compensation which shall not be increased nor diminished during his continuance in office.

10. There shall be elected, in the same manner as is provided for the election of governor, a lieutenant governor, who shall continue in office for the same term of time. Whenever the office of governor shall become vacant by death, resignation, removal from office, or otherwise, the lieutenant governor shall exercise the office of governor until another governor shall be duly qualified.

11. Whenever the offices of governor and lieutenant governor shall both become vacant, by death, resignation, removal from office, or otherwise, the president of the Senate shall exercise the office of governor until a governor be duly qualified; and should such vacancies occur during a recess of the General Assembly, and there be no president of the Senate, the secretary of state shall, by proclamation, convene the Senate, that a president may be chosen to exercise the office of governor.

12. Whenever the lieutenant governor or president of the Senate shall exercise the office of governor, he shall receive the compensation of governor only; and his duties as president of the Senate shall cease while he shall continue to act as governor; and the Senate shall fill the vacancy by an election from their own body.

13. In case of a disagreement between the two

Houses of the General Assembly respecting the time or place of adjournment, the person exercising the office of governor may adjourn them to such time or place as he shall think proper; provided that the time of adjournment shall not be extended beyond the first day of the next stated session.

14. The person exercising the office of governor may, in cases of special necessity, convene the General Assembly at any town or city in this state at any other time than hereinbefore provided. And, in case of danger from the prevalence of epidemic or contagious diseases, or from other circumstances, in the place in which the General Assembly are next to meet, he may, by proclamation, convene the Assembly at any other place within the state.

15. A secretary of state, a general treasurer, and an attorney general, shall also be chosen annually, in the same manner, and for the same time, as is herein provided respecting the governor. The duties of these officers shall be the same as are now, or may hereafter be, prescribed by law. Should there be a failure to choose either of them, or should a vacancy occur in either of their offices, the General Assembly shall fill the place by an election in joint committee.

16. The electors in each county shall, at the annual elections, vote for an inhabitant of the county to be sheriff of said county for one year, and until a successor be duly qualified. In case no person shall have a majority of the electoral votes of his county for sheriff, the General Assembly, in joint committee, shall elect a sheriff from the two candidates who shall have the greatest number of votes in such county.

17. All commissions shall be in the name of the State of Rhode Island and Providence Plantations, sealed with the seal of the state, and attested by the secretary.

Art. IX.—General Provisions.

1. This constitution shall be the supreme law of the state; and all laws contrary to or inconsistent with the same, which may be passed by the General Assembly, shall be null and void.

2. The General Assembly shall pass all necessary laws for carrying this constitution into effect.

3. The judges of all the courts, and all other officers, both civil and military, shall be bound by oath or affirmation to the due observance of this constitution, and of the constitution of the United States.

4. No jurisdiction shall, hereafter, be entertained by the General Assembly in cases of insolvency, divorce, sale of real estate of minors, or appeal from judicial decisions, nor in any other matters appertaining to the jurisdiction of judges and courts of law. But the General Assembly shall confer upon the courts of the state all necessary powers for affording relief in the cases herein named; and the General Assembly shall exercise all other jurisdiction and authority which they have heretofore entertained, and which is not prohibited by, nor repugnant to, this constitution.

5. The General Assembly shall, from time to time, cause estimates to be made of the ratable property of the state, in order to the equitable apportionment of state taxes.

6. Whenever a direct tax is laid by the state, one sixth part thereof shall be assessed on the polls of the qualified electors: provided that the tax on a poll shall never exceed the sum of fifty cents; and that all persons who actually perform military duty, or duty in the fire department, shall be exempted from said poll tax.

7. The General Assembly shall have no power hereafter to incur state debts to an amount exceeding the sum of fifty thousand dollars, except in time of war, or in case of invasion, without the express consent of the

people. Every proposition for such increase shall be submitted to the electors at the next annual election, or on some day to be set apart for that purpose ; and shall not be further entertained by the General Assembly, unless it receive the votes of a majority of all the persons voting. This section shall not be construed to refer to any money that now is, or hereafter may be, deposited with this state by the general government.

8. The assent of two thirds of the members elected to each House of the General Assembly shall be requisite to every bill appropriating the public moneys, or property, for local or private purposes ; or for creating, continuing, altering, or renewing any body politic or corporate, banking corporations excepted.

9. Hereafter, when any bill creating, continuing, altering, or renewing any banking corporation, authorized to issue its promissory notes for circulation, shall pass the two Houses of the General Assembly, instead of being sent to the governor, it shall be referred to the electors for their consideration, at the next annual election, or on some day to be set apart for that purpose, with printed tickets containing the question, " Shall said bill " (with a brief description thereof,) " be approved, or not ?" and if a majority of the electors voting shall vote to approve said bill, it shall become a law ; otherwise not.

10. All grants of incorporation shall be subject to future acts of the General Assembly, in amendment or repeal thereof, or in any wise affecting the same; and this provision shall be inserted in all acts of incorporation hereafter granted.

11. The General Assembly shall exercise, as heretofore, a visitatorial power over corporations. Three bank commissioners shall be chosen at the June session for one year, to carry out the powers of the General Assembly in this respect. And commissioners for the visitation of other corporations, as the General Assembly

may deem expedient, shall be chosen at the June session, for the same term of office.

12. No city council, or other government, in any city, shall have power to vote any tax upon the inhabitants thereof, excepting the amount necessary to meet the ordinary public expenses in the same, without first submittiug the question of an additional tax, or taxes, to the electors of said city; and a majority of all who vote shall determine the question. But no elector shall be entitled to vote, in any city, upon any question of taxation thus submitted, unless he shall be qualified by the possession, in his own right, of ratable property to the amount of one hundred and fifty dollars, and shall have been assessed thereon to pay a city tax, and shall have paid the same, as provided in section fourth of Article II. Nothing in that article shall be so construed as to prevent any elector from voting for town officers, and, in the city of Providence, and other cities, for mayor, aldermen, and members of the common council.

13. The General Assembly shall not pass any law, nor cause any act or thing to be done, in any way to disturb any of the owners or occupants of land in any territory now under the jurisdiction of any other state or states, the jurisdiction whereof may be ceded to, or decreed to belong to, this state; and the inhabitants of such territory shall continue in the full, quiet, and undisturbed enjoyment of their titles to the same, without interference in any way on the part of this state.

Art. X. — Of Elections.

1. The election of the governor, lieutenant governor, secretary of state, general treasurer, attorney general, and also of senators and representatives to the General Assembly, and of sheriffs of the counties, shall be held on the third Wednesday of April annually.

2. The names of the persons voted for as governor, lieutenant governor, secretary of state, general treasurer, attorney general, and sheriffs of the respective counties, shall be put upon one ticket; and the tickets shall be deposited by the electors in a box by themselves. The names of the persons voted for as senators and as representatives shall be put upon separate tickets, and the tickets shall be deposited in separate boxes. The polls for all the officers named in this section shall be opened at the same time.

3. All the votes given for governor, lieutenant governor, secretary of state, general treasurer, attorney general, sheriffs, and also for senators, shall remain in the ballot boxes till the polls be closed. These votes shall then, in open town and ward meetings, and in the presence of at least ten qualified voters, be taken out and sealed up, in separate envelopes, by the moderators and town clerks, and by the wardens and ward clerks, who shall certify the same, and forthwith deliver or send them to the secretary of state, whose duty it shall be securely to keep the same, and to deliver the votes for state officers and sheriffs to the speaker of the House of Representatives, after the House shall be organized, at the June session of the General Assembly. The votes last named shall, without delay, be opened, counted, and declared, in such manner as the House of Representatives shall direct; and the oath of office shall be administered to the persons who shall be declared to be elected, by the speaker of the House of Representatives, and in the presence of the House : provided that the sheriffs may take their engagement before a senator, judge, or justice of the peace. The votes for senators shall be counted by the governor and secretary of state within seven days from the day of election; and the governor shall give certificates to the senators who are elected.

4. The boxes containing the votes for representatives

to the General Assembly in the several towns shall not be opened till the polls for representatives are declared to be closed. The votes shall then be counted by the moderator and clerk, who shall announce the result, and give certificates to the person selected. If there be no election, or not an election of the whole number of representatives to which the town is entitled, the polls for representatives may be reopened, and the like proceedings shall be had, until an election shall take place: provided, however, that an adjournment of the election may be made to a time not exceeding seven days from the first meeting.

5. In the city of Providence, and other cities, the polls for representatives shall be kept open during the whole time of voting for the day; and the votes in the several wards shall be sealed up, at the close of the meeting, by the wardens and ward clerks, in the presence of at least ten qualified electors, and delivered to the city clerks. The mayor and aldermen of said city or cities shall proceed to count said votes within two days from the day of election; and if no election, or an election of only a portion of the representatives whom the representative districts are entitled to elect, shall have taken place, the mayor and aldermen shall order a new election to be held, not more than ten days from the day of the first election; and so on, till the election of representatives shall be completed. Certificates of election shall be furnished to the persons chosen by the city clerks.

6. If there be no choice of a senator or senators at the annual election, the governor shall issue his warrant to the town and ward clerks of the several towns and cities in the senatorial district or districts that may have failed to elect, requiring them to open town or ward meetings for another election, on a day not more than fifteen days beyond the time of counting the votes for senators. If, on the second trial, there shall be no

choice of a senator or senators, the governor shall certify the result to the speaker of the House of Representatives; and the House of Representatives, and as many senators as shall have been chosen, shall forthwith elect, in joint committee, a senator or senators, from the two candidates who may receive the highest number of votes in each district.

7. If there be no choice of governor at the annual election, the speaker of the House of Representatives shall issue his warrant to the clerks of the several towns and cities, requiring them to notify town and ward meetings for another election, on a day to be named by him, not more than thirty nor less than twenty days beyond the time of receiving the report of the committee of the House of Representatives, who shall count the votes for governor. If on this second trial there shall be no choice of a governor, the two Houses of the General Assembly shall, at their next session, in joint committee, elect a governor from the two candidates having the highest number of votes, to hold his office for the remainder of the political year, and until his successor be duly qualified.

8. If there be no choice of governor and lieutenant governor at the annual election, the same proceedings for the choice of a lieutenant governor shall be had as are directed in the preceding section: provided, that the second trial for the election of governor and lieutenant governor shall be on the same day: and also provided, that, if the governor shall be chosen at the annual election, and the lieutenant governor shall not be chosen, then the last-named officer shall be elected in joint committee of the two Houses, from the two candidates having the highest number of votes, without a further appeal to the electors. The lieutenant governor, elected as is provided in this section, shall hold his office as is provided in the preceding section respecting the governor.

9. All town, city, and ward meetings for the choice of representatives, justices of the peace, sheriffs, senators, state officers, representatives to Congress, and electors of president and vice president, shall be notified by the town, city, and ward clerks, at least seven days before the same are held.

10. In all elections held by the people under this constitution, a majority of all the electors voting shall be necessary to the choice of the person or persons voted for.

11. The oath, or affirmation, to be taken by all the officers named in this article, shall be the following: You, being elected to the place (of governor, lieutenant governor, secretary of state, general treasurer, attorney general, or to the places of senators or representatives, or to the office of sheriff or justice of the peace,) do solemnly swear, or severally solemnly swear, or affirm, that you will be true and faithful to the State of Rhode Island and Providence Plantations, and that you will support the constitution thereof; that you will support the constitution of the United States; and that you will faithfully and impartially discharge the duties of your aforesaid office, to the best of your abilities and understanding: so help you God! or, this affirmation you make and give upon the peril of the penalty of perjury.

Art. XI. — Of the Judiciary.

1. The judicial power of this state shall be vested in one Supreme Court, and in such other courts, inferior to the Supreme Court, as the legislature may, from time to time, ordain and establish; and the jurisdiction of the Supreme and of all other courts may, from time to time, be regulated by the General Assembly.

2. Chancery powers may be conferred on the Supreme Court; but no other court exercising chancery powers shall be established in this state, except as is now provided by law.

3. The justices of the Supreme Court shall be elected in joint committee of the two Houses, to hold their offices for one year, and until their places be declared vacant by a resolution to that effect, which shall be voted for by a majority of all the members elected to the House in which it may originate, and be concurred in by the same vote of the other House, without revision by the governor. Such resolution shall not be entertained at any other than the annual session for the election of public officers; and in default of the passage thereof at the said session, the judge, or judges, shall hold his or their place or places for another year. But a judge of any court shall be removable from office, if, upon impeachment, he shall be found guilty of any official misdemeanor.

4. In case of vacancy by the death, resignation, refusal, or inability to serve, or removal from the state, of a judge of any court, his place may be filled by the joint committee, until the next annual election; when, if elected, he shall hold his office as herein provided.

5. The justices of the Supreme Court shall receive a compensation which shall not be diminished during their continuance in office.

6. The judges of the courts inferior to the Supreme Court shall be annually elected in joint committee of the two Houses, except as herein provided.

7. There shall be annually elected by each town, and by the several wards in the city of Providence, a sufficient number of justices of the peace, or wardens resident therein, with such jurisdiction as the General Assembly may prescribe. And said justices or wardens (except in the towns of New Shoreham and Jamestown) shall be commissioned by the governor.

8. The General Assembly may provide that justices of the peace, who are not reëlected, may hold their offices for a time not exceeding ten days beyond the day of the annual election of these officers.

9. The courts of probate in this state, except the Supreme Court, shall remain as at present established by law, until the General Assembly shall otherwise prescribe.

Art. XII. — Of Education.

1. All moneys which now are, or may hereafter be, appropriated, by the authority of the state, to public education, shall be securely invested, and remain a perpetual fund for the maintenance of free schools in this state; and the General Assembly are prohibited from diverting said moneys or fund from this use, and from borrowing, appropriating, or using the same, or any part thereof, for any other purpose, or under any pretence whatsoever. But the income derived from said moneys or fund shall be annually paid over, by the general treasurer, to the towns and cities of the state, for the support of said schools, in equitable proportions: provided, however, that a portion of said income may, in the discretion of the General Assembly, be added to the principal of said fund.

2. The several towns and cities shall faithfully devote their portions of said annual distribution to the support of free schools; and, in default thereof, shall forfeit their shares of the same to the increase of the fund.

3. All charitable donations for the support of free schools, and other purposes of public education, shall be received by the General Assembly, and invested and applied agreeably to the terms prescribed by the donors: provided the same be not inconsistent with the constitution, or with sound public policy; in which case the donation shall not be received.

Art. XIII. — Amendments.

The General Assembly may propose amendments to this constitution by the vote of a majority of all the

APPENDIX. 341

members elected to each House. Such propositions
shall be published in the newspapers of the state ; and
printed copies of said propositions shall be sent by the
secretary of state, with the names of all the members
who shall have voted thereon, with the yeas and nays, to
all the town and city clerks in the state ; and the said
propositions shall be, by said clerks, inserted in the
notices by them issued for warning the next annual
town and ward meetings in April ; and the town and
ward clerks shall read said propositions to the electors,
when thus assembled, with the names of all the representatives and senators who shall have voted thereon,
with the yeas and nays, before the election of representatives and senators shall be had. If a majority of
all the members elected at said annual meetings, present
in each House, shall approve any proposition thus
made, the same shall be published as before provided,
and then sent to the electors in the mode provided in
the act of approval ; and if then approved by a majority
of the electors who shall vote in town and ward meetings, to be specially convened for that purpose, it shall
become a part of the constitution of the state.

ART. XIV. — OF THE ADOPTION OF THE CONSTITU-
TION.

1. This constitution shall be submitted to the people,
for their adoption or rejection, on Monday, the 27th
day of December next, and on the two succeeding
days ; and all persons voting are requested to deposit
in the ballot boxes printed or written tickets in the following form : I am an American citizen, of the age of
twenty-one years, and have my permanent residence, or
home, in this state. I am (or not) qualified to vote
under the existing laws of this state. I vote for (or
against) the constitution formed by the convention of
the people, assembled at Providence, and which was

proposed to the people by said convention on the 18th day of November, 1841.

2. Every voter is requested to write his name on the face of his ticket; and every person entitled to vote as aforesaid, who, from sickness or other causes, may be unable to attend and vote in the town or ward meetings assembled for voting upon said constitution, on the days aforesaid, is requested to write his name upon a ticket, and to obtain the signature, upon the back of the same, of a person who has given in his vote, as a witness thereto. And the moderator, or clerk, of any town or ward meeting convened for the purpose aforesaid, shall receive such vote, on either of the three days next succeeding the three days before named for voting on said constitution.

3. The citizens of the several towns in this state, and of the several wards in the city of Providence, are requested to hold town and ward meetings on the days appointed, and for the purpose aforesaid; and also to choose, in each town and ward, a moderator and clerk, to conduct said meetings and receive the votes.

4. The moderators and clerks are required to receive, and carefully to keep, the votes of all persons qualified to vote as aforesaid, and to make registers of all the persons voting; which, together with the tickets given in by the voters, shall be sealed up, and returned by said moderators and clerks, with certificates signed and sealed by them, to the clerks of the convention of the people, to be by them safely deposited and kept, and laid before said convention, to be counted and declared at their next adjourned meeting, on the 12th day of January, 1842.

5. This constitution, except so much thereof as relates to the election of the officers named in the sixth section of this article, shall, if adopted, go into operation on the first Tuesday of May, in the year one thousand eight hundred and forty-two.

6. So much of the constitution as relates to the election of the officers named in this section shall go into operation on the Monday before the third Wednesday of April next preceding. The first election, under this constitution, of governor, lieutenant governor, secretary of state, general treasurer, and attorney general, of senators and representatives, of sheriffs for the several counties, and of justices of the peace for the several towns, and the wards of the city of Providence, shall take place on the Monday aforesaid.

7. The electors of the several towns and wards are authorized to assemble on the day aforesaid, without being notified, as is provided in Section 9 of Article X., and without the registration required in Section 7 of Article II., and to choose moderators and clerks, and proceed in the election of the officers named in the preceding section.

8. The votes given in at the first election for representatives to the General Assembly, and for justices of the peace, shall be counted by the moderators and clerks of the towns and wards chosen as aforesaid; and certificates of election shall be furnished by them to the representatives and justices of the peace elected.

9. Said moderators and clerks shall seal up, certify, and transmit to the House of Representatives all the votes that may be given in at said first election for governor and state officers, and for senators and sheriffs; and the votes shall be counted as the House of Representatives may direct.

10. The speaker of the House of Representatives shall, at the first session of the same, qualify himself to administer the oath of office to the members of the House, and to other officers, by taking and subscribing the same oath in the presence of the House.

11. The first session of the General Assembly shall be held in the city of Providence on the first Tuesday of May, in the year one thousand eight hundred and

forty-two, with such adjournments as may be necessary; but all other sessions shall be held as is provided in Article IV. of this constitution.

12. If any of the representatives, whom the towns or districts are entitled to choose at the first annual election aforesaid, shall not be then elected, or if their places shall become vacant during the year, the same proceedings may be had to complete the election, or to supply vacancies, as are directed concerning elections in the preceding sections of this article.

13. If there shall be no election of governor or lieutenant governor, or of both of these officers, or of a senator or senators, at the first annual election, the House of Representatives, and as many senators as are chosen, shall forthwith elect, in joint committee, a governor or lieutenant governor, or both, or a senator or senators, to hold their offices for the remainder of the political year; and, in the case of the two officers first named, until their successors shall be duly qualified.

14. If the number of justices of the peace determined by the several towns and wards on the day of the first annual election shall not be then chosen, or if vacancies shall occur, the same proceedings shall be had as are provided for in this article in the case of a non-election of representatives and senators, or of vacancies in their offices. The justices of the peace thus elected shall hold office for the remainder of the political year, or until the second annual election of justices of the peace, to be held on such day as may be prescribed by the General Assembly.

15. The justices of the peace elected in pursuance of the provisions of this article may be engaged by the persons acting as moderators of the town and ward meetings, as herein provided; and said justices, after obtaining their certificates of election, may discharge the duties of their office, for a time not exceeding **twenty days**, without a commission from the governor.

APPENDIX. 345

16. Nothing contained in this article, inconsistent with any of the provisions of other articles of the constitution, shall continue in force for a longer period than the first political year under the same.

17. The present government shall exercise all the powers with which it is now clothed, until the said first Tuesday of May, one thousand eight hundred and forty-two, and until their successors, under this constitution, shall be duly elected and qualified.

18. All civil, judicial, and military officers now elected, or who shall hereafter be elected by the General Assembly, or other competent authority, before the said first Tuesday of May, shall hold their offices, and may exercise their powers, until that time.

19. All laws and statutes, public and private, now in force, and not repugnant to this constitution, shall continue in force until they expire by their own limitation, or are repealed by the General Assembly. All contracts, judgments, actions, and rights of action shall be as valid as if this constitution had not been made. All debts contracted, and engagements entered into, before the adoption of this constitution, shall be as valid against the state as if this constitution had not been made.

20. The Supreme Court, established by this constitution, shall have the same jurisdiction as the Supreme Judicial Court at present established; and shall have jurisdiction of all causes which may be appealed to, or pending in the same; and shall be held at the same times and places in each county, as the present Supreme Judicial Court, until the General Assembly shall otherwise prescribe.

21. The citizens of the town of New Shoreham shall be hereafter exempted from military duty, and the duty of serving as jurors in the courts of this state. The citizens of the town of Jamestown shall be forever hereafter exempted from military field duty.

22. The General Assembly shall, at their first session

after the adoption of this constitution, propose to the electors the question, whether the word "white," in the first line of the first section of Article II. of the constitution, shall be stricken out. The question shall be voted upon at the succeeding annual election; and if a majority of the electors voting shall vote to strike out the word aforesaid, it shall be stricken from the constitution; otherwise, not. If the word aforesaid shall be stricken out, Section 3 of Article II. shall cease to be a part of the constitution.

23. The president, vice presidents, and secretaries shall certify and sign this constitution, and cause the same to be published.

Done in convention, at Providence, on the 18th day of November, in the year one thousand eight hundred and forty-one, and of American independence the sixty-sixth.

JOSEPH JOSLIN, *President of the Convention.*
WAGER WEEDEN, } *Vice Presidents.*
SAMUEL H. WALES,
Attest:
WILLIAM H. SMITH, } *Secretaries.*
JOHN S. HARRIS,

CONSTITUTION OF THE STATE OF RHODE ISLAND AND PROVIDENCE PLANTATIONS,

ADOPTED NOVEMBER, 1842.

WE, the people of the State of Rhode Island and Providence Plantations, grateful to Almighty God for the civil and religious liberty which he hath so long permitted us to enjoy, and looking to him for a blessing upon our endeavors to secure and to transmit the same, unimpaired, to succeeding generations, do ordain and establish this constitution of government.

ART. I. — DECLARATION OF CERTAIN CONSTITUTIONAL RIGHTS AND PRINCIPLES.

In order effectually to secure the religious and political freedom established by our venerated ancestors, and to preserve the same for our posterity, we do declare that the essential and unquestionable rights and principles hereinafter mentioned shall be established, maintained, and preserved, and shall be of paramount obligation in all legislative, judicial, and executive proceedings.

SECTION 1. In the words of the Father of his Country, we declare that "the basis of our political systems is the right of the people to make and alter their constitutions of government; but that the constitution which at any time exists, till changed by an explicit and authentic act of the whole people, is sacredly obligatory upon all."

SEC. 2. All free governments are instituted for the protection, safety, and happiness of the people. All laws, therefore, should be made for the good of the whole; and the burdens of the state ought to be fairly distributed among its citizens.

SEC. 3. Whereas Almighty God hath created the mind free; and all attempts to influence it by temporal punishments or burdens, or by civil incapacitations, tend to beget habits of hypocrisy and meanness: and whereas a principal object of our venerable ancestors, in their migration to this country, and their settlement of this state, was, as they expressed it, to hold forth a lively experiment that a flourishing civil state may stand and be best maintained with full liberty in religious concernments: We therefore declare that no man shall be compelled to frequent or to support any religious worship, place, or ministry whatever, except in fulfilment of his own voluntary contract; nor enforced, restrained, molested, or burdened in his body or goods, nor disqualified from holding any office, nor otherwise suffer, on account of his religious belief; and that every man shall be free to worship God according to the dictates of his own conscience, and to profess, and by argument to maintain, his opinion in matters of religion; and that the same shall in no wise diminish, enlarge, or affect his civil capacity.

SEC. 4. Slavery shall not be permitted in this state.

SEC. 5. Every person within this state ought to find a certain remedy, by having recourse to the laws, for all injuries or wrongs which he may receive in his person, property, or character. He ought to obtain right and justice freely and without purchase, completely and without denial, promptly and without delay, comformably to the laws.

SEC. 6. The right of the people to be secure in their persons, papers, and possessions, against unreasonable searches and seizures, shall not be violated; and no warrant shall issue but on complaint in writing, upon probable cause supported by oath or affirmation, and describing as nearly as may be the place to be searched, and the persons or things to be seized.

SEC. 7. No person shall be held to answer for a capital or other infamous crime, unless on presentment or indictment by a grand jury, except in cases of impeachment, or of such offences as are cognizable by a justice of the peace; or in cases arising in the land or naval forces, or in the militia, when in actual service in time of war or public danger. No person shall, after an acquittal, be tried for the same offence.

SEC. 8. Excessive bail shall not be required, nor excessive fines imposed, nor cruel punishments inflicted; and all punishments ought to be proportioned to the offence.

SEC. 9. All persons imprisoned ought to be bailed by

APPENDIX. 349

sufficient surety, unless for offences punishable by death or by imprisonment for life, when the proof of guilt is evident or the presumption great. The privilege of the writ of habeas corpus shall not be suspended, unless when in cases of rebellion or invasion the public safety shall require it; nor ever, without the authority of the General Assembly.

SEC. 10. In all criminal prosecutions, the accused shall enjoy the right to a speedy and public trial by an impartial jury, to be informed of the nature and cause of the accusation, to be confronted with the witnesses against him, to have compulsory process for obtaining them in his favor, to have the assistance of counsel in his defence, and shall be at liberty to speak for himself; nor shall he be deprived of life, liberty, or property, unless by the judgment of his peers, or the laws of the land.

SEC. 11. The person of a debtor, when there is not strong presumption of fraud, ought not to be continued in prison after he shall have delivered up his property for the benefit of his creditor, in such manner as shall be prescribed by law.

SEC. 12. No ex-post-facto law, or law impairing the obligation of contracts, shall be passed.

SEC. 13. No man in a court of common law shall be compelled to give evidence criminating himself.

SEC. 14. Every man being presumed innocent until he is pronounced guilty by the law, no act of severity which is not necessary to secure an accused person shall be permitted.

SEC. 15. The right of trial by jury shall remain inviolate.

SEC. 16. Private property shall not be taken for public uses without just compensation.

SEC. 17. The people shall continue to enjoy and freely exercise all the rights of fishery, and the privileges of the shore, to which they have been heretofore entitled under the charter and usages of this state. But no new right is intended to be granted, nor any existing right impaired, by this declaration.

SEC. 18. The military shall be held in strict subordination to the civil authority. And the law martial shall be used and exercised in such cases only as occasion shall necessarily require.

SEC. 19. No soldier shall be quartered in any house, in time of peace, without the consent of the owner ; nor in time of war, but in manner to be prescribed by law.

SEC. 20. The liberty of the press being essential to the security of freedom in a state, any person may publish his sentiments on any subject, being responsible for the abuse of that liberty ; and in all trials for libel, both civil and criminal, the truth, unless published from malicious motives, shall be sufficient defence to the person charged.

SEC. 21. The citizens have a right in a peaceable manner to assemble for their common good, and to apply to those invested with the powers of government for redress of grievances, or for other purposes, by petition, address, or remonstrance.

SEC. 22. The right of the people to keep and bear arms shall not be infringed.

SEC. 23. The enumeration of the foregoing rights shall not be construed to impair or deny others retained by the people.

ART. II. — OF THE QUALIFICATION OF ELECTORS.

SECTION 1. Every male citizen of the United States, of the age of twenty-one years, who has had his residence and home in this state for one year, and in the town or city in which he may claim a right to vote six months next preceding the time of voting, and who is really and truly possessed, in his own right, of real estate in such town or city, of the value of one hundred and thirty-four dollars over and above all encumbrances, or which shall rent for seven dollars per annum over and above any rent reserved, or the interest of any encumbrances thereon, being an estate in fee simple, fee tail, for the life of any person, or an estate in reversion or remainder, which qualifies no other person to vote, the conveyance of which estate, if by deed, shall have been recorded at least ninety days, shall thereafter have a right to vote in the election of all civil officers, and on all questions in all legal town or ward meetings, so long as he continues so qualified. And if any person hereinbefore described shall own any such estate within this state, out of the town or city in which he resides, he shall have a right to vote in the election of all general officers, and members of the General Assembly, in the town or city in which he shall have had his residence and home for the term of six months next preceding the election, upon producing a certificate from the clerk of the town or city in which his estate lies, bearing date within ten days of the time of his voting, setting forth that such person has a sufficient estate therein to qualify him as a voter; and that the deed, if any, has been recorded ninety days.

SEC. 2. Every [ ] male native citizen of the United States, of the age of twenty-one years, who has had his residence and home in this state two years, and in the town or city in which he may offer to vote six months next preceding the time of voting, whose name is registered pursuant to the act calling the convention to frame this constitution, or shall be registered in the office of the clerk of such town or city at least seven days before the time he shall offer to vote, and before the last day of December in the present year, and who has paid or shall pay a tax or taxes assessed upon his estate within this state, and within a year of the time of voting, to the amount of one dollar, or who shall voluntarily pay at least seven days before the time he shall offer to vote, and before said last day of December, to the clerk or treasurer of the town or city where he resides, the sum of one dollar, or such sum as, with his other taxes, shall amount to one dollar, for the support of public schools therein, and shall make proof of the same, by the certificate of the clerk, treasurer, or collector of any town or city where such payment is made; or who, being so registered, has been enrolled in any military company in this state, and done military service or duty therein, within the present year, pursuant to law, and shall (until other proof is required by law) prove by the certificate of the officer legally commanding the regiment, or chartered or legally authorized volunteer company, in which he may have served or done duty, that he has been equipped and done duty according to law, or, by the certificate of the commissioners upon military claims, that he has performed military service, shall have a right to vote in the election of all civil officers, and on all questions in all legally organized town or ward meetings, until the end of the first year after the adoption of this constitution, or until the end of the year eighteen hundred and forty-three.

From and after that time, every such citizen who has had the residence herein required, and whose name shall be registered in the town where he resides, on or before the last day of December, in the year next preceding the time of his voting, and who shall show, by legal proof, that he has, for and within the year next preceding the time he shall offer to vote, paid a tax or taxes assessed against him in any town or city in this state, to the amount of one dollar, or that he has been enrolled in a military company in this state, been equipped and done duty therein according to law, and at least for one day during such year, shall have a right to vote in the election of all civil officers, and on all questions in all legally organized town or ward meetings: *Provided*, That no person shall at any time be allowed to vote in the election of the city council of the city of Providence, or upon any proposition to impose a tax, or for the expenditure of money in any town or city, unless he shall, within the year next preceding, have paid a tax assessed upon his property therein, valued at least at one hundred and thirty-four dollars.

SEC. 3. The assessors of each town or city shall annually assess upon every person whose name shall be registered, a tax of one dollar, or such sum as with his other taxes shall amount to one dollar; which registry tax shall be paid into the treasury of such town or city, and be applied to the support of public schools therein. But no compulsory process shall issue for the collection of any registry tax: *Provided*, That the registry tax of every person who has performed military duty according to the provisions of the preceding section, shall be remitted for the year he shall perform such duty; and the registry tax assessed upon any mariner, for any year while he is at sea, shall, upon his application, be remitted; and no person shall be allowed to vote whose registry tax, for either of the two years next preceding the time of voting, is not paid or remitted as herein provided.

SEC. 4. No person in the military, naval, marine, or any other service of the United States, shall be considered as having the required residence by reason of being employed in any garrison, barrack, or military or naval station in this state; and no pauper, lunatic, person *non compos mentis*, person under guardianship, or member of the Narragansett tribe of Indians, shall be permitted to be registered or to vote. Nor shall any person convicted of bribery, or of any crime deemed infamous at common law, be permitted to exercise that privilege, unless he be expressly restored thereto by act of the General Assembly.

SEC. 5. Persons residing on lands ceded by this state

to the United States shall not be entitled to exercise the privileges of electors.

SEC. 6. The General Assembly shall have full power to provide for a registry of voters, to prescribe the manner of conducting the elections, the form of certificates, the nature of the evidence to be required in case of a dispute as to the right of any person to vote, and generally to enact all laws necessary to carry this article into effect, and to prevent abuse, corruption, and fraud in voting.

ART. III. — OF THE DISTRIBUTION OF POWERS.

The powers of government shall be distributed into three departments — the legislative, executive, and judicial.

ART. IV. — OF THE LEGISLATIVE POWER.

SECTION 1. This constitution shall be the supreme law of the state, and any law inconsistent therewith shall be void. The General Assembly shall pass all laws necessary to carry this constitution into effect.

SEC. 2. The legislative power under this constitution shall be vested in two Houses — the one to be called the Senate, the other the House of Representatives; and both together, the General Assembly. The concurrence of the two Houses shall be necessary to the enactment of laws. The style of their laws shall be, *It is enacted by the General Assembly as follows.*

SEC. 3. There shall be two sessions of the General Assembly holden annually — one at Newport, on the first Tuesday of May, for the purposes of election and other business; the other on the last Monday of October, which last session shall be holden at South Kingstown once in two years, and the intermediate years alternately at Bristol and East Greenwich; and an adjournment from the October session shall be holden annually at Providence.

Sec. 4. No member of the General Assembly shall take any fee, or be of counsel in any case pending before either House of the General Assembly, under penalty of forfeiting his seat, upon proof thereof to the satisfaction of the House of which he is a member.

Sec. 5. The person of every member of the General Assembly shall be exempt from arrest, and his estate from attachment in any civil action, during the session of the General Assembly, and two days before the commencement, and two days after the termination thereof; and all process served contrary hereto shall be void. For any speech in debate, in either House, no member shall be questioned in any other place.

Sec. 6. Each House shall be the judge of the elections and qualifications of its members, and a majority shall constitute a quorum to do business; but a smaller number may adjourn from day to day, and may compel the attendance of absent members, in such manner and under such penalties as may be prescribed by such House, or by law. The organization of the two Houses may be regulated by law, subject to the limitations contained in this constitution.

Sec. 7. Each House may determine its rules of proceeding, punish contempts, punish its members for disorderly behavior, and, with the concurrence of two thirds, expel a member; but not a second time for the same cause.

Sec. 8. Each House shall keep a journal of its proceedings. The yeas and nays of the members of either House shall, at the desire of one fifth of those present, be entered on the journal.

Sec. 9. Neither house shall, during a session, without the consent of the other, adjourn for more than two days, nor to any other place than that in which they may be sitting.

Sec. 10. The General Assembly shall continue to exercise the powers they have heretofore exercised, unless prohibited in this constitution.

Sec. 11. The senators and representatives shall receive the sum of one dollar for every day of attendance, and eight cents per mile for travelling expenses in going to and returning from the General Assembly. The General Assembly shall regulate the compensation of the governor and all other officers, subject to the limitations contained in this constitution.

Sec. 12. All lotteries shall hereafter be prohibited in this state, except those already authorized by the General Assembly.

Sec. 13. The General Assembly shall have no power hereafter, without the express consent of the people, to incur state debts to an amount exceeding fifty thousand dollars, except in time of war, or in case of insurrection or invasion; nor shall they in any case, without such consent, pledge the faith of the state for the payment of the obligations of others. This section shall not be construed to refer to any money that may be deposited with this state by the government of the United States.

Sec. 14. The assent of two thirds of the members elected to each House of the General Assembly shall be required to every bill appropriating the public money or property for local or private purposes.

Sec. 15. The General Assembly shall, from time to time, provide for making new valuations of property for the assessment of taxes, in such manner as they may deem best. A new estimate of such property shall be taken before the first direct state tax after the adoption of this constitution shall be assessed.

Sec. 16. The General Assembly may provide by law for the continuance in office of any officers of annual election or appointment, until other persons are qualified to take their places.

Sec. 17. Hereafter, when any bill shall be presented to either House of the General Assembly, to create a corporation for any other than for religious, literary, or charitable purposes, or for a military or fire company, it shall be continued until another election of members of the General Assembly shall have taken place; and such public notice of the pendency thereof shall be given as may be required by law.

Sec. 18. It shall be the duty of the two Houses, upon the request of either, to join in grand committee for the purpose of electing senators in Congress, at such times, and in such manner, as may be prescribed by law for said elections.

Art. V. — Of the House of Representatives.

Section 1. The House of Representatives shall never exceed seventy-two members, and shall be constituted on the basis of population, always allowing one representative for a fraction exceeding half the ratio; but each town or city shall always be entitled to at least one member; and no town or city shall have more than one sixth of the whole number of the members to which the House is hereby limited. The present ratio shall be one representative to every fifteen hundred and thirty inhabitants; and the General Assembly may, after any new census taken by the authority of the United States or of this state, reapportion the representation by altering the ratio; but no town or city shall be divided into districts for the choice of representatives.

Sec. 2. The House of Representatives shall have authority to elect its speaker, clerks, and other officers. The senior member from the town of Newport, if any be present, shall preside in the organization of the House.

Art. VI. — Of the Senate.

Section 1. The Senate shall consist of the lieutenant governor, and of one senator from each town or city in the state.

Sec. 2. The governor, and, in his absence, the lieutenant governor, shall preside in the Senate and in grand committee. The presiding officer of the Senate and grand committee shall have a right to vote in case of equal division, but not otherwise.

Sec. 3. If, by reason of death, resignation, absence, or other cause, there be no governor or lieutenant governor present, to preside in the Senate, the Senate shall elect one of their own members to preside during such absence or vacancy; and until such election is made by the Senate, the secretary of state shall preside.

Sec. 4. The secretary of state shall, by virtue of his office, be secretary of the Senate, unless otherwise provided by law; and the Senate may elect such other officers as they may deem necessary.

Art. VII.— Of the Executive Power.

Section 1. The chief executive power of this state shall be vested in a governor, who, together with a lieutenant governor, shall be annually elected by the people.

Sec. 2. The governor shall take care that the laws be faithfully executed.

Sec. 3. He shall be captain general and commander-in-chief of the military and naval forces of this state, except when they shall be called into the service of the United States.

Sec. 4. He shall have power to grant reprieves, after conviction, in all cases except those of impeachment, until the end of the next session of the General Assembly.

Sec. 5. He may fill vacancies in office not otherwise provided for by this constitution or by law, until the same shall be filled by the General Assembly or by the people.

Sec. 6. In case of disagreement between the two Houses of the General Assembly, respecting the time or place of adjournment, certified to him by either, he may adjourn them to such time and place as he shall think proper : *Provided*, That the time of adjournment shall not be extended beyond the day of the next stated session.

SEC. 7. He may, on extraordinary occasions, convene the General Assembly at any town or city in this state, at any time not provided for by law ; and in case of danger from the prevalence of epidemic or contagious disease in the place in which the General Assembly are by law to meet, or to which they may have been adjourned, or for other urgent reasons, he may, by proclamation, convene said Assembly at any other place within this state.

SEC. 8. All commissions shall be in the name and by authority of the State of Rhode Island and Providence Plantations ; shall be sealed with the state seal, signed by the governor, and attested by the secretary.

SEC. 9. In case of vacancy in the office of governor, or of his inability to serve, impeachment, or absence from the state, the lieutenant governor shall fill the office of governor, and exercise the powers and authority appertaining thereto, until a governor is qualified to act, or until the office is filled at the next annual election.

SEC. 10. If the offices of governor and lieutenant governor be both vacant, by reason of death, resignation, impeachment, absence, or otherwise, the person entitled to preside over the Senate for the time being, shall, in like manner, fill the office of governor during such absence or vacancy.

SEC. 11. The compensation of the governor and lieutenant governor shall be established by law, and shall not be diminished during the term for which they are elected.

SEC. 12. The duties and powers of the secretary, attorney general, and general treasurer, shall be the same under this constitution as are now established, or as, from time to time, may be prescribed by law.

Art. VIII. — Of Elections.

Section 1. The governor, lieutenant governor, senators, representatives, secretary of state, attorney general, and general treasurer, shall be elected at the town, city, or ward meetings, to be holden on the first Wednesday of April, annually; and shall severally hold their offices for one year, from the first Tuesday of May next succeeding, and until others are legally chosen and duly qualified to fill their places. If elected or qualified after the said first Tuesday of May, they shall hold their offices for the remainder of the political year, and until their successors are qualified to act.

Sec. 2. The voting for governor, lieutenant governor, secretary of state, attorney general, general treasurer, and representatives to Congress, shall be by ballot; senators and representatives to the General Assembly, and town or city officers, shall be chosen by ballot, on demand of any seven persons entitled to vote for the same; and in all cases where an election is made by ballot, or paper vote, the manner of balloting shall be the same as is now required in voting for general officers, until otherwise prescribed by law.

Sec. 3. The names of the persons voted for as governor, lieutenant governor, secretary of state, attorney general, and general treasurer, shall be placed upon one ticket; and all votes for these officers shall, in open town or ward meetings, be sealed up by the moderators and town clerks, and by the wardens and ward clerks, who shall certify the same, and deliver or send them to the secretary of state, whose duty it shall be securely to keep and deliver the same to the grand committee after the organization of the two Houses at the annual May session; and it shall be the duty of the two Houses, at said session, after their organization, upon the request of either House, to join in grand committee, for the purpose of counting and declaring said votes, and of electing other officers.

SEC. 4. The town and ward clerks shall also keep a correct list or register of all persons voting for general officers, and shall transmit a copy thereof to the General Assembly on or before the first day of said May session.

SEC. 5. The ballots for senators and representatives in the several towns shall, in each case, after the polls are declared to be closed, be counted by the moderator, who shall announce the result, and the clerk shall give certificates to the persons elected. If in any case there be no election, the polls may be reopened, and the like proceedings shall be had until an election shall take place: *Provided, however,* That an adjournment or adjournments of the election may be made to a time not exceeding seven days from the first meeting.

SEC. 6. In the city of Providence, the polls for senator and representatives shall be kept open during the whole time of voting for the day, and the votes in the several wards shall be sealed up at the close of the meeting by the wardens and ward clerks in open ward meeting, and afterwards delivered to the city clerk. The mayor and aldermen shall proceed to count said votes within two days from the day of election; and if no election of senator and representatives, or if an election of only a portion of the representatives, shall have taken place, the mayor and aldermen shall order a new election, to be held not more than ten days from the day of the first election, and so on until the election shall be completed. Certificates of election shall be furnished by the city clerk to the persons chosen.

SEC. 7. If no person shall have a majority of votes for governor, it shall be the duty of the grand committee to elect one by ballot from the two persons having the highest number of votes for the office, except when such a result is produced by rejecting the entire vote of any town, city, or ward, for informality or illegality; in which case, a new election by the electors throughout the state shall be ordered; and in case no person shall have a majority of votes for lieutenant governor, it shall be the duty of the grand committee to elect one by ballot from the two persons having the highest number of votes for the office.

SEC. 8. In case an election of the secretary of state, attorney general, or general treasurer should fail to be made by the electors at the annual election, the vacancy or vacancies shall be filled by the General Assembly, in grand committee, from the two candidates for such office having the greatest number of the votes of the electors. Or in case of a vacancy in either of said offices from other causes, between the sessions of the General Assembly, the governor shall appoint some person to fill the same until a successor elected by the General Assembly is qualified to act; and in such case, and also in all other cases of vacancies not otherwise provided for, the General Assembly may fill the same in any manner they may deem proper.

SEC. 9. Vacancies from any cause in the Senate or House of Representatives may be filled by a new election.

SEC. 10. In all elections held by the people under this constitution, a majority of all the electors voting shall be necessary to the election of the persons voted for.

ART. IX. — OF QUALIFICATIONS FOR OFFICE,

SECTION 1. No person shall be eligible to any civil office (except the office of school committee) unless he be a qualified elector for such office.

SEC. 2. Every person shall be disqualified from holding any office to which he may have been elected, if he be convicted of having offered, or procured any other person to offer, any bribe to secure his election, or the election of any other person.

Sec. 3. All general officers shall take the following engagement before they act in their respective offices, to wit: You ———, being by the free vote of the electors of this State of Rhode Island and Providence Plantations, elected unto the place, of ———, do solemnly swear (or affirm) to be true and faithful unto this state, and to support the constitution of this state and of the United States; that you will faithfully and impartially discharge all the duties of your aforesaid office to the best of your abilities, according to law: so help you God. Or, This affirmation you make and give upon the peril of the penalty of perjury.

Sec. 4. The members of the General Assembly, the judges of all the courts, and all other officers, both civil and military, shall be bound by oath or affirmation to support this constitution, and the constitution of the United States.

Sec. 5. The oath, or affirmation, shall be administered to the governor, lieutenant governor, senators, and representatives, by the secretary of state, or, in his absence, by the attorney general. The secretary of state, attorney general, and general treasurer shall be engaged by the governor, or by a justice of the Supreme Court.

Sec. 6. No person holding any office under the government of the United States, or of any other state or country, shall act as a general officer, or as a member of the General Assembly, unless, at the time of taking his engagement, he shall have resigned his office under such government. And if any general officer, senator, representative, or judge, shall, after his election and engagement, accept any appointment under any other government, his office under this shall be immediately vacated; but this restriction shall not apply to any person appointed to take depositions or acknowledgments of deeds, or other legal instruments, by the authority of any other state or country.

ART. X. — OF THE JUDICIAL POWER.

SECTION 1. The judicial power of this state shall be vested in one Supreme Court, and in such inferior courts as the General Assembly may, from time to time, ordain and establish.

SEC. 2. The several courts shall have such jurisdiction as may, from time to time, be prescribed by law. Chancery powers may be conferred on the Supreme Court, but on no other court, to any greater extent than is now provided by law.

SEC. 3. The judges of the Supreme Court shall, in all trials, instruct the jury in the law. They shall also give their written opinion upon any question of law, whenever requested by the governor, or by either House of the General Assembly.

SEC. 4. The judges of the Supreme Court shall be elected by the two Houses in grand committee. Each judge shall hold his office until his place be declared vacant by a resolution of the General Assembly to that effect; which resolution shall be voted for by a majority of all the members elected to the House in which it may originate, and be concurred in by the same majority of the other House. Such resolution shall not be entertained at any other than the annual session for the election of public officers; and, in default of the passage thereof at said session, the judge shall hold his place as herein provided. But a judge of any court shall be removed from office, if, upon impeachment, he shall be found guilty of any official misdemeanor.

SEC. 5. In case of vacancy by death, resignation, removal from the state, or from office, refusal or inability to serve, of any judge of the Supreme Court, the office may be filled by the grand committee, until the next annual election, and the judge then elected shall hold his office as before provided. In cases of impeachment, or temporary absence or inability, the governor may appoint a person to discharge the duties of the office during the vacancy caused thereby.

SEC. 6. The judges of the Supreme Court shall receive a compensation for their services which shall not be diminished during their continuance in office.

SEC. 7. The towns of New Shoreham and Jamestown may continue to elect their wardens as heretofore. The other towns, and the city of Providence, may elect such number of justices of the peace, resident therein, as they may deem proper. The jurisdiction of said justices and wardens shall be regulated by law. The justices shall be commissioned by the governor.

ART. XI. — OF IMPEACHMENTS.

SECTION 1. The House of Representatives shall have the sole power of impeachment. A vote of two thirds of all the members elected shall be required for an impeachment of the governor. Any officer impeached shall thereby be suspended from office until judgment in the case shall have been pronounced.

SEC. 2. All impeachments shall be tried by the Senate; and, when sitting for that purpose, they shall be under oath or affirmation. No person shall be convicted except by vote of two thirds of the members elected. When the governor is impeached, the chief or presiding justice of the Supreme Court, for the time being, shall preside, with a casting vote in all preliminary questions

SEC. 3. The governor, and all other executive and judicial officers, shall be liable to impeachment; but judgment in such cases shall not extend further than to removal from office. The person convicted shall, nevertheless, be liable to indictment, trial, and punishment, according to law.

Art. XII.— Of Education.

Section 1. The diffusion of knowledge, as well as of virtue, among the people, being essential to the preservation of their rights and liberties, it shall be the duty of the General Assembly to promote public schools, and to adopt all means which they may deem necessary and proper to secure to the people the advantages and opportunities of education.

Sec. 2. The money which now is, or which may hereafter be, appropriated by law for the establishment of a permanent fund for the support of public schools, shall be securely invested, and remain a perpetual fund for that purpose.

Sec. 3. All donations for the support of public schools, or for other purposes of education, which may be received by the General Assembly, shall be applied according to the terms prescribed by the donors.

Sec. 4. The General Assembly shall make all necessary provisions by law for carrying this article into effect. They shall not divert said money, or fund, from the aforesaid uses; nor borrow, appropriate, or use the same, or any part thereof, for any other purpose, under any pretence whatsoever.

Art. XIII.— Of Amendments.

The General Assembly may propose amendments to this constitution by the votes of a majority of all the members elected to each House. Such propositions for amendment shall be published in the newspapers, and printed copies of them shall be sent to the secretary of state, with the names of all the members who shall have voted thereon, with the yeas and nays, to all the town and city clerks in the state. The said propositions shall be, by said clerks, inserted in the warrants or notices by them issued, for warning the next annual town and ward meetings, in April; and the clerks shall read said propositions to the electors when thus assembled, with the names of all the representatives and senators who shall have voted thereon, with the yeas and nays, before the election of senators and representatives shall be had. If a majority of all the members elected to each House, at said annual meeting, shall approve any proposition thus made, the same shall be published and submitted to the electors in the mode provided in the act of approval; and if then approved by three fifths of the electors of the state present, and voting thereon in town and ward meetings, it shall become a part of the constitution of the state.

ART. XIV.—OF THE ADOPTION OF THIS CONSTITUTION.

SECTION 1. This constitution, if adopted, shall go into operation on the first Tuesday of May, in the year one thousand eight hundred and forty-three. The first election of governor, lieutenant governor, secretary of state, attorney general, and general treasurer, and of senators and representatives under said constitution, shall be had on the first Wednesday of April next preceding, by the electors qualified under said constitution; and the town and ward meetings therefor shall be warned and conducted as is now provided by law. All civil and military officers now elected, or who shall be hereafter elected, by the General Assembly, or other competent authority, before the said first Wednesday of April, shall hold their offices, and may exercise their powers, until the said first Tuesday of May, or until their successors shall be qualified to act. All statutes, public and private, not repugnant to this constitution, shall continue in force until they expire by their own limitation, or are repealed by the General Assembly. All charters, contracts, judgments, actions, and rights of action, shall be as valid as if this constitution had not been made. The present government shall exercise all the powers with which it is now clothed, until the said first Tuesday of May, one thousand eight hundred and forty-three, and until the government under this constitution is duly organized.

SEC. 2. All debts contracted, and engagements entered into, before the adoption of this constitution, shall be as valid against the state as if this constitution had not been adopted.

SEC. 3. The Supreme Court, established by this constitution, shall have the same jurisdiction as the Supreme Judicial Court at present established; and shall have jurisdiction of all causes which may be appealed to, or pending in the same; and shall be held at the same times and places, and in each county, as the present Supreme Judicial Court, until otherwise prescribed by the General Assembly.

SEC. 4. The towns of New Shoreham and Jamestown shall continue to enjoy the exemptions from military duty which they now enjoy, until otherwise prescribed by law.

Done in convention at East Greenwich, this fifth day of November, 1842.

JAMES FENNER, *President.*
HENRY Y. CRANSTON, *Vice President.*
THOMAS A. JENCKES, } *Secretaries.*
WALTER W. UPDIKE,